CW01024199

CURRENT MARINE ENVIRONMENTAL ISSUES AND THE INTERNATIONAL TRIBUNAL FOR THE LAW OF THE SEA

HAMBURG PAPERS

Current Marine Environmental Issues and the International Tribunal for the Law of the Sea is part of a series of publications on oceans law and policy associated with the Center for Oceans Law and Policy, University of Virginia School of Law. This volume is based on presentations made at the Center's Twenty-Fifth Annual Conference held at the International Tribunal for the Law of the Sea in Hamburg from March 16-19, 2001.

CENTER FOR OCEANS LAW AND POLICY

CURRENT MARINE ENVIRONMENTAL ISSUES AND THE INTERNATIONAL TRIBUNAL FOR THE LAW OF THE SEA

Edited by

Myron H. Nordquist

and

John Norton Moore

MARTINUS NIJHOFF PUBLISHERS

THE HAGUE / LONDON / NEW YORK

Library of Congress Cataloging-in-Publication Data

ISBN 90-411-1715-6

Published by Kluwer Law International,
P.O. Box 85889, 2508 CN The Hague, The Netherlands.

Sold and distributed in North, Central and South America
by Kluwer Law International,
101 Philip Drive, Norwell, MA 02061, U.S.A.
kluwerlaw@wkap.com

In all other countries, sold and distributed
by Kluwer Law International, Distribution Centre,
P.O. Box 322, 3300 AH Dordrecht, The Netherlands.

Printed on acid-free paper

Printed in the Netherlands

This book is respectfully dedicated to

The Honorable Elliot L. Richardson

(1920 - 1999)

CONTENTS

Panel VII: Perspectives on Maritime Disasters
Michael Lodge, Moderator

Closing Remarks

PREFATORY NOTE

The Center for Oceans Law and Policy, University of Virginia School of Law ("COLP"), has sponsored an annual conference at various locales for the past twenty-five years. The focus of the conferences has often been on topical themes of international importance. Several years ago, however, the Center decided to use the annual conferences as a means to highlight the new or existing international organizations most impacted by the 1982 UN Convention on the Law of the Sea. The conference series with this theme began in Montego Bay, Jamaica, in the very room where the 1982 Convention was signed. The panelists at the twenty-second annual conference in 1998 covered the activities to date of the International Seabed Authority, the International Tribunal for the Law of the Sea, and the Commission on the Continental Shelf. The following year, on the occasion of the fiftieth anniversary of the International Maritime Organization, the twenty-third conference was co-hosted at IMO's headquarters in London. The range of IMO's activities and its interface with the Law of the Sea Convention was impressive indeed. The logical next step after the IMO was to co-host a conference with the Food and Agriculture Organization at its headquarters in Rome. The fulsome record of the twenty-fourth meeting in 2000 stands as visible tribute to the FAO's work on global fisheries and the fundamental changes underway as fishermen transition from hunting to farming living resources in the world's oceans.

The capstone to COLP's four year review of the key international organizations associated with the 1982 Convention is contained in this volume. The twenty-fifth annual conference was co-hosted from March 16-19, 2001, at the magnificent new headquarters of the International Tribunal for the Law of the Sea ("ITLOS") in Hamburg, Germany. Since the Rule of Law in the world's oceans is epitomized by ITLOS and is a fundamental tenet of COLP, it was deemed fitting that the twenty-fifth conference and its proceeding be dedicated to the memory of The Honorable Elliot L. Richardson. The dedication was given by a close, personal friend of Secretary Richardson, Secretary-General Satya N. Nandan. The co-editors cannot think of any two individuals who have done more to promote the Rule of Law in the world's oceans. We are honored to report many of the key contributions of these consummate gentlemen and scholars in this volume.

The Hamburg meeting began with opening remarks by the President of the International Tribunal for the Law of the Sea, P. Chandrasekhara Rao. President Rao noted the unique role of the Tribunal concerning the interpretation and application of the 1982 Convention. The Tribunal consists of twenty-one judges with in-depth expertise who are devoted exclusively to the law of the sea. The jurisdiction of the court has both obligatory and consensual aspects and its scope is not limited to the four corners of the 1982 Convention.

Professor John Norton Moore welcomed participants as the Director of the Center and introduced the keynote speaker: Satya N. Nandan, the Secretary-General of the International Seabed Authority. The Director highlighted the seminal role that the Rule of Law must play and the enormous contribution that Ambassador Nandan continues to make to world order in the oceans. The Secretary-General had led the efforts to re-negotiate the deep seabed regime to make it acceptable to developed States as the Under Secretary-General of the United Nations for the Law of the Sea. His speech in Hamburg discussed the new regulations for prospecting and exploration for polymetallic nodules adopted by the International Seabed Authority in July 2000, in effect providing an update on the principal work of the ISA since the reporting from the Center's Jamaica meeting in 1998. The new regulations now mean that the ISA is ready to do business by issuing exploration permits to the seven pioneer investors. Nandan explained that the regulations only deal with the prospecting and exploration of polymetallic nodules.

The Hamburg conference was divided into two distinct phases. The program on Saturday, March 17, focused on the work of ITLOS. The program on Monday, March 19, was directed towards maritime transport and the consequences of marine disasters. The reason for the division was that the judges were available to speak about the activities of the court on Saturday, bringing COLP's coverage of the relationship to key law of the sea organizations to a close. The Monday meeting reverted to the usual COLP format of bringing expertise to bear on a topical issue of significance to the international legal community.

The first panel consisted of a roundtable discussion of the origins and purposes of ITLOS. The former president of the Tribunal, Judge Thomas A. Mensah presided as moderator. Judge Hugo Caminos led off with a background analysis of specialized cases and the various types of international dispute settlement organs created to settle such cases. The First Registrar of the Tribunal, Gritakumar E. Chitty, then addressed himself to the history of the post conference development of the Tribunal as an international judicial body. As an aside, the co-editors note that this was our good friend Kumar's last public appearance in this capacity since the Tribunal announced his retirement in 2001 after many years of international public service. Judge Mohamed Mouldi Marsit next spoke on the difficulties encountered during the initial phases of ITLOS' establishment. The last speaker was Judge Gudmundur Eiriksson who spoke on the difficulties encountered during the initial phase of ITLOS' establishment.

The members of Panel II were introduced by the former Vice President of the Tribunal, Judge Rüdiger Wolfrum. Judge David H. Anderson covered the deliberations, judgments, and separate opinions in ITLOS' practice to date. The issue of the question of time-limits in urgent proceedings before the Tribunal was discussed by Judge Joseph Akl. The President of the Seabed Disputes Chamber, Judge Tullio Treves, dealt with advisory opinions under the Law of the Sea Convention. Judge Tafsir Malick Ndiaye addressed himself to the topic of provisional measures and the International Tribunal for the Law of the Sea. Judge Wolfrum then spoke on implementing the decisions of international courts. Lastly, Judge Edward Arthur Laing looked at the role played by bonds in ITLOS procedures and practices.

Professor John Norton Moore, the Director of the Center for Oceans Law and Policy, moderated Panel III, which was oriented around the theme of private practice before the Tribunal. The

General Editor of the Virginia Commentary on the 1982 Convention, Ambassador Shabtai Rosenne, gave an overview of the case law of ITLOS from 1997 to 2001 to begin the panel. Thereafter, Professor Philippe Sands from the University of London provided his perspective on the tribunal's decision-making process. The perspective of a private practitioner was then given by Nick Howe, a London solicitor. Donald L. Morgan of the Washington, D.C., bar then critiqued the order granting provisional measures in the Southern Bluefin Tuna cases that was decided by the Tribunal in August 1999.

The moderator for the roundtable discussion in Panel IV was the Vice President of the Tribunal, Judge Dolliver Nelson. Judge Budislav Vukas pointed out some of the main problems arising with using compulsory dispute settlement under the 1982 Convention. Judge Alexander Yankov focused on current fisheries disputes and the issues raised in recent ITLOS cases. Judge Anatoly L. Kolodkin discussed the evolution in national legislation in light of the 1982 Convention and the practice of ITLOS. The Deputy Registrar for the Tribunal, Philippe Gautier, analyzed the interim measures of protection concept as applied in the cases that had come before the Tribunal. Judge Nelson spoke last on the role of the Commission on the Limits of the Continental Shelf in the interpretation and application of the 1982 Convention.

The Associate Director of the Center, Myron H. Nordquist, opened the second part of the twenty-fifth conference program as the moderator of Panel V dealing with the subjects of accidents, insurance and classification in the context of maritime disasters. Henrik Ringbom of the Directorate General for Energy and Transport, European Commission, covered in detail the developments on EU maritime regulations as a result of the Erika accident. Hans G. Payer, the Past-Chairman of the International Association of Classification Societies and of the Executive Board, Germanischer Lloyd, then provided the carrier's perspective on insurance and class and marine accidents.

The moderator for Panel VI, Barbara S. Moore, showed a series of slides with data on accidental oil spills, comparing them both in time and volume. Joseph Angelo, the Head of the U.S.

Delegation to the Marine Environmental Protection Committee at IMO, traced the developments at IMO on double hulls in the aftermath of the Erika spill in late 1999. C. Thomas Burke, a former U.S. Panama Canal Commissioner, discussed the changes that had occurred in Panama since the departure of the United States and identified a number of problems that may arise in the future. Professor Nilufer Oral from the Maritime Studies Research Centre in Istanbul analyzed recent measures taken by the Turkish government to cope with the export of oil from the Caspian Sea through the Turkish straits.

The final panel of the Conference, Panel VII, was moderated by Michael Lodge, the Legal Advisor to the International Seabed Authority. The former Legal Adviser to the U.S. Department of State, Davis R. Robinson, utilized an innovative technique of role-playing to bring out the issues surrounding a maritime disaster such as the Erika. He pretended that he was a legal advisor to a foreign minister in Europe who was required to give his opinions on short notice about recourse against flag States for breaches of their international obligations under the 1982 Convention. The last speaker of the conference was Dr. Klaus Ramming who delivered a paper prepared by Dr. Christian Breitzke about the advice that a maritime lawyer in private practice would give to his client to help cope with a marine disaster.

The Closing Remarks for the twenty-fifth conference were delivered by Judge Alexander Yankov on behalf of the President of the Tribunal. Judge Yankov graciously noted the long tradition of the City of Hamburg in maritime affairs. He praised the Center for Oceans Law and Policy and noted that reviewers of the Virginia Commentary on the 1982 Convention refer to it as "the most authoritative source of information on the new law of the sea." Judge Yankov concluded with a special tribute to the late Elliot L. Richardson noting his "political vision, human touch, and exemplary integrity. . . ."

NOTE BY THE EDITORS

The Twenty-Fifth Annual Conference of the Center for Oceans Law and Policy, University of Virginia School of Law, was held from March 16-19, 2001, in Hamburg, Germany. The site for the conference was the beautiful new headquarters for the International Tribunal for the Law of the Sea. The warm welcome and active participation by the Judges ensured that the academic value of this program would equal similar conferences co-hosted at the headquarters of the Food and Agriculture Organization in Rome and the International Maritime Organization in London. A principal objective of the 2001 conference was to help explain what the Tribunal is all about, and we believe that these proceedings achieve that result. The Center is especially appreciative of the kind cooperation of the President of the International Tribunal for the Law of the Sea, P. Chandrasekhara Rao, as well as the Vice President, Dolliver Nelson. Many practical arrangements were made with the guidance of Judge Rüdiger Wolfrum, a longtime friend of the Center for Oceans Law and Policy. The actual organization of the conference was accomplished through the Good Offices of Gritakumar E. Chitty, the First Registrar of the Tribunal, who was assisted by Antje Vorbeck.

The Center's Executive Administrator, Donna D. Ganoe, was truly the single point of contact on all matters. She was ably assisted by Kathy H. Wood, Kay W. Wood, and Ana Cecilia Porte Petit A. A particular note of gratitude is due to Joanna C. Murdick, the Center's Editorial Assistant, who organized, collected, and largely edited the papers in this book. The co-editors are well-aware that collegiate efforts are required in undertakings such as this and in that spirit we extend our heartfelt thanks to all who contributed to this successful volume.

Myron H. Nordquist
Co-editors

John Norton Moore
July 2001

DEDICATION TO ELLIOT L. RICHARDSON

Satya N. Nandan [*]

Distinguished colleagues, this is a very special moment, because I have been asked to dedicate this Conference to the memory of Elliot L. Richardson. Elliot Richardson served as Ambassador at Large and Special Representative of the President of the United States to the Law of the Sea Conference from 1977-1980. He made a historic contribution to the development of the rule of law for the world's oceans. A glance at his résumé reveals a long and distinguished career dedicated to public service. He held four different cabinet posts, more than anyone else in the history of the United States. Anyone who knew Elliot could testify to his gifts as an administrator, motivator, and a friend who made great contributions in whatever field he served. Elliot became nationally known as a model of integrity when he chose to resign his position as Attorney General of the United States under President Nixon rather than carry out White House orders to fire Special Prosecutor Archibald Cox, the leading government investigator of the Watergate break-in.

On October 21, 1973, the date of Elliot's resignation, he assumed an important place in the history of the United States and became a symbol for the kind of public servant that has sadly become all too rare, one who will place his honor before ambition and duty before partisanship. Many of us had the privilege of working with Elliot, and I was very privileged indeed to share that honor. I am, therefore, very pleased that the Center for Oceans Law and Policy chose to dedicate this Conference on the "Current Marine Environmental Issues and the International Tribunal for the Law of the Sea" to Elliot Richardson. This is a mark of high respect and an acknowledgement of Elliot's remarkable

---

[*] Secretary-General, International Seabed Authority. For more information on Secretary-General Nandan, please see "Introduction to Ambassador Satya N. Nandan" given by Professor John Norton Moore.

contribution to the law of the sea as well as a recognition of Elliot as an outstanding individual.

Elliot would be very proud to be associated with our efforts in Hamburg to promote the rule of law through increased use of the International Tribunal for the Law of the Sea. As one dedicated to law, he strongly supported the establishment of ITLOS and used this as an example of a very positive aspect of the Convention in his attempt to persuade the United States to become a party to the Convention.

Elliot Richardson passed away in 1999, leaving a unique legacy of personal and professional achievements. He was a descendant from New England's earliest settlers and inherited the strong work ethic and sense of public responsibility characteristic of his ancestors. He grew up in Boston and earned his Bachelor's Degree from Harvard University in 1941. He served in the United States Army during World War II and received a Bronze Star and two Purple Hearts for bravery in combat. He returned to the United States and graduated from Harvard Law School in 1947. He clerked for Judge Learned Hand of the U.S. Court of Appeals and Supreme Court Justice Felix Frankfurter. In 1964, he was elected Lieutenant Governor of Massachusetts, then served as the state's Attorney General from 1967 until 1969. Elliot also held a variety of offices in the Nixon administration prior to his resignation as United States Attorney General. These included, Under-Secretary of State, Secretary of Health, Education, and Welfare, and Secretary of Defense. In 1975, he became the United States Ambassador to the Court of St. James in Great Britain. And two years later served as President Ford's Secretary of Commerce. He received the Presidential Medal for Freedom, the United States' highest civilian honor, in 1998.

Elliot was also a fine artist and an inveterate doodler, producing wonderful watercolor illustrations as well as the occasional pen and ink work, usually during, I believe, Cabinet meetings. We witnessed him doodle during the Third United Nations Conference on the Law of the Sea especially during some of the very important and critical informal negotiations that were held in small groups. Many of us were recipients of his doodles. They were remarkable pieces of work.

As we struggle to resolve the legal issues facing the world's oceans, it is appropriate that we contemplate those who have wrestled with these issues in the past. As we remember these colleagues of ours, for me Elliot would be first on the list of those who inspired peoples around the globe to promote world order in the oceans.

Despite his outstanding career and achievements, Elliot was a humble, sincere, and uncomplicated person. He was a friend to all and he respected everyone. He would meet with ambassadors, permanent representatives, counsellors, first secretaries, second secretaries, whoever needed to be spoken to or to be seen, or was dealing with a particular issue that Elliot needed to discuss. He would explain the United States' position to them as he tried to understand the positions of other delegations. In this sense he was remarkable, because prior to Elliot, United States Chief Delegates basically came, made their statements, and disappeared, apart from Ambassador Jack Stevenson, who was also a person of similar characteristics as Elliot. Most of the other representatives would disappear after they had spoken and there was no dialogue between them and other delegations. But Elliot changed all of that.

Elliot came to the Conference at a time when the die was cast on most issues. He basically came to try to retrieve certain things that the United States felt was lost to them. The Part XI negotiations were difficult negotiations, and the text of Part XI at that time was such that it was an anathema to the United States and indeed to other industrialized countries. Having come somewhat in the middle of the Conference, he had to try to renegotiate these and do so delicately without upsetting everybody in the process. He would go to great lengths to persuade us all that his government would not be able to accept the Convention as it was drafted at that time and that we needed to make a number of essential changes. He was making great headway before he left the Conference when the Reagan administration came and decided to distance itself from the Convention. Elliot was a friend to all of us. He was a very personal friend; even after he left the Law of the Sea Conference, we kept in contact.

In spite of the fact that Elliot had left the law of the sea some time ago, he was nevertheless continuing with his efforts to try to get the United States to become a party to the Convention. He was very happy when we finally resolved the outstanding issues. We had several meetings with him and he would ask us what he could do to help the United States become a party. When was the right time to move forward? Elliot was the Chairman of the Council for Oceans Law in Washington and through that council he made a tremendous effort to keep the United States, or at least the key players in the Senate and Congress, informed of the developments in relation to the Convention and to try to keep the interest in the Convention simmering, as it were, and not let it be lost altogether.

About a month before he died, his secretary called me to say that Elliot wanted to come to New York to visit with me. At that time I was about to travel to Asia. I knew that he was not too well, so I changed my program and returned earlier and invited him to come to lunch at my residence in New York. I also invited a number of his old friends from the Law of the Sea. This was in November of 1999. Elliot, who had been having some health problems, was somewhat frail by this time, but he came and he was in great form. He talked about all kinds of things, but mostly about the Law of the Sea. It was interesting that he remembered all his colleagues and friends at the Conference and exchanged anecdotes about the Conference.

For a number of years I was one of the lucky recipients of Elliot's Christmas cards. These were hand-drawn cards. They came usually in January, because he would draw them over Christmas. The last card I received was from the previous January. In that he had made a very nice doodle on the cover page and inside there was the usual Christmas greetings. But there was a very interesting little P.S. "What are we going to do about Jesse Helms this year?" So you can see, Elliot never got Law of the Sea out of his mind and one of his dying wishes was that the United States should become a party to the Convention. I hope that his wish will one day come true. But let me say how privileged and pleased I am that I have been asked to dedicate this Conference to Elliot L. Richardson. Elliot will be long remembered for being a very fine person, a wonderful human being, and above all, a major contributor to the process that led to the Law of the Sea Convention. I am very pleased to dedicate this Conference to his memory.

WELCOMING REMARKS

WELCOMING REMARKS

P. Chandrasekhara Rao[*]

I am thankful to Professor John Norton Moore of the University of Virginia Center for Oceans Law and Policy for inviting me to make welcoming remarks on this occasion.

This magnificent building in which the present seminar is being held, was opened officially on July 3, 2000. The Tribunal moved into this building in the second half of November 2000. To celebrate that event, the Max-Planck Institute for Comparative Public Law and International Law held a symposium here on "The International Dispute Settlement System." It was followed by the conference "Pacem in Maribus 2000" in December 2000. This is the third seminar being held in this building. The Tribunal would gladly offer its facilities to similar seminars in the future; they will be of interest not only to us but also to the legal community as a whole.

There are persons in this gathering who contributed in significant measure to the making of the Convention. It is not, therefore, necessary for me to trace the historical background of the International Tribunal for the Law of the Sea. The compulsory procedures entailing binding decisions under Part XV of the United Nations Convention on the Law of the Sea include the Tribunal, the International Court of Justice, the arbitral tribunal under Annex VII, and the special arbitral tribunal under Annex VIII to the Convention.

The International Tribunal for the Law of the Sea is unique in a number of respects. The General Assembly of the United Nations referred to the "important role and authority" of this Tribunal concerning the interpretation and application of the Convention. Why is this so? The reasons for this are set out in the Convention itself. The Tribunal is a standing court of twenty-one judges dealing exclusively with the law of the sea. The judges of the

---

[*] President, International Tribunal for the Law of the Sea.

M.H. Nordquist and J.N. Moore (eds.),
Current Marine Environmental Issues and the International Tribunal for the Law of the Sea, 3–8.
© 2001 *Kluwer Law International. Printed in the Netherlands.*

Tribunal are all specialists in the field of the law of the sea. Unless parties agree otherwise, the Tribunal's jurisdiction becomes obligatory in respect of prompt release of vessels under article 292 and provisional measures under article 290, paragraph 5, of the Convention. The Seabed Disputes Chamber of the Tribunal enjoys almost exclusive jurisdiction in relation to activities in the international seabed area. This Chamber is the only body that is competent to give advisory opinions at the request of the Assembly or the Council of the Seabed Authority. The jurisdiction of the Tribunal is not confined to disputes under the Convention; it extends to other disputes under other agreements that confer jurisdiction on the Tribunal. The Seabed Disputes Chamber is open to non-State entities in disputes with respect to activities in the area. The Tribunal as a whole is also open to non-State entities in any case submitted pursuant to any agreement conferring juris-diction on the Tribunal that is accepted by all the parties to that case. The Tribunal is competent to give an advisory opinion if an international agreement related to the purposes of the Convention provides for the submission of a request for such an opinion. Thus, two or more States could seek an advisory opinion of the Tribunal; this is a unique feature. Further, if all the parties to a convention already in force and concerning the subject matter covered by the convention so agree, any disputes concerning such convention may be submitted to the Tribunal. There are thus a number of important reasons that render the Tribunal a special institution.

The Tribunal may also, under article 15 of the Statute, form special chambers. The Tribunal forms annually a Chamber of Summary Procedure under article 15, paragraph 3, of the Statute. In prompt release cases under article 292 of the Convention, it would be more appropriate in time to come if such cases were referred to the Chamber of Summary Procedure. The Tribunal has formed two other chambers, one to deal with fisheries disputes and the other with marine environment disputes. No cases have yet been submitted to these Chambers.

Very recently, at the request of Chile and the European Community, the Tribunal, under article 15, paragraph 2, of its Statute, formed a special chamber to deal with a dispute concerning the conservation and sustainable exploitation of swordfish stocks in the Southeastern Pacific Ocean, of which I am the President. Judges Caminos, Yankov, Wolfrum and *ad hoc* Judge Orrego Vicuña, are the other members of this special chamber. This is a unique case between an international organization and a State that has been attracted by the contentious jurisdiction of a world court. After this Chamber was constituted, the parties entered into a bilateral arrangement whereby they decided to resolve this matter outside the framework of the court and approached the Special Chamber for obtaining adequate time for this purpose. On April 15, 2001, the Chamber gave time to the parties for this purpose. However, either party could at any time approach the Special Chamber to recommence the proceedings.

The Tribunal began to work in October 1996. It had a brief organizational phase of one year. During this period, it elaborated the Rules of the Tribunal, a Resolution on the Internal Judicial Practice of the Tribunal, and Guidelines concerning the Preparation and Presentation of Cases before the Tribunal. While preparing its Rules, the Tribunal took into account the practice of other judicial bodies, especially that of the ICJ, and the comments of practicing international lawyers before such bodies. The Tribunal had, however, departed from the practice of other bodies in important respects. The Rules lay down strict time-limits for filing of pleadings. The Resolution on the Internal Judicial Practice does not prescribe a strict system of note writing by judges during internal deliberations. In the preparation of the Guidelines, the Tribunal took into account the practice of municipal courts. There are guidelines even in relation to the ICJ. The Tribunal's Guidelines are, however, much more elaborate. They contain several new features with regard to the length, format and presentation of written and oral proceedings and use of electronic means of communication. In practice, the Tribunal enforces strict time limits in respect of presentation of oral arguments. Of course, these time limits are specified in consultation with the parties. I am very glad to inform you that the parties have never asked us for more time. They have been able to complete their arguments within the time given to them.

The Tribunal has decided six cases so far. One case is pending now and we have received notice that a new case is likely to be filed in the course of next week. Of these cases, three cases related to prompt release proceedings under article 292 of the Convention. One case, the M/V "SAIGA" no. 2 Case, was decided on merits. Though the number of cases decided by the Tribunal was very limited, the Tribunal made important contributions towards clarifying the jurisprudence on the law of the sea. In the M/V "SAIGA" No. 2 Case, the Tribunal has had occasion to deal with rights and jurisdiction of coastal States, freedom of navigation, hot pursuit, etc. The Tribunal has heard cases filed by New Zealand and Australia for prescription of provisional measures under article 290, paragraph 5, concerning southern bluefin tuna. Under the Convention, and this is a unique feature of the Convention, provisional measures can be prescribed not only to preserve the respective rights of the parties, but also to "prevent serious harm to the marine environment," pending the final decision. The Tribunal held in that case that the parties should act with "prudence and caution to ensure that effective conservation measures are taken to prevent serious harm to the stock of southern bluefin tuna." The Tribunal also declared that "the conservation of the living resources of the sea is an element in the protection and preservation of the marine environment." This declaration has been commented upon extensively in academic writings. The question was whether the Tribunal had endorsed the so-called precautionary approach as a principle of law. On your list, I see speakers who will be commenting on this question later on.

The Tribunal has also been making use of new developments in technology. In the "Camouco" Case, the Tribunal was willing to record the evidence of a witness through a video conference. However, the party did not find it feasible to arrange this facility. The Tribunal has also been using courtroom multi-media facilities during hearings of cases to facilitate better presentation of arguments and evidence of parties.

The Tribunal has delivered its orders and judgments in remarkably short periods. The Tribunal makes special efforts to make this possible, keeping in view the need for achieving expeditious settlement of international disputes. The parties to prompt release proceedings under article 292 of the Convention have, however, underlined the difficulties they face in complying with the tine-limits fixed in the Rules of the Tribunal in the matter of filing of a statement in response by the respondent and examination of that statement by the applicant before commencing its arguments.

The Tribunal reviewed its Rules in the light of the experience gained in handling prompt release cases. On March 15, 2001, it amended articles 111 and 112 of its Rules. Prior to the amendments, applications under article 292 are required to be disposed of within a period not exceeding twenty-one days; after the amendments, an application is required to be disposed of within a period of thirty days. While the Tribunal is keen to render its judgments within as short period as possible, it will have to bear in mind the difficulties of each case and the requirements of parties.

Enforcement of decisions of international courts and tribunals is a matter that needs to be looked at very closely. The record in this regard does not appear to be very satisfactory. In the case of the ICJ, the Charter of the United Nations entrusts the enforcement role to the Security Council. The hitherto limited invocation of this enforcement process, which is essentially political in character, has not yet tested the full utility of the process. It is, however, obvious that in practice this process may not be of much help in respect of any of the permanent members of the Security Council.

The Convention provides that a decision rendered by a court or tribunal having jurisdiction under section 2 of Part XV is final and shall be complied with by all the parties to the dispute. Compliance itself is left solely to the parties submitting themselves to the jurisdiction of such courts and tribunals. There is, however, a good faith obligation undertaken by them to comply with the decision. It is open to the injured State to secure compliance by its own means permitted by international law in this regard, as also by recourse to more general diplomatic steps. Third States could also validly act in support of the court decision.

It is encouraging to note that the United Nations Millennium Declaration found it appropriate to call upon Members of the United Nations to "ensure compliance" with the decisions of the ICJ, in compliance with the Charter of the United Nations, in cases to which they are parties. Though not explicitly stated, this applies with equal force to decisions of all international courts and tribunals, whether within the framework of the United Nations system or outside. In fact, the General Assembly, while dealing with "oceans and the law of the sea," also noted the obligation of States to ensure prompt compliance with decisions of a court or tribunal referred to in article 287 of the Convention, in cases to which they are parties. The Tribunal decided that in its reports to the States Parties, it should give on account of the complaints it received regarding non-enforcement of the Tribunal's judgments.

There is also the question of proliferation of Tribunals. It has been suggested that there should be only one apex international judicial body and that other judicial bodies should be subordinate to it. I do not think that this is the correct approach to the issue. The General Assembly welcomed the establishment of tribunals as representing a significant event within the United Nations Decade of International Law. I do not think that the fears expressed with regard to fragmentation of international law are based on any past experience or are otherwise well-founded.

I thank the organizers again for giving me the opportunity to speak on this occasion.

WELCOMING REMARKS

John Norton Moore [*]

President Rao, distinguished judges of the International Tribunal for the Law of the Sea, the Secretary-General of the International Seabed Authority, the Registrar of the Tribunal, and Ladies and Gentlemen.

Over twenty-five hundred years of human experience have demonstrated the importance of the rule of law. Indeed, the rule of law, both nationally and internationally, may well be *the* crucial fundament in unleashing the boundless creativity of mankind. From war avoidance and protection of human rights through economic growth and the protection of the very planet we are blessed to inhabit, no other factor has proven to correlate more strongly with the achievement of human aspirations.

Against this background of the special significance of the rule of law, and in the setting of the beautiful and historic city of Hamburg, the Center for Oceans Law and Policy is honored to hold its annual Conference at the site of this International Tribunal for the Law of the Sea, one of the newest international institutions dedicated to the rule of law.

ITLOS and the distinguished judges and staff of this institution can take great pride in the achievements of this important new participant in the struggle for law.

In the less than five years since becoming operational, the Court has:

- Established its rules of procedure and access embodying both tried and true procedures and new innovations in judicial fairness and efficiency. Only last week in Charlottesville at another conference I was running, we had a former President of the International Court of Justice who

---

[*] Walter L. Brown Professor of Law and Director, Center for Oceans Law and Policy, University of Virginia School of Law.

M.H. Nordquist and J.N. Moore (eds.),
Current Marine Environmental Issues and the International Tribunal for the Law of the Sea, 9–11.
© 2001 *Kluwer Law International. Printed in the Netherlands.*

was lauding the new procedures adopted by the Tribunal and commending the excellence of innovation in those procedures.

- The Tribunal has, through the generous support of Germany, its host government, moved into the beautiful modern facility we see around us.

- And, perhaps of greatest importance, it has, by its excellence in the law of the sea and fairness to all, already developed a robust record, with seven entries in its list of cases and an eighth, we have just heard, on its way.

- If I can also echo one of the points just made by President Rao, there is a particularly unique setting for the new Tribunal in the extraordinary expertise and participation in negotiation of the underlying law itself of the members of this Tribunal during the formative phase of this Court. Very few Tribunals are blessed by this kind of extraordinary participation of judges in the development of normative principles themselves that the Court will apply. When I think back, for example, as to the great importance of the early decisions in the United States Supreme Court, I think of *Marbury vs. Madison*, and the importance of those early decisions. Surely to have this kind of firsthand knowledge of the LOS Convention is a unique advantage of this Tribunal.

As we look a mere century into the future, all of us can readily imagine the great contribution of the Tribunal to the rule of law in the world's oceans and beyond. We may, however, as easily underestimate what is likely to be the workload of this robust institution. As we have seen with other of mankind's institutions in the struggle for law, for example the European Court of Human Rights, or within my country, the United States Supreme Court, early beginnings may be but a shadow of the Institution to come.

I agree also with a very important theme of President Rao: As we look at this next century of the development of international law, including the law of the sea, that enforcement, indeed perhaps most broadly, compliance, is going to be one of the most important sets of issues for the international community. In my course in international law at the University of Virginia, I routinely tell my students we have a great deal of normative law. For the most part, it is good law. The problem is one of compliance. And the issue for your generation is compliance, compliance, compliance.

ITLOS also builds on the 1982 United Nations Convention on the Law of the Sea, itself a remarkable contribution to the rule of law in the world's oceans. Many in this room, including Satya Nandan, the former Under Secretary-General for the Law of the Sea, Alexander Yankov, the Chairman of Committee III of the Conference, and other framers of the Convention in this room who are too numerous to list here, but are known to all of us, have contributed greatly to that remarkable success that in turn led to this Tribunal.

I am pleased to say that my country, the United States, played a seminal role in the development of the UNCLOS success, including, we may forget, serving as perhaps the principal advocate in the creation of this Tribunal. It was my pleasure, as a then United States Ambassador to the UNCLOS negotiations, to have been present at the creation, that is, at the time of the Montreux formulae, the real diplomatic genesis of this Tribunal. I remember well the passion of the United States Delegation on behalf of the idea that became this Court.

That following the successful renegotiation of Part XI, the United States is not yet a party to UNCLOS III is a matter of regret. I am confident, however, that ultimate United States adherence to the Treaty is a matter of when, and not of whether. With a new administration, I am also hopeful that the when will be now.

Distinguished participants, colleagues in the quest for a rule of law in the world's oceans, and ladies and gentlemen, may our deliberations at this Conference, in the tradition of academic integrity and the search for truth, add impetus to the development of this great new institution.

KEYNOTE ADDRESS

INTRODUCTION FOR AMBASSADOR SATYA N. NANDAN

John Norton Moore[*]

Historians sometimes debate whether history is the product of great men or great events. Ambassador Nandan is living proof that great men are a key part of any answer.

We all know Satya Nandan, but it is important that we acknowledge just how important Satya has been to the Law of the Sea. Satya was the Foreign Secretary of Fiji before he became the Ambassador to the European Union. Then began an extraordinary set of events for the Law of the Sea and for the whole world. Satya became the Ambassador of Fiji to the Third United Nations Conference on the Law of the Sea, where we came to know his great accomplishments and success. In that setting, he was the Rapporteur of Committee II. And I can say from personal experience, and I believe many others in this room would agree, that Satya was one of a handful of key individuals who facilitated the core underlying political compromise in the Law of the Sea. Basically that compromise was a recognition of coastal State resource rights in return for full navigational freedom, and he, as the Rapporteur of Committee II, was essentially responsible for getting the single negotiating text out that was the critical breakthrough in that core compromise.

Subsequently, when we had some problems concerning Part XI on deep seabed mining preventing global acceptance of the Law of the Sea Convention after it had been adopted in 1982, it was Satya Nandan in his role as the Under Secretary-General of the United Nations for the Law of the Sea, who persevered year after year to ensure that serious renegotiation of Part XI would take place. And he personally not only led the initiatives that created those negotiations, but he then led the negotiations themselves that

---

[*] Walter L. Brown Professor of Law and Director, Center for Oceans Law and Policy, University of Virginia School of Law.

M.H. Nordquist and J.N. Moore (eds.),
Current Marine Environmental Issues and the International Tribunal for the Law of the Sea, 15–16.
© 2001 *Kluwer Law International. Printed in the Netherlands.*

enabled all nations to come together in support of the Law of the Sea Treaty.

Later when we began to have problems in global fisheries beyond 200 miles concerning straddling and highly migratory stock issues that had not been finalized as appropriately as they should have been in the initial Law of the Sea Convention, he led the negotiations on straddling stocks and highly migratory species that once again led to successful results that *are* making a difference in the preservation of fish stocks around the world.

And yet again Satya is in a position that makes a difference on an important issue. He is the Secretary-General of the International Seabed Authority. And in that setting he is again providing leadership for the world to try to bring all of the countries together to adhere to a regime that has been put together with extraordinary skill, care, and diplomacy.

Ladies and Gentlemen, please join me in welcoming a leader who has truly made a difference, Ambassador Satya N. Nandan.

KEYNOTE ADDRESS

Satya N. Nandan[*]

I am delighted to be in Hamburg in the company of such a distinguished gathering of eminent international lawyers and judges, and I would like to express my appreciation to Professor John Norton Moore of the University of Virginia, Center for Oceans Law and Policy, and to the President, judges, and the Registrar of the International Tribunal for the Law of the Sea for their generosity in hosting this year's seminar on the premises of the Tribunal. I am sure you have been impressed, as I have, by the sumptuous splendor of the palatial new premises of the Tribunal, the gift of the Federal Republic of Germany.

I have been asked to speak on the new regulations for prospecting and exploration for polymetallic nodules in the international seabed area adopted by the International Seabed Authority in July 2000. The regulations are, indeed, an integral part of the Convention and the 1994 Agreement for the implementation of Part XI. Their significance lies in the fact that they complete and give effect to the scheme laid out in Part XI and Annex III of the Convention, and the Agreement, enabling the Authority to issue contracts for exploration to those entities listed in article 153 of the Convention, which are eligible to carry out activities in the Area. The adoption of the regulations, following three years of work by the Legal and Technical Commission and the Council of the Authority, means that the Authority may finally enter into exploration contracts with the seven investors who were registered as pioneer investors by the Preparatory Commission under Resolution II of the Third United Nations Conference on the Law of the Sea, thus bringing those registered pioneer investors within the single and definitive regime established by the Convention and the 1994 Agreement.

---

[*] Secretary-General of the International Seabed Authority.

M.H. Nordquist and J.N. Moore (eds.),
Current Marine Environmental Issues and the International Tribunal for the Law of the Sea, 17–26.
© 2001 *Kluwer Law International. Printed in the Netherlands.*

The regulations deal only with the prospecting and exploration phases and are applicable only to polymetallic nodules. This is in accordance with article 162, paragraph 2(o)(ii), of the Convention, and the Agreement, which required the Authority to give priority to the adoption of rules, regulations, and procedures for exploration for polymetallic nodules, despite the fact that since the Convention was adopted in 1982, commercial interest in deep seabed polymetallic nodules has dwindled to the point where commercial exploitation of these resources seems farther off than before. Much of the content of the regulations, however, would be equally applicable to prospecting and exploration for other mineral resources in the Area, so the fact that the prospects for commercial exploitation appear remote at this time does not in any way diminish the significance of the regulations, nor has it deterred the pioneer investors from seeking to enter into fifteen-year exploration contracts with the Authority based on the provisions of the regulations.

Under the Convention and the Agreement, a plan of work for exploration must be drawn up in the form of a contract between the Authority and the entity that wishes to carry out exploration activities. The basic format of the regulations describes the way in which a prospective contractor may apply for approval of a plan of work, the form and content of that application, the procedure for approval of the plan of work, and the form and content of the contract.

The part of the regulations dealing with procedural matters is drawn largely from the provisions of Annex III of the Convention, elaborating upon those provisions as necessary, for example, by defining the nature and scope of the obligations of a sponsoring State, as envisaged by article 4 of Annex III. The objective, however, was to make the procedure for application relatively simple and straightforward, while at the same time transparent.

Perhaps the most interesting aspect of the regulations is the contract for exploration itself. At an early stage of its discussions, the Legal and Technical Commission decided to promulgate standard terms and conditions for all contractors. It decided that the best way to achieve this would be to draft standard clauses that could be annexed to the regulations. These standard clauses would be common to all contractors and would thus remove the need for the Authority to negotiate with each potential contractor individually.

The contract itself is a short, two-page document, which merely sets out the names of the parties to the contract, describes the subject matter of the contract, its duration and date of commencement, and states that the standard clauses shall be incorporated in the contract and shall have effect as if set out at length. In order to reflect the differences between individual contractors, the contract contains a number of schedules. Schedule 1 defines the exploration area allocated to the contractor. Schedule 2 is the contractor's program of activities, and schedule 3 is the contractor's training program, as required under article 144 and Annex III, article 15, of the Convention. The idea of standard clauses of contracts is not new and, in fact, is reflected in the national legislation of a number of countries in the case of offshore oil and gas licensing. In the context of the Authority's relations with its contractors, this is an extremely useful approach that helps remove any doubt over the application of the provisions of the regulations to individual contractors and promotes efficiency by removing the need for further negotiation.

Among the most contentious issues to be discussed in formulating the regulations were the matters of confidentiality of the data and information submitted to the Authority and the protection of the marine environment. Neither of these matters is dealt with extensively in the Convention or the Agreement, although, of course, Part XII of the Convention deals in more general terms with the obligations of States to protect and preserve the marine environment. Since the Convention was adopted, however, the question of the protection of the marine environment has assumed greater importance. This preoccupation with the marine environment is reflected in the 1994 Agreement itself, which, *inter alia*, requires that the rules, regulations, and procedures adopted by the Authority incorporate applicable standards for the protection and preservation of the marine environment and that applications for approval of plans of work for exploration are accompanied by an assessment of the potential environmental impacts of the proposed exploration activities and a program for oceanographic and environmental baseline studies.

The regulations make reference to a general duty on the part of contractors, pursuant to article 145 of the Convention, to take necessary measures to prevent, reduce, and control pollution and other hazards to the marine environment arising from their activities in the Area as far as reasonably possible using the best technology available to them. The specific content of this general duty, as far as the exploration phase is concerned, is outlined in the regulations as well as in the standard clauses for exploration contracts. Thus, the contractor is required to gather environmental baseline data as exploration activities progress and to establish environmental baselines against which to assess the likely effects of its activities on the marine environment. It is important to note that the obligations on the contractor are progressive in nature. It is widely accepted that during the initial phase of exploration, there would be little, if any, impact on the marine environment. Most exploration work would be non-invasive, relying primarily on remote sensing and standard sampling techniques. However, the standard clauses recognize that a secondary phase of exploration begins with the commencement of testing of collecting systems and processing operations. At this time, the contractor will be required to submit a site-specific environmental impact assessment and a proposal for a monitoring program to determine the effect on the marine environment of the equipment that will be used during the mining tests. In recognition of the dynamic and progressive nature of exploration, the regulations also permit the Legal and Technical Commission to issue from time to time recommendations of a technical or administrative nature for the guidance of contractors to assist them in the implementation of the regulations. Although, strictly speaking, not legally binding, it is anticipated that such recommendations will form the basis of an acceptable code of conduct for contractors. The first set of such recommendations, relating to environmental baseline studies, is currently under consideration by the Legal and Technical Commission.

The issue of confidentiality of data and information from seabed exploration was a matter of the greatest concern both to seabed mining States and non-seabed mining States. On the one hand, the seabed miners had legitimate concerns over protecting the confidentiality of data and information submitted to the Authority given the enormous expense of exploration work and the commercial sensitivity of much of that data and information. On the other hand, many members of the Authority had equally legitimate concerns over the need for transparency and ensuring access to sufficient data and information to enable the various organs of the Authority, including the Council, Secretariat, and Legal and Technical Commission, to carry out their functions under the Convention and the Agreement. Unfortunately, the only provision in Annex III of the Convention (Annex III, article 14) dealing with confidentiality of data and information is somewhat obscure and did not really satisfy either constituency.

The scheme that was finally adopted in the regulations gives a broad definition to confidential data and information. Much to the dismay of some member States, it also allows the contractor, in consultation with the Secretary-General, broad latitude to determine which data and information shall be designated as confidential. Such data and information may only be used by the Secretary-General and staff of the Secretariat and by the members of the Legal and Technical Commission as necessary for and relevant to the effective exercise of their powers and functions. Procedures are established, which it is the Secretary-General's duty to carry out, to maintain confidentiality.

While several seabed mining States would have liked to maintain confidentiality indefinitely, this was not acceptable to the majority of member States. Instead, drawing on precedents from national mining legislation, the regulations prescribe an initial period of ten years from the date of submission during which data and information will remain confidential. At that time, and every five years thereafter, the contractor and the Secretary-General are to review the data and information to determine whether there is a need for it to remain confidential. The test that is to be applied is whether the contractor can establish that there is a substantial risk of serious and unfair economic prejudice if the data were to be released. Of course, if the contractor decides to proceed to exploitation, the data and information would remain confidential in accordance with the contract for exploitation.

The regulations were drafted over a period of three years. A draft of the regulations was formulated first by the Legal and Technical Commission, based on an initial draft prepared by the Secretariat. The draft formulated by the Commission was submitted to the Council for approval in August 1998 and the Council then considered the regulations in detail during the 1999 and 2000 sessions of the Authority. At the end of the process, I am pleased to say that the regulations were adopted by consensus in the Council and approved by the Assembly without any amendment. Following the adoption of the regulations, and acting on the instructions of the Council, I immediately took steps to prepare draft contracts for each of the registered pioneer investors, and it is expected that the first three of these contracts will be signed in Kingston before the end of March 2001 and the remaining four by the end of June. In many respects, the signature of the contracts for exploration will mark the end of a long process of negotiation that began during the Third United Nations Conference on the Law of the Sea, which included the adoption of Resolution II, and was continued throughout the Preparatory Commission and the first six sessions of the International Seabed Authority. Over more than twenty years, negotiators have come and gone, political, social, and economic situations have changed for many countries and, indeed, for the world as a whole, but I believe that the contractual relationship between the Authority as the custodian of the common heritage of mankind and those wishing to carry out exploration activities in the deep seabed remains fully consistent with the basic principles set out in Part XI of the Convention and the Agreement.

I might add, parenthetically, that the need to appreciate the development of the deep seabed mining regime in its historical perspective is an illustration of why the University of Virginia's Law of the Sea Commentary Project is so important. The *Commentary* is virtually the only place where one can find a complete and impartial record of the negotiations that took place on each individual article of the Convention during the Conference, including the various proposals that were put forward by individual delegations or negotiating groups and that helped to influence and shape the final draft of each article. It is indeed regrettable that owing to financial and other constraints, organizations such as the United Nations have been unable to give sufficient priority to the preservation and publication of the *travaux preparatoires* and related notes and documentation of a negotiating process that has contributed so much to the preservation of international peace and security.

During the drafting of the Authority's regulations and at many other times during the establishment of the Authority, it has been essential to refer back to the records of the Conference and even the records of the Seabed Committee, in order to fully understand the reasoning behind the sometimes obscure provisions of Part XI and Annex III and thereby to give effect to Annex III in the spirit in which it was intended and preserve the integrity of the Convention as a whole. I have noted with much satisfaction that the Tribunal itself has referred to the Commentary on several occasions in the course of its judgments. The international community owes a debt of gratitude to the University of Virginia for sponsoring this important academic work over so many years.

In 1998, the Authority was requested by a member State to adopt regulations to cover prospecting and exploration for certain other kinds of mineral resources in the Area, specifically cobalt-rich crusts and polymetallic sulphides. As a first step in understanding the nature of these resources, the Authority held a workshop in June 2000 at which eminent scientists and researchers from around the world were invited to give presentations on the nature and occurrence of these resources, their resource potential, and prospects for future development.

Cobalt crusts, or more accurately, cobalt-rich ferromanganese crusts, occur throughout the global oceans on seamounts, ridges, and plateaus. The crusts precipitate out of cold ambient seawater onto hard rock substrates forming pavements up to 250 millimeters thick. These crusts form at water depths of between 400 to 4,000 meters, with the thickest and most cobalt-rich occurring at depths of 800 to 2,500 meters. Crusts are important as a potential resource for cobalt, but also contain titanium, cerium, nickel, platinum, manganese, thallium, tellurium, and other rare earth elements.

Polymetallic sulphides in the form of high-temperature black smokers, were first discovered in 1979 on the East Pacific Rise off Baja, California. Since then, polymetallic massive sulphides have been discovered at water depths of up to 3,700 meters in a variety of tectonic settings at the modern seafloor, including mid-ocean ridges, sedimented ridges, back-arc rifts, and seamounts. Many of these deposits consist of a so-called black smoker complex on top of a sulphide mound. Precipitation of massive sulphides takes place in response to mixing of the high-temperature metal-rich hydrothermal seawater fluid with ambient seawater. Seafloor polymetallic sulphide deposits can reach a considerable size and often carry high concentrations of copper, zinc, and lead in addition to gold and silver. More than 100 sites of hydrothermal mineralization are known at the seafloor, including at least twenty-five sites with high-temperature black smoker venting. The majority of sites so far have been located at the East Pacific Rise, the Southeast Pacific Rise, and the Northeast Pacific Rise. However, it is estimated that only about five percent of the 60,000 kilometers of oceanic ridges worldwide have been surveyed in any detail.

Based on the discussions during the workshop, the Secretariat has been giving thought to the kind of regime that would be most appropriate in order to best encourage future development of these resources. The resources of the Area are the common heritage of mankind. However, at the heart of the regime for the Area established in Part XI of the Convention and the Agreement is the so-called "parallel" system. This is elaborated in article 153 of the Convention. The essential elements of the parallel system include assured access for States Parties and their nationals to seabed mineral resources along with the idea of site-banking, whereby reserved areas are to be set aside for the conduct of activities by the Authority, through the Enterprise—either by itself or in association with developing States. In the case of polymetallic nodules, the regulations require the prospective contractor to provide the Authority with a so-called reserved area, and this was done by the registered pioneer investors in accordance with the provisions of Resolution II. As a result of the 1994 Agreement, however, the Authority is not in a position to make use of those reserved areas until such time as someone is willing to propose a joint-venture operation with the Enterprise.

In the case of crusts and sulphides, the very nature of the resources makes it unrealistic to expect the prospective contractor necessarily to carry out the work required to offer two sites of equal estimated commercial value. Unlike polymetallic nodules, which are essentially two-dimensional, lying in fields upon the ocean floor, cobalt crusts and polymetallic sulphides are three-dimensional in nature. No two occurrences of such resources are the same, and there may be substantial variation in grade of deposits even within one seamount, which would make it very difficult for the prospector to determine two sites of equal estimated commercial value without substantial and costly exploration work.

One possibility that might, therefore, be considered is a two-track system, whereby a prospective contractor may choose to provide the Authority with a reserved area, or instead of providing the Authority with a reserved area that the Authority may never be in a position to utilize in any event, another possible option would be to require the contractor to give the Authority, through the Enterprise, a certain equity interest in the project with the right of first refusal to enter into a joint venture with the contractor, subject to certain specified terms and conditions.

Other important and potentially contentious issues that also need to be considered include the size of the areas to be given to contractors and appropriate provisions to prevent monopolization of the seabed resources.

Let me conclude by stating that the International Seabed Authority is a new organization established only as recently as 1994 upon the entry into force of the Convention. As you would have already noted, the Authority is engaged in earnest in discharging its responsibility to administer the resources of the deep seabed. Through its workshops and programs on environmental studies, it is becoming an important repository of information on the seabed and its resources as well as a catalyst for activities in the deep seabed area.

Once again, I would like to thank Professor John Norton Moore and the organizers of this Conference for inviting me to speak to this illustrious gathering.

PANEL I

Roundtable Comments on ITLOS Origins and Purposes

INTRODUCTORY REMARKS

*Thomas A. Mensah**

Professor John Norton Moore has rightly identified the "rule of law" as the defining characteristic of civilized society. It is a society based on the rule of law that founding fathers of the United Nations intended to establish for the world after the ravages of the first and second world wars. The peaceful settlement of disputes is one of the two main pillars of the international legal order that was established by the Charter of the United Nations. As stated in Article 1 of the Charter, one of the major objectives of the United Nations is to bring about by peaceful means, and in conformity with the principles of justice and international law, adjustment or settlement of international disputes and situations. To this end, all Member States of the Organization accept the obligation to settle their international disputes "by peaceful means in such a manner that international peace and security, and justice, are not endangered."

Specifically, the Charter enjoins States to settle their disputes through the procedures listed in article 33, paragraph 1, of the Charter, namely "negotiation, enquiry, mediation, conciliation, arbitration, judicial settlement, resort to regional agencies or arrangements, or other peaceful means of their own choice." This provision reflects the wide measure of choice that is available to States in selecting the procedures for the settlement of their disputes. As one commentator has succinctly put it:

> [T]he range of dispute settlement mechanisms in article 33 of the Charter represents an orderly progression from settlement-directed activity engaged in by the parties by themselves, through mechanisms which confer on third parties in varying degrees the authority to assist in resolving the dispute, and culminating in grant of authority to a judicial body to determine the legal rights and duties of

---

* Judge, International Tribunal for the Law of the Sea.

M.H. Nordquist and J.N. Moore (eds.),
Current Marine Environmental Issues and the International Tribunal for the Law of the Sea, 29–32.
© 2001 *Kluwer Law International. Printed in the Netherlands.*

the disputants (M.C.W. Pinto, "The Process of International Arbitration; Inter-State Disputes," in *International Arbitration: Past and Prospects*, A.H.A. Soons [Ed.] 1990, pp. 63-69 at p. 64).

International judicial institutions are established to provide to States "third-party" mechanisms for the settlement of disputes where the parties to the disputes are not able to settle such disputes by other means of their own choice. These institutions do not derogate from the fundamental right of states to settle their disputes among themselves. Rather, they respond to the universal recognition that there should be credible avenues for the conclusive settlement of international disputes, if and when the parties involved cannot agree on mutually acceptable procedures for settlement.

The wide choice given to States in regard to mechanisms for dispute settlement also takes account of the fact that States are not always willing to submit their disputes to standing judicial bodies. In particular, States tend to be reluctant to accept the mandatory jurisdiction of a single judicial body over all their disputes. Consequently, it has long been recognized by learned and influential commentators that it is neither realistic nor useful to restrict States to one or even a few mechanisms for dispute settlement. Rather, it has been urged that States should be given as many options as possible in the procedures that they may use for resolving their differences. It is for this reason that a large number and variety of judicial institutions have been established in recent years at the global, regional, and even sub-regional levels. These institutions have varying jurisdictions both as to subject matter and with regard to the number and types of entities over which they can exercise competence.

The International Tribunal for the Law of the Sea is one of several judicial mechanisms available to States for the settlement of disputes regarding the management and use of the resources of the seas and oceans. The drafters of the 1982 United Nations Convention on the Law of the Sea concluded that it was both necessary and useful to offer to the States Parties to the Convention a choice of procedures for the settlement of disputes that may arise between them concerning the interpretation or application of the Convention. To cater for the wider scope of coverage of the Convention, it was also considered necessary to have a dispute settlement mechanism that would be open to non-State entities in appropriate cases. The Tribunal is not the only judicial body for the settlement of disputes under the Convention, but it is a pivotal institution in the scheme of the Convention. It does not have automatic competence in every dispute, but it provides a residual means of resolving some of the disputes in the absence of agreement between the parties on other procedures of settlement.

The discussions this morning, and in the subsequent sessions today, will examine the rationale and origins of the Tribunal; the processes through which it was conceived, organized, and brought into being; the way in which it has operated in the nearly five years of its existence; and the prospects that one may envisage for it in the future.

The members of Panel I are all persons who have had a long and close association with the Tribunal in one capacity or another. Three of them are elected judges of the Tribunal who also happen to have participated actively in the negotiations that led to the development and adoption of the 1982 United Nations Convention on the Law of the Sea and the establishment of the Tribunal. The other member of the panel is the Registrar of the Tribunal. In an earlier capacity, he played a key role not only in the work on the development of the Convention and the Statute of the Tribunal, but also in the actual putting in place of the Tribunal as an operational body. He has subsequently guided the work of the Registry of the Tribunal in its formative stages.

By agreement between the panelists, presentations will be made in an order slightly different from the listing in the program. The first presentation will be made by Judge Hugo Caminos, who will speak about the rationale behind the idea of a tribunal to deal with disputes arising under the Convention on the Law of the Sea. He will be followed by Registrar Gritakumar Chitty, who will continue the historical setting with a record of the developments during and after the Conference, including the work of the Preparatory Commission, the election of the judges, and the physical establishment of the Tribunal in Hamburg. The next presentation will be by Judge Mouldi Marsit, who will introduce us to aspects of the work of the Tribunal, with particular reference to the difficulties and problems that have had to be overcome to facilitate the effective operation of the Tribunal. Finally, Judge Gudmundur Eiriksson will give us his insights into the prospects for the Tribunal and the role it can play in the development of a world legal not only for the oceans but also in other aspects of international life.

THE ESTABLISHMENT OF SPECIALIZED COURTS

*Hugo Caminos**

I. LEGAL BASIS

Almost eighty years ago, at precisely the same time of the creation of the first international judicial body—the Permanent Court of International Justice—the right of States to submit their disputes to other international tribunals was expressly acknowledged. Article 1 of the Statute of the Permanent Court and article 13 (3) of the Covenant of the League of Nations provided for the submission of legal disputes to the Permanent Court or to "any tribunal agreed by the parties to the dispute or stipulated in any convention existing between them."

The same principle is found in the Charter of the United Nations. As Judge Yankov has expressed:

> [M]ore than fifty years ago the drafters of the Charter in its Chapter XIV on the International Court of Justice with clear sightedness anticipated for States to make use of the plurality of options in choosing the appropriate means of dispute settlement, as embodied in Article 95, which reads:
>
> > Nothing in the present Charter shall prevent Members of the United Nations from entrusting the solution of their differences to other tribunals by virtue of agreements already in existence or which may be concluded in the future.[1]

In commenting on this provision, Kelsen has observed:

> Hence the Members are allowed to submit their disputes in accordance with pre-existing or newly concluded treaties to

---

* Judge, International Tribunal for the Law of the Sea.

33

M.H. Nordquist and J.N. Moore (eds.),
Current Marine Environmental Issues and the International Tribunal for the Law of the Sea, 33–40.
© 2001 *Kluwer Law International. Printed in the Netherlands.*

ad hoc tribunals of arbitration or to establish—for instance by regional arrangements—another court of Justice. According to Article 33, paragraph 1, and Article 95, of the Charter, they may establish a special court with compulsory jurisdiction, excluding the jurisdiction of any other tribunal, even the jurisdiction of the International Court of Justice established by the Charter.[2]

Another commentary states:

Clearly, the designation of the International Court of Justice as the principal judicial organ of the United Nations (Article 92) was not intended to preclude the establishment of other judicial organs under the auspices of the United Nations or outside the framework of the Organization.[3]

It is clear that neither of the two World Courts was created with a view to establishing a centralized international judicial system.

II. THE SEABED COMMITTEE PROPOSALS: THE ORIGINS OF THE INTERNATIONAL TRIBUNAL FOR THE LAW OF THE SEA

The first proposals for creating a tribunal for the settlement of law of the sea disputes were submitted to the Seabed Committee. Basically, these concerned disputes relating to seabed mining where the actors could not only be States, but also international organizations and natural or juridical persons. No existing tribunal was competent to decide these disputes.

As early as 1970, the United States submitted to the Seabed Committee a working paper containing a Draft United Nations Convention on the International Seabed Area,[4] which provided for the creation of a special tribunal as an organ of an International Seabed Resource Authority. The tribunal would decide all disputes and advise on all questions relating to the application of the seabed treaty and apply relevant principles of international law as well. Subject to an authorization under article 96 of the United Nations

Charter, it could request the International Court of Justice to give an advisory opinion on any question of international law.

In 1971, Malta proposed in the Committee, in the context of a draft ocean space treaty concerning not only the establishment of an international machinery for the seabed area, but also a broad range of related issues: high seas, continental shelf, territorial sea, straits, fisheries, preservation of the marine environment—among others—the creation of an international marine court "as the principal judicial organ of the International Ocean Space Institutions."[5] The court was competent to deal with all disputes arising in the ocean space.

Other proposals also envisaged the creation of a new tribunal. Canada, for instance, proposed that a tribunal "composed of a small body of legal (or perhaps technical) experts" should be part of the structure of an international machinery to give effect to the seabed regime.[6] In its proposals "for elements of a convention,"[7] the United Kingdom, after stating that "existing arrangements, including the International Court of Justice, might have a role to play" in the context of settlements of disputes between States Parties or between States Parties and the Authority, "it could also be agreed that the Convention should provide for a Tribunal to which parties to a dispute could have recourse in the absence of a solution by other methods." The Tribunal "would have to be entirely independent."

The Draft Statute for an international seabed authority presented by Tanzania[8] stated that disputes "in regard to the meaning or the scope of a licence shall be settled by negotiation, mediation or arbitration" and that any other disputes "regarding the exploration or exploitation of the area and its resources . . . shall be submitted if negotiation, mediation or arbitration fail, to the International Court of Justice." In commenting on this proposal, Professor Sohn observed that "many disputes will arise not between States but between a private person and that authority." The International Court of Justice, under the existing limitations in its Statute, cannot be conferred jurisdiction over such disputes.[9]

Professor Sohn's conclusion was that "without drastic changes in its procedure, functions and jurisdiction," the International

Court of Justice could not deal with most of the disputes relating to the operation of the seabed regime and that "a special tribunal could be needed for that purpose."[10]

The idea of establishing a tribunal with compulsory jurisdiction, to be established in an Annex to the Convention, to deal with law of the sea disputes in general was presented by the United States on the last day of the last session of the Seabed Committee in August 1973.[11] Thus, the United States expanded its 1970 proposal, which only related to seabed disputes. The new proposal consisted of nine articles in a document entitled "Draft Articles for a Chapter on the Settlement of Disputes." It contains the initial steps of some of the notions later developed in Part XV and Annex VI of the United Nations Convention on the Law of the Sea.

For example, the U.S. Draft provided that the tribunal could make binding interim orders in cases that have been submitted to arbitration; that the owner or operator of any vessel detained by any State would have the right to bring the question of the detention of the vessel before the tribunal in order to secure its prompt release in accordance with the provisions of the Convention, without prejudice to the merits of any case against the vessel; that the members of the tribunal would be of recognized competence in law of the sea matters; that in disputes involving technical questions the tribunal would be assisted by technical advisors sitting with it but without the right to vote; that decisions of the Tribunal would be binding upon the parties; that if the parties to a dispute had agreed in any general, regional, or special agreement to resort to arbitration, any party to the dispute should be entitled to refer it to arbitration in accordance with the agreement, in place of submitting the dispute to the tribunal.

As Professor Sohn explains,

[A]t the last stage of the preparations for the Law of the Sea Conference in 1973, several proposals were made dealing in a piecemeal fashion with disputes that might arise in various fields, and the United States became concerned that chaos might result from this multiplicity of proposals.

This prompted the United States to present its proposal practically when the Seabed Committee had finished its work.[12]

The United States' 1973 draft served as a basis for informal consultations in the latter part of the Caracas session in 1974. This marked the beginning of the long negotiating process on the subject of settlement of disputes in the Third United Nations Conference on the Law of the Sea.

III. The Growth of International Adjudication

In his well-known book "The Prospects of International Adjudication," published almost forty years ago, Wilfred Jenks envisaged the development of international adjudication. He stated that

[T]here will be . . . variations in the forms of adjudication which correspond more closely to the needs of successive phases of development. As international life becomes more complex, the relative importance of specialized tribunals and procedures may be expected to grow. . . .[13]

Human Rights regional tribunals, the International Tribunal for the Law of the Sea and the International Criminal Tribunals for the Former Yugoslavia and for Rwanda are examples of the developments foreseen by Jenks. Also, the International Criminal Court, created by the Rome Convention, which may be soon in place, will be the first permanent criminal court.

Quite recently, in analyzing the question of multiplication of international legal institutions, Judge Higgins mentions, among the main features of the present state of affairs, which reflects on international litigation, the vast corpus of norms of international law, the subject matters expanding indefinitely, and the effects of globalization that "have encouraged the realization that at least in certain . . . areas of international law, actors other than States have access to the legal procedures."[14] As a result,

[W]e have today a certain decentralization of some of the topics with which the ICJ *can* in principle deal to new highly specialized bodies, whose members are experts in a subject matter which becomes even more complex, which are open to non-State actors, and which can respond rapidly. I think this is an inevitable consequence of the busy and complex world in which we live and is not a cause of regret.

Should international lawyers see the growth of international adjudication as a step backwards in the development of international law?

In a lecture on "The Shortcomings of International Law" delivered at the University of Oxford in 1924, Brierly reminded us that "[L]aw, after all, is only a means to an end, and that end is to assist in solving the problems of the society in and for which it exists."[15] In an address delivered twenty years later, he referred to international customary law as consisting of rather vague general principles, and to the fact that the application of these generalities to facts had not been worked out as the application of English common law had been worked out by many generations of judges. He stated: "That is a defect which will, one may hope, be gradually reduced in importance by the growth of international adjudication to which every well-wisher of international law must look forward." And later, in the same address, affirming that the methods of mass production could not be applied to the growth of law, he observed: "Its growth can be stimulated, in fact if it is to develop beyond a very rudimentary stage it needs to be stimulated, by the purposive creation of specialized institutions such as courts through which it can perform its functions. . . ."[16]

Members of the specialized international tribunals should be conscious that the unity of international law might be at risk. On this point, I can conclude by endorsing the words of Jonathan Charney, one of the authors who has studied this subject extensively. He stated that:

[T]he coherence of international law does not appear to be significantly threatened by the increased number of international tribunals. However, all participants in the system need to be sensitive to the risks inherent in the decentralized system and be careful to avoid actions that might pull the system apart.[17]

Notes

[1] Alexander Yankov, "The International Tribunal for the Law of the Sea: Its place within the Dispute Settlement System of the UN Law of the Sea Convention," 37 *The Indian Journal of International Law* (July–September 1997): 365.

[2] *The Law of the United Nations* (New York, 1950), 477.

[3] Goodrich, Hambro, and Simons, *Charter of the United Nations, Commentary and documents*, 3d ed., rev. (Columbia University Press, 1969), 558-559.

[4] UN Doc. A/AC.138/25 (1970), GAOR, XXV, Supp.21 (A/8021), 130–176.

[5] UN Doc. A/AC.138/53 (1971), GAOR, XXV, Supp.21 (A/8021), 105–193.

[6] UN Doc. A/AC.138/59 (1971), GAOR, XXV, Supp.21 (A/8021), 205–225.

[7] UN Doc. A/AC.138/46 (1971), GAOR, XXV, Supp.21 (A/8021), 83–91.

[8] UN Doc. A/AC.138/33 GAUR, etc.

[9] Louis B. Sohn, *A Tribunal for the Sea-Bed or the Oceans*, Zeitschrift für ausländisches öffentliches Recht und Völkerrecht (1972), 258.

[10] Id., 263. Professor Sohn also considered desirable, since the tribunal would apply relevant principles of international law, to arrange, under Article 96 of the United Nations Charter, for an authorization enabling the tribunal to request advisory opinions from the International Court of Justice on any question of international law.

[11] UN Doc. A/AC.138/97 (1973), GAOR, XXVIII, Supp.21 (A/9021), Vol. II, 22–23.

[12] Louis B. Sohn, *Problems of Dispute Settlement in Law of the Sea: Conference Outcomes and Problems of Implementation*. Proceedings Law of the Sea Institute Tenth Annual Conference (June 22–25, 1976) Kingston, Rhode Island, 224.

[13] C. Wilfred Jenks, *The Prospects of International Adjudication* (1964), 775.

[14] Judge Rosalyn Higgins, "Respecting Sovereign States and Running a Tight Courtroom," 50 *International and Comparative Law Quarterly* (2001): 121.

[15] *The Basis of Obligation in International Law and Other Papers* by the late James Leslie Brierly, selected and edited by Sir H. Lauterpacht and C. H. M. Waldock (Oxford University Press, 1958), 72.

[16] Id., 312.

[17] Jonathan I. Charney, "The Impact on the International Legal System of the Growth of International Courts and Tribunals," 31 *New York Journal of International Law and Politics* (1999): 707–708.

A Brief History of the Post Conference Development of the Tribunal as an International Judicial Body

Gritakumar E. Chitty[*]

Mr. President, Professor John Norton Moore, Secretary-General Nandan, Moderator—and former President of the Tribunal—Judge Mensah, Judges of the Tribunal, Professor Nordquist, Ladies and Gentlemen.

Introduction

When dealing with the history of the Tribunal, it is difficult to decide where to start. Would it be better to start with UNCLOS I—the 1958 Convention and its optional protocol—or with the first session of the Third United Nations Conference?

Since Judge Caminos has covered the work of the Seabed Committee, I will start by pointing to the Declaration of Principles Governing the Seabed and the Ocean Floor and the Subsoil thereof, beyond the Limits of National Jurisdiction, adopted by the General Assembly of the United Nations at its 1933rd Plenary session on December 17, 1970. In the Declaration we find the first crystallization of approach to the resolution of disputes relating to the Seabed. The declaration provided that:

> [P]arties to any dispute relating to activities in the area and its resources shall resolve such disputes by the measures mentioned in Article 33 of the Charter of the United Nations and such procedures for settling disputes as may be agreed upon in the international régime to be established.[1]

---

[*] First Registrar of the International Tribunal for the Law of the Sea. The author wishes to thank Mr. Robert H. van Dijk, Legal Officer of the International Tribunal for the Law of the Sea, for his valuable assistance.

M.H. Nordquist and J.N. Moore (eds.),
Current Marine Environmental Issues and the International Tribunal for the Law of the Sea, 41–51.
© 2001 *Kluwer Law International. Printed in the Netherlands.*

THE UNITED STATES PROPOSAL

The initiative of the United States delegation to set up a group of more than thirty-five delegations, which held consultations towards the end of the 1974 Caracas session of the Third United Nations Conference on the Law of the Sea, is perhaps the starting point in the framework of the Conference.[2] The group had before it the proposal of the United States that had been submitted to the Seabed Committee in 1973,[3] to which Judge Caminos has already referred. The group's meeting was followed by the meeting in Montreal to which Professor Moore referred.

Other proposals also on the table, *inter alia*, were made by Malta, Japan, Canada, and Singapore. The U.S. proposal, however, stood out by its comprehensive nature. It consisted of nine articles. The first draft article enumerated the means for peaceful settlement listed in article 33 of the Charter—following the declaration of principles—and later leaving its trace in article 279 of the Convention.

Article 2 of the proposal foresaw that disputes falling under compulsory dispute settlement procedures would be submitted to the new, to-be-established Tribunal. The draft also provided for jurisdiction of the Tribunal in cases requiring urgent action including requests for prompt release of vessels by entities other than States Parties to the Convention.

THE NEGOTIATIONS

The result of the informal deliberations was a working paper on the settlement of disputes submitted to the Conference at the closing meeting of its second session in 1974.[4] The working paper included a draft Statute on the Tribunal in its Annex. Informal deliberations continued during the third session of the Conference in 1975, and after this session, the President of the Conference submitted an informal single negotiating text to the Conference. His text was based to a considerable extent on the work of the informal group. Comprehensive and detailed proposals were presented, including a more elaborate Statute of the Law of the Sea Tribunal. This provided the model for later drafts of the Statute.

The informal plenary of the Conference acted as the main committee on dispute settlement with its chairman, the President of the Conference, who formulated many of the draft articles. At the same time that the informal plenary negotiations were being held on a maritime court with general jurisdiction, negotiations were held in the First Committee of the Conference on a separate Seabed Tribunal with jurisdiction over the exploration and exploitation of the International Seabed Area. At the fifth session, the two concepts were merged with the approval of the proposal to establish a Seabed Disputes Chamber within the Tribunal.[5]

This merger severed the organic link that had been envisaged between the Seabed Tribunal and the International Seabed Authority. Thus, the new, to-be-established Tribunal was to be a completely independent body. The Tribunal's general procedures and powers would be along the lines of the Statute of the International Court of Justice and other international judicial tribunals, while taking into account the specific requirements of the Tribunal.[6]

ADOPTION OF THE CONVENTION

Finally, after years of negotiations, the United Nations Convention on the Law of the Sea was opened for signature on December 10, 1982. The Convention was unique in that it provided for the first time a comprehensive system for the settlement of disputes relating to uses of ocean space. The dispute settlement system was also flexible by providing for different fora suiting the international community's Cold War needs. Importantly, this dispute settlement system was made an integral part of the Convention and not an optional protocol to the Convention, thus guaranteeing the integrity of the Convention. Central to the dispute settlement regime was the establishment of the International Tribunal for the Law of the Sea.

The process of negotiations leading up to the final text of the Convention and especially the dispute settlement provisions has been heavily commented upon, particularly in the *Virginia Commentary*. However, the commentators omitted a twelve-year period of gestation between the adoption of the Convention and the inauguration of the Tribunal. This was the period in which the Preparatory Commission for the International Seabed Authority and the International Tribunal for the Law of the Sea carried out its work.

THE PREPARATORY COMMISSION FOR THE INTERNATIONAL SEABED AUTHORITY AND FOR THE INTERNATIONAL TRIBUNAL FOR THE LAW OF THE SEA

When adopting the Convention, the Third Conference on the Law of the Sea adopted Resolution I as part of its Final Act, which established the Preparatory Commission for the International Seabed Authority and the International Tribunal for the Law of the Sea.

The Preparatory Commission was first convened in 1983, and it established four special commissions at its first session.[7] Special Commission 4 was charged with preparing recommendations regarding practical arrangements for the establishment of the International Tribunal for the Law of the Sea. The Commission identified an all-encompassing list of items to be addressed to ensure that the Tribunal would be able to start functioning at the earliest possible date.[8] Throughout its existence, the work of Special Commission 4 was based on working papers presented by the Secretariat and of redrafts thereof taking into account the ongoing deliberations.

By the end of its existence, Special Commission 4 had formulated a series of work products comprising: a Draft Protocol on the Privileges and Immunities of the Tribunal; a Draft Headquarters Agreement to be entered into between the Tribunal and the host country, Germany; Draft Rules of the Tribunal establishing the procedural requirements for it to function; a Draft Relationship Agreement between the Tribunal and the United

Nations; and a comprehensive set of documentation regarding the administrative arrangements, structure, and financial implications of the establishment of the Tribunal.[9]

The Tribunal thus came into being equipped with the basic materials to commence its work and enter into its functions expeditiously. The Tribunal had the benefit of the legal instruments, administrative and institutional arrangements, and budgetary calculations that had been the subject of close scrutiny and evaluation by more than 100 States participating in the Preparatory Commission. This intergovernmental review carried out in advance provided an exceptional assessment of the materials needed for the new institution to commence its functions early, effectively, and on the basis of general intergovernmental support.

It is interesting now, four years after the Tribunal was inaugurated, to look back and see what has been achieved from the perspective of what was done by the Preparatory Commission.

On matters of Judicial Procedure, the Preparatory Commission formulated the Draft Rules of the Tribunal. It formulated a comprehensive set of provisions, including those concerning the composition of the Tribunal and its chambers, the working languages, the internal judicial practice, and the question of access by States not parties to the Convention.

These Draft Rules of the Tribunal greatly facilitated the start-up of the Tribunal. In order to be able to deal with a case if submitted before formally adopting its Rules, the Tribunal decided to apply the Preparatory Commission's draft Rules on a provisional basis.[10] In addition, the Tribunal's discussions of its Rules took place on the basis of the Preparatory Commission draft, which in turn was based on the well-established model of the International Court of Justice and other international judicial institutions, taking into account that there had to be rules for dealing with matters for which there was no precedent, such as for cases of prompt release of vessels and crews.

The Preparatory Commission also formulated draft international agreements. For example, when the Tribunal started functioning, it had before it a Draft Headquarters Agreement and a Draft Protocol on the Privileges and Immunities of the Tribunal. The Draft Agreement was the result of detailed deliberations over several sessions with the active participation of the host country delegation. In the negotiations between the Tribunal and the host country, it was this Draft Headquarters Agreement provided by the Preparatory Commission that served as the basis for the negotiations.

When the Tribunal took up its seat in Hamburg, direct negotiations between the Tribunal and the host country on the Headquarters Agreement still had to commence. Until such time that a Headquarters Agreement would be agreed upon, the Federal Republic of Germany enacted a bill to provide for the essential Privileges and Immunities of the new Institution, its Judiciary, and Registry upon its commencing functioning in Germany.

The Preparatory Commission had also prepared a draft agreement on Cooperation and Relationship between the United Nations and the Tribunal. This draft enabled the Tribunal to formalize its relationship with the United Nations very expeditiously. As early as 1997, the Agreement was signed by Secretary-General Kofi Annan on behalf of the United Nations. The arrangements with the United Nations, *inter alia*, enable the Tribunal to use the United Nations Laissez-Passer. On December 17, 1997, the Tribunal was given observer status at the General Assembly of the United Nations, and on September 8, 1998, that arrangement entered into force. Interestingly, in these arrangements, the Relationship Agreement does not render the Tribunal a Specialized Agency of the United Nations. This kind of relationship was not regarded as appropriate in the case of the Tribunal. A relationship arrangement between the Tribunal and the International Seabed Authority has yet to be worked out.

On administrative arrangements for the Tribunal, the Preparatory Commission made recommendations concerning the administrative structure and the financial implications of the constitution of the Tribunal, such as the recommendations concerning the initial phasing-in of the Tribunal. Draft Financial Rules and Staff Regulations were discussed, but no solutions were provided. Finally, there were recommendations concerning the location of the headquarters and the building requirements.

The twelve years of work of Special Commission 4 were concluded, as was the work of the whole Preparatory Commission, with the imminent entry into force of the Convention thirty days after the receipt of the sixtieth instrument of ratification.[11]

The Preparatory Commission recommended that a Meeting of States Parties to the Convention be convened as soon as possible after the date of entry into force of the Convention.

Almost no industrialized countries had ratified the Convention at that time. To achieve as wide a participation in the Convention as possible, the Preparatory Commission proposed to defer the first election of Members of the Tribunal, which, pursuant to article 4 of the Statute, was to be held within six months after the entry into force of the Convention. The deferral was to give States Parties in the process of ratifying the Convention the opportunity to nominate candidates and to participate in the election of judges that was scheduled for August 1, 1996, and also to secure the required representation of the geographical regions in the election of judges.

On November 21, 1994, the States Parties first convened and decided along the lines proposed by the Preparatory Commission.

The Preparatory Commission also recommended that the first Meeting of States Parties request the Secretary-General to make preparations of a practical nature for the organization of the Tribunal.[12] Acting on the recommendation, the final process of planning for the establishment of the Tribunal and the construction of the headquarters got under way.[13]

The Preparatory Commission also provided the first Meeting of States Parties with a provisional agenda, draft rules of procedure for the Meeting, and a review of the possible geographic distribution of the seats of the Tribunal after taking into account the need for geographic distribution.

I have tried to identify some of the results of the work of the Preparatory Commission, but it left two important issues pending that it could not resolve. Most importantly, the question was left open as to whether the Tribunal would have six official working languages or less than that, and if so, what treatment should be accorded to the other languages. The second issue was that the Statute of the Tribunal provides for judges who may not be occupied on a year-round basis. An arrangement for the phasing-in of the Tribunal and adjustment to the workload of the Tribunal had to be worked out. In both cases, the Meeting of States Parties found solutions.

INAUGURATION

On August 1, 1996, the second Meeting of States Parties elected twenty-one judges, and 100 States Parties participated in that election. Each judge required a two-thirds majority. The elected judges met for the first time in Hamburg on October 1, 1996, at its temporary headquarters located in the center in Hamburg. During this first session, the Tribunal was inaugurated in the splendid ornamental halls of Hamburg's City Hall.

When the establishment of the Tribunal was contemplated at the Conference, it had been more than fifty years since a totally new world court had been created. The constitution of the Tribunal, however, followed shortly after the constitution of the International Criminal Tribunal for the Former Yugoslavia. Not surprisingly, the initial meetings of the Tribunal closely followed the pattern set by the Yugoslav Tribunal. In both instances the Secretary-General of the United Nations was represented by the Legal Counsel of the United Nations who presided over the first meetings, until a President had been elected.

Four organizational sessions were held during the first year of the Tribunal's existence. One of the most important matters discussed at these sessions was the rules of procedure that the Tribunal would apply when a case was submitted to it. Within two weeks after the Tribunal had adopted its Rules, it received its first case concerning the prompt release of the vessel M/V "Saiga." Six other cases have followed and the Secretary-General of the United

Nations has expressed his great satisfaction on the work that has been carried out by the Tribunal.[14]

CONCLUSION

The establishment of the Tribunal is a step in a gradually maturing effort to responsibly and justly administer and preserve the most important domain of the globe—its oceans. The Tribunal exists to settle disputes relating to the use of ocean space in a rational, orderly, and authoritative way and to protect the unity of the Convention. The Conference was aware of the need to protect its delicate, carefully negotiated compromises and, therefore, created a forum with truly global representation to do so.

The Tribunal is a new institution with traditional form, consisting of its twenty-one member judiciary and an independent executive arm, the Registry or secretariat of this institution. It combines tried and tested rules with the unique jurisdictional powers given to it by the Convention.

To understand the mandate of the Tribunal, it is crucial to understand the geopolitical relations at the time of the Conference, the calls for a modern effective court that would reflect the interests of the world community, and to keep in mind that the Tribunal is the result of the merger of two different concepts—that of a forum for the resolution of traditional law of the sea disputes and a forum for a whole new range of disputes that would be submitted to it.

Over the past four and a half years, the Tribunal has proven the effectiveness of the dispute settlement system set up by the Convention. Interesting in this respect is the decision of parties in two instances to agree to adjudication by the Tribunal after arbitral proceedings under Annex VII of the Convention had commenced.

Notes

[1] GA Resolution 2749 (XXV), para. 15. Article 33 of the Charter provides that: *"(1). The parties to any dispute, the continuance of which is likely to endanger the maintenance of international peace and security, shall, first of all, seek a solution by negotiation, enquiry, mediation, conciliation, arbitration, judicial settlement, resort to regional agencies or arrangements, or other peaceful means of their own choice. (2). The Security Council shall, when it deems necessary, call upon the parties to settle their dispute by such means."*

[2] See A. O. Adede, "The System for Settlement of Disputes under the United Nations Convention on the Law of the Sea" (The Netherlands: Martinus Nijhoff Publishers, 1987), 13.

[3] A/AC.138/97.

[4] S. Rosenne, "UNCLOS III—The Montreux (Riphagen) Compromise," in A. Bos and H. Siblesz, "Realism in Law-Making," Essays on international law in honour of Wellem Riphagen (The Netherlands: Martinus Nijhoff Publishers, 1986), 171.

[5] See Doc. A/CONF.62/WP.9/Rev.2, in "United Nations Conferences on the Law of the Sea," Official Records, Third Conference, vols. 5-7, 1976-1977, (New York: William S. Hein & Co., Inc., 2000), 144, 151.

[6] M. H. Nordquist, ed., *United Nations Convention on the Law of the Sea 1982, A Commentary*, Vol. V, Center for Oceans Law and Policy, University of Virginia (The Netherlands: Martinus Nijhoff Publishers, 1989), 336. (Hereafter referred to as the *Virginia Commentary*.)

[7] The Preparatory Commission was in accordance with paragraph 1 of Resolution I, to be convened no sooner than sixty days and no later than ninety days after the signature of or accession to the Convention by fifty States. This requirement was fulfilled on the first day of the opening for signature, on which 119 States signed the Convention.

[8] See LOS/PCN/SCN.4/WP.1 reproduced in Volume II of the Report of the Preparatory Commission, LOS/PCN/152.

[9] The work of the Preparatory Commission is fully documented in LOS/PCN/152, which details the work of the Commission and the result of that work.

[10] See Press Release ITLOS/Press 5.

[11] On November 14, 1993, Guyana was the sixtieth State to ratify the Convention thereby triggering the entering into force of the Convention twelve months later. See article 308 of the Convention.

[12] GA Resolution 49/28, operative para. 11.

[13] See SPLOS/3, Report of first meeting (November 21-22, 1994); Report of second meeting (May 15-19, 1995); SPLOS/5, Report of third meeting (November 27-December 1, 1995); SPLOS/8, Report of fourth meeting (March 4-8, 1996); SPLOS/14, Report of fifth meeting (July 24-August 2, 1996);

SPLOS/20, Report of the sixth meeting (March 10-14, 1997); SPLOS/24, Report of seventh meeting (May 19/23, 1997).
[14] See Press Release ITLOS/Press36/Add.1.

THE INTERNATIONAL TRIBUNAL FOR THE LAW OF THE SEA AND THE DIFFICULTIES ENCOUNTERED DURING THE INITIAL PHASE OF ITS ESTABLISHMENT[1]

*Mohamed Mouldi Marsit**

It would be difficult to imagine that the International Tribunal for the Law of the Sea could commence its activity without experiencing difficulties of various natures. What were the difficulties encountered?

START-UP DIFFICULTIES

Composition

The Tribunal is composed in accordance with the principle of geographical distribution. The difficulty related to the application of such a principle is the responsibility of State Parties and not that of the Tribunal. However, the Tribunal cannot ignore this question when taking various steps, such as selection of members of the Tribunal chambers, committees, and working groups. The same principle is to be taken into consideration when staff members of the Tribunal are to be appointed, etc.

Scatter of Members of the Tribunal

Judges of the Tribunal are not obliged to reside in Hamburg. Due to the remuneration they receive, judges cannot *de facto* reside in Hamburg. Therefore, they are bound to undertake travel, usually on short notice, which makes the situation difficult for the Registry and the judges themselves.

---

* Judge, International Tribunal for the Law of the Sea.

M.H. Nordquist and J.N. Moore (eds.),
Current Marine Environmental Issues and the International Tribunal for the Law of the Sea, 53–55.
© 2001 *Kluwer Law International. Printed in the Netherlands.*

DIFFICULTIES RELATED TO THE APPLICATION AND THE INTERPRETATION OF TEXTS RESULTING FROM A COMPROMISE

Difficulties emanating from the Convention are, by far, more important. It is difficult to apply a text of compromise.

However, Members of the Tribunal who are very familiar with the Third Conference and its specific methods run the risk of encountering other forms of difficulties, not to mention those who are not familiar with the new law of the sea, its techniques, and its innovative spirit. Some learned commentators have already underscored this very peculiar situation. Other commentators must be careful before criticizing the Tribunal and the way it is facing problems in applying the Convention.

CONCLUSION

The difficulties encountered by the Tribunal during this initial phase of its establishment are not limited to these few problems. The situation of nationals of developing countries also needs to be taken into consideration.

Notes

[1] This is a short summary based on the more extensive text delivered in French at the conference.

COMMENTS ON THE ORIGINS AND PURPOSES OF ITLOS

Gudmundur Eiriksson[*]

Following the comments of Registrar Chitty and Judge Caminos on the origins of the Tribunal for the Law of the Sea, I have chosen to deal with some aspects of the negotiating process, which was developed at the Law of the Sea Conference. A study of the black-letter law and a recounting of the various proposals and counter-proposals cannot give the flavor of the negotiations. In my view, it is from the spirit that guided the negotiations that we can learn the most lessons for the future.

I find such a presentation timely, since I have recently come to feel that the work of the Law of the Sea Conference is not being fully appreciated in certain international circles.

Although I will be arguing today that the law of the sea negotiations were characterized by a significant degree of community interest, I don't turn a blind eye to other motivations of States involved in the process: national interests and what could often be seen as selfish economic interests. I would appear naïve if I did. I maintain, nonetheless, that had these interests not been embroidered in a general fabric of equity and accommodation of the entire international community, the end result of the Law of the Sea Conference would not have been the success it has proven to be. The law of the sea would be far different today. In particular, the Tribunal would be a far different and less forward-looking institution than it is, if, indeed, it would have been established at all.

We must remember that the Convention is unique among the major lawmaking treaties in providing for a comprehensive regime for the settlement of disputes. In this respect, it represents a major departure from the trends of the 1970s and 1980s against third party dispute settlement. In fact, it was a miracle of sorts that such a system was adopted in the climate of the times. And I think all of

---

[*] Judge, International Tribunal for the Law of the Sea.

M.H. Nordquist and J.N. Moore (eds.),
Current Marine Environmental Issues and the International Tribunal for the Law of the Sea, 57–60.
© 2001 *Kluwer Law International. Printed in the Netherlands.*

these thoughts must be put in the context of the development of international law as a whole.

At the time when the Law of the Sea Conference was starting its work, I think it is fair to say that in the developing world there was a general disenchantment with international law as a discipline. One strongly held view was that international law was the tool of the European countries, dominated in its formation and implementation by colonial and big power interests. These sentiments gave rise to efforts to establish new international law modalities, certainly much more political and (at least I would argue) much less "legal," such as the concept of the new international economic order. Then along came the law of the sea negotiations, where the traditional international law subjects needed to be addressed from new perspectives, with new concepts emerging that had to be accommodated within the existing legal order.

These sentiments were perhaps most pronounced in the field of the settlement of disputes. The attitude in the developing world towards international law had been crystallized in an attitude of disapproval of the work of the International Court of Justice and the idea of recourse to international adjudication as a whole.

Quite fortuitously, the most influential molders of thought in international law were drawn to the law of the sea process both from developing countries as well as industrialized nations. While the law of the sea negotiations were a preeminently political process involving the sovereign rights and vital interests of States, in most cases the leaders of the negotiations were experts in international law. In many cases, delegations included prominent professors of international law. Indeed, I venture to say that there has never been such a gathering of leading international lawyers in international negotiations. Some of them are here today, and, in fact, as I think about these matters, I am recalling those who are no longer with us. In my case, I served under the leadership of: Hans Anderson, the leader of the Icelandic delegation; Andres Aguilar, Chairman of the Second Committee; Shirley Amerasinghe, first President of the Conference; and Under-Secretaries-General Stavropoulous and Zuleta.

The experts assembled at the Conference were able to find common ground in the search for innovative solutions to international law questions. I am convinced that the success of their attempts inspired confidence in the Third World in the very discipline of international law. As I mentioned earlier, a firm indication of this was the inclusion in the Convention of the comprehensive system for the settlement of disputes, including the Law of the Sea Tribunal.

I can only agree with Judge Caminos when he spoke so convincingly in support of the new firmament of international courts of which the Tribunal is a part. I particularly endorse the comments he cited of Judge Rosalyn Higgens. My point of departure is quite simple: the more opportunities there are available for the peaceful settlement of disputes, the better. And I would have thought that all international lawyers would share this view. Certainly, in the case of the Law of the Sea Tribunal, at least, the contrary view represents a lack of appreciation of those great international lawyers I have mentioned who set up this institution.

But I go even one step further. As a continuation of what I was saying before about the impact of the law of the sea on the development of international law, I am prepared to argue that the process I described earlier—which Judge Caminos and Registrar Chitty developed in more detail and which led to the establishment of the Tribunal—has resulted in an environment strengthening the classical regime of the settlement of disputes, not vice versa.

We see signs everywhere of growing respect for the rule of law in international relations. Specifically in the field of the peaceful settlement of disputes, we have seen increased interest in and resort to the International Court of Justice and enhanced institutional arrangements for existing international human rights courts. It is in this environment that we witness the establishment of new international courts in the fields of criminal law and trade law.

To me, this current state of affairs is the lasting legacy of the law of the sea negotiations. I have come to believe that in the end what characterized the law of the sea negotiations and the subsequent and still ongoing implementation of the principles elaborated was a recognition that we were not throwing up our tents for one night only, as we say in my country, but rather were laying the groundwork for a legal regime to last for the foreseeable future.

I hope it is clear to all serious observers of the work of the Law of the Sea Tribunal that we are carrying on in that spirit.

PANEL II

Roundtable Comments on
ITLOS Procedures and Practices

DELIBERATIONS, JUDGMENTS, AND SEPARATE OPINIONS IN THE PRACTICE OF THE INTERNATIONAL TRIBUNAL FOR THE LAW OF THE SEA

*David H. Anderson**

INTRODUCTION

This paper examines the internal judicial practice of the Tribunal in handling its first six judgments and reasoned orders.[1] The practice in deliberating, in drafting its judgments and orders, and in permitting the delivery of separate opinions is based upon the *Resolution on Internal Judicial Practice of the Tribunal* adopted in October 1997.[2] While the terms of the Resolution are similar in many respects to those of the Resolution of the International Court of Justice,[3] there are some differences, as mentioned below.

The judgments and orders were delivered in the period of three years between December 1997 and December 2000. All six applications succeeded substantially, although not in the precise terms requested. Five of the six applications were made in urgent proceedings: three judgments upon applications for the prompt release of vessels and crews under article 292 of the Convention[4] and two orders issued in response to applications for provisional measures under article 290.[5] All five of these urgent cases were dealt with in short periods of time. In the three prompt release cases, the period was as little as twenty-two days from start to finish. The two applications for provisional measures were dealt with in twenty-nine days and fifty-eight days. All this meant Herculean efforts by the judges and the entire staff of the Registry. The remaining judgment was regarding the merits of the Saiga (No. 2) Case, where the Tribunal dealt with a large number of separate issues after full argument and deliberations. Even so, the

---

* Judge, International Tribunal for the Law of the Sea.

M.H. Nordquist and J.N. Moore (eds.),
Current Marine Environmental Issues and the International Tribunal for the Law of the Sea, 63–73.
© 2001 *Kluwer Law International. Printed in the Netherlands.*

entire proceedings lasted only eighteen months. This was the best test of the Tribunal's procedures and practice.

DELIBERATIONS

The Tribunal begins its deliberations on a case at an earlier stage in the proceedings than does the Court. In accordance with article 3 of its Resolution, the Tribunal deliberates once the written pleadings have been completed. This is in order to ascertain collectively which issues have been fully covered and those which have not. The early start to deliberations has the incidental advantage of assisting the judges to appreciate together, in something often approaching a common learning process, the scope and nature of the issues in a case.

After a discussion, an agreed paper is drawn up for use by the President. Needless to say, in such discussions opinions vary, and there is often a good deal of give and take over what is included in the paper. This process enables the President to inform the Agents in advance of the opening of the oral proceedings of two matters: first, issues on which the Tribunal considers it has received sufficient information; and secondly, issues on which it would like more information or questions to which it would like answers. So far, each paper has been treated as an informal indication of the Tribunal's initial reactions. It has not always been specified to whom the questions were directed. In responding to questions, Counsel have sometimes referred to the informal paper and sometimes not. Occasionally, a question has passed unanswered by both parties. In the future, a higher status could be given to the paper. For example, it could become a document in the case, part of the record.

In practice, to date all questions have been posed by the President in the name of the Tribunal as a whole. In a body as large as the Tribunal, restraint is called for on the part of individual judges. No individual questions have been posed. While this demonstrates a collegial approach, there may still be a need in a future case for individual questions. For example, if a judge has a different approach from the majority or considers as relevant some different aspects from those picked out by his colleagues, it may be necessary in the future for an individual question to be posed in order for that judge to reach a decision upon how to vote or how to formulate a separate opinion.

A second difference with the practice in The Hague Court concerns the method of exchanging views. The procedure followed by the Tribunal for deliberations is based primarily upon an informed oral debate, possibly supplemented by written notes by individual judges, whereas the practice in The Hague is to concentrate to a greater extent upon written notes, except in urgent cases such as interim measures of protection.

For an oral debate to be effective in a body as large as twenty-one, careful preparation and strong chairmanship are required. There has to be agreement at an early stage upon the list of questions that the Tribunal is to answer in order to dispose of the case and a structured debate in which the questions are taken in a logical order. For instance, jurisdiction should be considered first and then admissibility, before proceeding to the merits. This progression can be seen in the judgment on the merits of the Saiga (No. 2) case and, for the first time in a prompt release case, in the decision in the Monte Confurco case. There may well be several issues under each heading, especially the merits. There should be a full *tour de table*, so that all points of view, including doubts and hesitations as well as strongly held opinions, are heard before any tentative conclusions are reached. There should be the opportunity for a confrontation of opposing views across the table in order to enable a majority view to emerge and decisions to be reached.

Written notes have the advantage of requiring each judge to address all the issues for decision, to do so in some depth, and to share thoughts with all colleagues. However, the writing of the notes may have the disadvantage in some instances of entrenching positions or closing minds to new thinking ahead of the oral debates.[6]

The Tribunal's Resolution on Internal Judicial Practice was designed to foster a spirit of collegiality in deliberating.

Collegiality is a valuable commodity in a body as large as twenty-one. The Tribunal has not gone as far as the Appellate Body under the Dispute Settlement Procedures of the World Trade Organization and inscribed the principle of collegiality into the Rules or its Resolution.[7] Nonetheless, the Resolution does encourage collegiality. For example, an interchange between the majority opinion and other tentative opinions held by individual judges is encouraged, with a view to reaching the broadest possible consensus or majority. The Drafting Committee is mandated by article 7(2) to "*prepare a draft judgment which not only states the opinion of the majority as it appears then to exist but which may also attract wider support within the Tribunal.*" The members of the Tribunal benefit from a warm collegial spirit.

A further point to note is that the standard procedures for deliberations are modified in article 11(2) for urgent cases. There just is not sufficient time to prepare written notes upon the issues for decision, especially when there is a need for translation before any discussion. Thus, the normal procedures specified in the Resolution have been applicable in practice only in the merits phase of the Saiga (No. 2) Case. In the other five decisions, there was urgency, which meant telescoping the time scales for all phases. This factor has meant that the initial debates, the indicative voting, the initial drafting, the oral deliberations on the draft, its revision, the interplay between the majority and the minority, and the preparation of separate opinions have all been compressed. It is important to ensure, even in urgent cases, that sufficient time is available for a thorough debate on the issues for decision and also on the reasoning to be given in the judgment or order.

A final difference with The Hague: for deliberations, a circular table is better than a rectangular one. The excellent book about the Court shows the evolution from the rectangular table of 1946 in the Ferdinand Bol Room to the circular table in the New Wing.[8] Each judge should be able not only to hear the others but also to see them. Each judge needs to be able to catch the eye of the President without having to compete with better-placed colleagues and without having to stretch forward. A large square room is best.

Plenty of space is needed at or under the table for the files of each judge. Architects please note!

JUDGMENTS AND ORDERS

At the end of the deliberations on the issues for decision, the President calls for votes on the agreed list of issues. These are provisional votes, usually by a show of hands. Once the provisional votes have been cast, attention turns to the drafting of the judgment. The general style followed by the Tribunal is that followed by the Court. As in The Hague, judgments are drafted by Drafting Committees, not a single juge rapporteur. Given the greater size of the Tribunal, our Resolution provides in article 6 that Drafting Committees have five members, which is often the total membership of an *ad hoc* arbitral tribunal. The members have been nominated by the President (assuming he has been in the majority) on a representative basis. The primary consideration should be to represent the mainstream of opinion on the issues for determination rather than to achieve regional balance. In practice, there have even been six members in order to ensure consistency between the two working languages by including one or two of the Francophone judges.

In appropriate cases, the decision of the Tribunal has been given in both English and French.[9] An early decision in principle has been taken, and the two versions have been drafted together. While this practice may give rise to questions of linguistic concordance,[10] it is the case that treaties (including the Convention on the Law of the Sea) are routinely concluded in six languages at the United Nations. The Vienna Convention on the Law of Treaties contains rules on the interpretation of plurilingual treaties that may provide guidance should discrepancies be detected in bilingual judgments. In urgent cases, the task of the Drafting Committee is to produce an excellent draft in little or no time. In many instances, the work on the first draft is shared out and, as a result, draft contributions are often produced by judges who are working under time pressure and in a language that is not their first working language.

The Tribunal greatly appreciates the views expressed by learned commentators, whether positive or negative. Academic and professional opinions are always instructive. The most common criticism of commentators of the Tribunal's decisions has been that of brevity.[11] The Tribunal does aim to be efficient, which means that overly long explanations are avoided.[12] It is the task of a court to dispose of the case before it, not to write learned essays on the law.

At the same time, the Tribunal cannot claim infallibility: in certain instances, and with the benefit of hindsight, a fuller set of reasons could have been provided. There are several explanations. First, it should be recalled that five of the six reasoned decisions have been given in urgent cases where the Tribunal has worked night and day, seven days a week, including Saturday night and Sunday morning. The time pressure may have affected the drafting process.

Secondly, brevity can be an unintended result of working by way of consensus. It is often easier in practice to gain general assent by omitting sentences that one or more colleagues do not like than by adding extra sentences.

A third point is that the two reasoned orders prescribing provisional measures were drafted in the classic French style, made up of recitals beginning with "whereas" and "considering." This style has many virtues, especially when penned by a master. It can produce orders that can be said to be elegant, even poetic. At the same time, this style imposes restraints of a technical nature and the constant repetition of "considering" can become tedious. The style may not be best suited to the recapitulation of complicated facts or the resolution of complex issues, requiring many pages. The formal structure begins to disappear under a welter of facts and legal arguments.

Governments wish to be assured that the Tribunal has weighed all their arguments, which in practice means summarizing them in the decision. That process can all too easily result, when it comes to the turn of the Tribunal to state its own position, in somewhat terse paragraphs. Orders may then appear to be elliptical, especially when compared with a more normal prose style. In the matter of style, the Tribunal has followed the practice of the Court so far. However, in the future it may depart from this style and use prose instead of poetry.

A final point: in the end, it is the dispositif that really counts. The reasoning leads up to the operative provisions. Great care has to be taken with the scope and content of the dispositif.

DISSENTING AND SEPARATE OPINIONS

According to the terms of the Resolution on Internal Judicial Practice, dissenting and separate opinions are to concentrate on the points of difference with the judgment.[13] In other words, the separate opinions should hold up mirrors to the judgment, casting light on it by indicating the crucial points of controversy. In that light, they are part of the collegial process. There are some incidental effects, in that outsiders, especially learned commentators, are given some additional indications as to what the controversial issues were during the deliberations.

As was pointed out many years ago by Professor Scerni, separate opinions should not be written as materials for casebooks.[14] They should not be any longer than is needed to explain differences with the judgment, nor, as Manfred Lachs pointed out, cover some completely extraneous issue not raised and discussed in the deliberations.[15]

Shabtai Rosenne has observed, in regard to the Saiga (No. 2) Merits Case, that: "Some of the opinions appended to this (and other) pronouncements of the Tribunal are long and expansive and to some readers may appear not to conform to . . ." article 8(6) of the Resolution.[16] Due note has been taken! Separate concurring opinions are permissible when a judge has voted for a paragraph in a judgment for reasons that differ from those of the majority. The separate opinion gives the second reason for supporting the paragraph. Separate opinions by members of the Drafting

Committee tend to be rare, although a brief Declaration on a discrete issue may be permissible.

What are the statistics on dissents and separate opinions? A table can show the bare statistics of votes, together with separate and dissenting opinions, in the six cases. Like all statistics, they do not tell the full story and, since deliberations must remain secret, neither does this paper. The table[17] shows all the votes in the operative paragraphs of the decisions in the six cases, a grand total of forty-two. What conclusions emerge from these statistics? First, the Tribunal has been deeply divided in some instances, notably in its very first decision. However, overall the majorities have been high. Out of a total of 862 votes cast, 766 have been concurring votes or about eighty-nine percent, and ninety-six have been dissenting or about eleven percent. One decision was unanimous on all points. Even where there have been divisions on one or more paragraphs in the dispositif, other points of decision have been unanimous.

Secondly, almost all dissents have been explained in individual or collective dissenting opinions. This is good practice. Even so, sometimes in urgent cases, judges preparing separate opinions have had hardly any time.

Thirdly, some judges have dissented more than others, but no judge has dissented more than half of the time. At the opposite extreme, three judges have maintained their record of voting with the majority on all occasions, and six judges have each made just a single dissent.

CONCLUDING REMARKS

1. The Tribunal's method of (mainly oral) debates is well-suited to handling cases without unnecessary delay. To work effectively, there must be an agreed list of issues for decision and a well-structured debate on each issue.

2. A little more time would be desirable in future cases, including urgent ones. More time should produce fuller and more persuasive reasoning, which means better judgments.

3.   The method also works satisfactorily in normal, non-urgent cases. Here more written notes on an agreed list of issues for decision would be helpful and would assist the process.

4.   The Tribunal's good collegial spirit is an asset. During our discussions, a frequently asked question is: "Are we together?" The answer is in the affirmative. Long may this spirit last!

Notes

[1] Substantive legal questions are beyond the scope of this paper.

[2] *International Tribunal for the Law of the Sea: Basic Texts* (The Hague: Kluwer, 1998). For general surveys of the internal judicial practice, see 38 *Indian Journal of International Law* (1998): 410, and the chapter on the topic in Khan, ed., *International Tribunal for the Law of the Sea: Law and Practice* (2001).

[3] Jennings, "The Collegiate Responsibility of the International Court of Justice," in *International Law at a Time of Complexity: Essays in honour of Shabtai Rosenne* (1983); and Jennings, "The Internal Judicial Practice of the International Court," 59 *BYBIL* (1988): 43.

[4] Saiga Case, *ITLOS Reports* (1997), 16; Camouco Case, *ITLOS Reports* (2000), xx; Monte Confurco Case, *ITLOS Reports* (2000), yy.

[5] Saiga (No. 2) Case, *ITLOS Reports* (1998), xx; Southern Bluefin Tuna Case, *ITLOS Reports* (1999), xx.

[6] A point made by Judge Higgins in her comments on the Report of a study group entitled *The International Court of Justice: Process, Practice and Procedure* (British Institute of International and Comparative Law, 1996).

[7] Petersmann, ed., *International Trade Law and the GATT/WTO Dispute Settlement System* (1997).

[8] Eyffinger, *International Court of Justice* (1996).

[9] The judgments in the Saiga (No. 2) (Merits) Case, the Camouco Case, and the Monte Confurco Case were delivered in both languages.

[10] As pointed out by Rosenne, "The International Tribunal for the Law of the Sea: Survey for 1999," 15 *IJMCL* 443 (2000): 451.

[11] For example, L. de la Fayette, "ITLOS and the Saga of the Saiga," 15 *IJMCL* (2000): 355.

[12] Article 49 of the Rules of the Tribunal reads: "The proceedings before the Tribunal shall be conducted without unnecessary delay or expense."

[13] Article 8(6) of the Resolution.

[14] Scerni, "Les opinions individuelles et dissidentes des juges des tribunaux internationales," 68 *RGDIP* (1964): 281.

[15] Lachs, "Le juge international á visage découvert (Les Opinions et la vote)," in *Estudios de Derecho Internacional (Essays in honour of Professor M. de la Muela)*, vol. II (1979), 951.

[16] 15 *IJMCL* 443 (2000): 463.

[17] See table on next page.

Judge	Saiga PR	Saiga No 2 PMs	Saiga No 2 Merits	SBT PMs	Camouco	Monte Confurco	Total dissents	Total SOs etc	Total concurrent votes	Total Votes cast
Op Paras	5	4	12	8	5	8				
Judge Zhao*			SO	1D		DNS	1	1	33	34
Caminos			1D/JDec	JDecl			1	2	41	42
Marotta Rangel				JDecl			0	1	42	42
Yankov			1D/JDec	JDecl			1	2	41	42
Yamamoto	4D/JDO		DNS	1D/JSO			5	2	25	30
Kolodkin					1D		1	0	41	42
Park	4D/JDO			JSO			4	2	38	42
Bamela Engo							0	0	42	42
Nelson	4D/JDO		SO		SO	SO	4	4	38	42
Mensah	4D/DO		SO		Decl	Decl	4	4	38	42
Chandra-sekhara Rao	4D/JDO		SO				4	2	38	42
Akl			1D/JDecl				1	1	41	42
Anderson	4D/DO		1D/JDec/SO	JDecl	4D/DO	4D/DO	13	6	29	42
Vukas	4D/JDO	Decl	2D/JDec/SO	8D/DO	4D/DO	Decl	18	7	24	42
Wolfrum	4D/JDO		SO	JDecl	1D/DO		5	4	37	42
Laing		SO	SO	SO	Decl	1D/DO	1	5	41	42
Treves			1D/JDecl	SO	1D/DO		2	3	40	42
Marsit							0	0	42	42
Eiriksson			1D/JDecl	2D/DO			3	2	39	42
Ndiaye	4D/JDO		10D/DO		Decl	Decl	14	4	28	42
Jesus	DNS	DNS	DNS	DNS	2D/DO	Decl	2	1	11	13
Warioba	DNS	Decl	10D/DO	2D/DO	DNS	DNS	12	3	17	29
Totals							96	56	766	862

Key

PR= Prompt Release	Blank box means concurrent votes	SO=separate opinion	DO=dissenting opinion
PMs=provisional measures	Decl=Declaration	J=joint	D=dissent
		DNS=Did not sit	* deceased Oct 2000

The votes of judge ad hoc Shearer have not been included in this table.

QUESTION OF TIME-LIMITS IN
URGENT PROCEEDINGS BEFORE THE TRIBUNAL

Joseph Akl[*]

The topic of my presentation relates to the question of time-limits in urgent proceedings before the Tribunal with particular focus on time-limits in prompt release proceedings under article 292 of the Convention, in the light of the most recent discussions and decisions of the Tribunal on this matter.

Urgent proceedings before the Tribunal provided for under the Convention, the Statute, and the Rules pertain either to incidental proceedings such as preliminary proceedings, preliminary objections, intervention and prescription of provisional measures, or to a specific and independent proceeding, the proceeding for prompt release of a vessel and its crew pursuant to article 292 of the Convention. Moreover, the Seabed Disputes Chamber, in the context of its contentious or consultative jurisdiction, may be seized with urgent proceedings such as applications for the prescription of provisional measures (article 290 of the Convention) or requests for advisory opinions on legal questions arising out of the activity of the Assembly or Council of the Authority (article 191 of the Convention and article 132 of the Rules). The special chambers provided for in article 15 of the Statute may also hear applications for the prescription of provisional measures.

For all of these urgent proceedings, with the exception of that pertaining to prompt release of a vessel or its crew, the Rules do not lay down a maximum time-limit for the reading of the Tribunal's decision at a public sitting, other than that provided for in article 8 of the Resolution on the Internal Judicial Practice of the Tribunal concerning the beginning of deliberations on the draft judgment. The various time-limits laid down by the Rules throughout the various phases of procedure are generally of one

---

[*] Judge, International Tribunal for the Law of the Sea.

M.H. Nordquist and J.N. Moore (eds.),
Current Marine Environmental Issues and the International Tribunal for the Law of the Sea, 75–80.
© 2001 *Kluwer Law International. Printed in the Netherlands.*

month or more. They are, for that matter, flexible so that the Tribunal, or the President if the Tribunal is not sitting, has latitude to change them in light of the nature and urgency of the case and the circumstances.

Therefore, the focus of this presentation will be confined to the question of deadlines in proceedings for prescription of provisional measures, which are urgent by their very nature, and deadlines in prompt release proceedings.

Article 90 of the Rules provides that "Subject to article 112, paragraph 1, a request for the prescription of provisional measures has priority over all other proceedings before the Tribunal" and that "The Tribunal, or the President if the Tribunal is not sitting, shall fix the earliest possible date for a hearing." Article 112, paragraph 1, provides that the Tribunal, when seized of an application for prompt release and of a request for the prescription of provisional measures, shall take the necessary measures to ensure that both the application and the request are dealt with without delay.

Article 292, paragraph 3, of the Convention provides that the Tribunal shall deal without delay with an application for release. For the purposes of this proceeding, unlike the proceeding concerning provisional measures, the Rules lay down fixed and rigid deadlines. Article 112, paragraph 3, provides that the Tribunal or the President "shall fix the earliest possible date, but not exceeding ten days from the date of receipt of the application, for a hearing. . . ." Article 111, paragraph 4, authorizes the detaining State to submit a statement in response no later than twenty-four hours before the hearing. Paragraph 4 of article 112 provides that "The judgment . . . shall be read at a public sitting of the Tribunal to be held not later than ten days after the closure of the hearing."

The Resolution on the Internal Judicial Practice of the Tribunal provides that deliberations concerning applications for the prescription of provisional measures and applications for prompt release "are conducted in accordance with [the same] principles and procedures" as those applying to other cases "taking account of the nature and urgency of the case" (article 11, paragraph 2).

"The Tribunal may decide to vary the procedures and arrangements set out above in a particular case for reasons of urgency or if circumstances so justify" (article 11, paragraph 1).

These procedures normally include several stages. First, the Tribunal proceeds to initial deliberations after the oral proceedings and to the examination of the issues that need to be decided in order to establish a majority opinion. Then a Drafting Committee is established, which should prepare a draft judgment. After a first reading, during which outlines of separate or dissenting opinions are put forward, a revised draft judgment is submitted to a second reading before the final voting procedure.

Thus far, the Tribunal has dealt with two requests for the prescription of provisional measures and three applications for prompt release and has been able to follow the time-limits laid down.

In the M/V "Saiga" (prompt release) case, the "Camouco" (prompt release) case, and the "Monte Confurco" (prompt release) case, the duration of each proceeding from the date of submission of the application to the Tribunal to the date of the reading of the judgment at public sitting was twenty-two days.

The efficiency and zeal with which the Tribunal has discharged its functions in these prompt release cases have elicited commendation from representatives of States parties to the Convention, scholars, agents, and practitioners of international litigation. However, this result was achieved only at the expense of enormous efforts in overcoming the difficulties that short and rigid deadlines imply for parties, members of the Tribunal, and staff of its Registry.

For the respondent State, the period of nine days to appear at the opening of the oral proceeding (eight days for submission of the statement in response) presents significant disadvantages, considering that those days include one or more official holidays. Within that time-lapse, the respondent must prepare its case and coordinate with various administrative departments, some of which may be quite remote from the capital. Nor should we lose sight of the time-zone differences and great distances between many States

Parties to the Convention and Hamburg, which may necessitate two days' travel time. In the first prompt release case, the Tribunal had to defer the opening of the hearing for six days at the request of the Guinean Government, which reported difficulties in receiving certain documents. It should also be noted that the legal services of many countries, particularly developing countries, are not adequately equipped to respond to an international jurisdictional proceeding with the required promptness.

At the same time, the applicant State for practical purposes receives the statement in response of the respondent State only on the eve of the opening of the hearing, which represents a distinct disadvantage.

Nor do the difficulties created by the time-tables laid down in the Rules spare the President and the Members of the Tribunal, particularly the members of the Drafting Committee, in their efforts to apply the principles laid down in the Resolution on the Internal Judicial Practice of the Tribunal to the deliberations and to the drafting and adoption of the judgment.

(a) The statement in response of the respondent and supporting documents are received, in one of the official languages of the Tribunal, only on the eve of the opening of the hearing. This renders more difficult the preparation of the President's working paper, which serves as a basis for the deliberations of judges before the oral proceedings. The judges do not have sufficient time to give careful attention to the respondent's arguments, evaluate the facts, and fully satisfy the purposes of these deliberations.

(b) Some cases may present facts that need to be elucidated or complex points of law that require in-depth examination.

(c) The distinct phases of initial deliberations after the oral proceedings, formation of the drafting committee, and deliberations on the draft judgment have to be excessively accelerated owing to the pressure of time.

(d) The deadlines in force oblige the President and judges to remain in session for thirteen consecutive days, including Saturdays and Sundays, and sometimes in night meetings.

This pace of work by the Tribunal weighs heavily upon the staff of the Registry, especially upon interpreters and translators, since the Tribunal's work must be conducted in both official languages. In this respect, it should be borne in mind that, at the present time, the staff of the Registry is relatively small and, at certain times of year, it proves difficult to make provision for the prompt translation of pleadings and various documents into one language or the other.

The difficulties described above would no doubt be exacerbated if the Tribunal were to be seized at the same time of an application for prompt release and of a request for provisional measures or of two applications for prompt release. This has not yet occurred, but its occurrence in the future cannot be ruled out.

In light of the foregoing considerations and of the experience thus far gained, the Tribunal adopted amendments to articles 111 and 112 of the Rules, which entered into force on March 15, 2001.

 a) In paragraph 4 of article 111, the detaining state may submit a statement in response to be filed "as soon as possible but no later than 96 hours" before the hearing.

 b) In paragraph 3 of article 112, the Tribunal or the President shall fix the earliest possible date "within a period of 15 days commencing with the first working day following the date on which the application is received" for a hearing.

 c) In paragraph 4 of article 112, the Judgement shall be read at a public sitting of the Tribunal to be held not later than "14" days after the closure of the hearing.

Adoption of the foregoing amendments to the Rules does not imply that the length of a prompt release proceeding will necessarily be extended by nine days. Expeditiousness remains the main characteristic of prompt release proceedings. The newly adopted deadlines are maximum deadlines. They provide some degree of flexibility and a useful safeguard in the event that a case were to prove highly complex and in the event that unforeseen special circumstances were to arise. In these special circumstances, they allow the parties a few more days to prepare their evidence and arguments and the judges a little more time to refine their judgments.

ADVISORY OPINIONS UNDER THE LAW OF THE SEA CONVENTION

Tullio Treves[*]

INTRODUCTION: ADVISORY OPINIONS UNDER THE CONVENTION AND THE RULES OF THE TRIBUNAL

A perusal of the United Nations Convention on the Law of the Sea immediately shows that the Convention does not provide for any form of advisory jurisdiction of the Tribunal in its full composition. Nor does it entrust with such jurisdiction the International Court of Justice or arbitral tribunals. Advisory jurisdiction is nonetheless entrusted to the Seabed Disputes Chamber of the Law of the Sea Tribunal. The Chamber can give advisory opinions under two provisions of the Convention. According to article 191, such opinions can be given at the request of the Assembly or the Council "on legal questions arising within the scope of their activities." According to article 159, paragraph 10, the Chamber can give advisory opinions at the request of the Assembly, if certain procedural requirements are satisfied, "on the conformity with th[e] Convention of a proposal before the Assembly on any matter" (article 159, para. 10).

These provisions may be considered in the light of article 96 of the UN Charter, which reserves to the General Assembly and the Security Council the right to request the International Court of Justice (ICJ) to issue an advisory opinion "on any legal question." Other organs of the United Nations and Specialized Agencies may be authorized by the General Assembly to request such opinions "on legal questions arising within the scope of their activities." As there is no other organization, apart from the International Seabed Authority, which is directly created by the Law of the Sea Convention, it seems broadly consistent with the precedent of article 96 that only this organization (through its Assembly and

---

[*] Judge, International Tribunal for the Law of the Sea; President, Seabed Disputes Chamber; and Professor, University of Milan.

M.H. Nordquist and J.N. Moore (eds.),
Current Marine Environmental Issues and the International Tribunal for the Law of the Sea, 81–93.
© 2001 *Kluwer Law International. Printed in the Netherlands.*

Council) should be entitled to request an advisory opinion to the Seabed Disputes Chamber of the Tribunal, which is the judicial body specifically competent for disputes concerning the field of activity of the Authority. Even taking into account the above illustrated consistency with the logic of article 96 of the Charter, one might nonetheless express regret that the power to request advisory opinions has not been given to other organizations that are entrusted with particular functions under the Convention. It may seem odd, for instance, that a United Nations Specialized Agency, such as the International Maritime Organization, should be entitled to request the International Court of Justice for an advisory opinion on whether it is the "competent international organization" mentioned in various provisions of the Law of the Sea Convention, while on such a question arising within the scope of its activities and so intimately connected with the interpretation of the Convention it cannot request the opinion of the International Tribunal for the Law of the Sea.

The request for an advisory opinion of The Hague Court has sometimes been described as a device that international organizations can use in order to circumvent, to a certain extent, the rule of article 34 of the Court's Statute, under which only States can be parties to cases before the Court. In the case of the Authority and the Seabed Disputes Chamber, such description is less accurate. Under the Convention, the Authority and the Enterprise, as well as organizations parties to the Convention such as the European Community, can be parties to disputes against States parties as well as against non-State entities. It follows that advisory proceedings may be resorted to not in order to substitute for contentious proceedings involving the Authority, but rather to perform authentic advisory functions in order to overcome genuine legal difficulties encountered by the Assembly or the Council of the Authority in performing their tasks. Nevertheless, such difficulties would, in all likelihood, arise from the clash of divergent legal views held by members of the Authority. Agreement within one of the main organs of the Authority to request an advisory opinion may be a way to prevent such difference of legal opinion being exacerbated and for avoiding deciding it through a vote, namely by the force of the majority and not by that of the law.

Even though such possibility is not mentioned in the Convention, in preparing its Rules, the Law of the Sea Tribunal felt that resorting to it in its plenary formation to obtain advisory opinions should not be ruled out. This was done in article 138 of the Rules by envisaging that future agreements could provide for such possibility.

I: ADVISORY PROCEEDINGS BEFORE THE SEABED DISPUTES CHAMBER OF THE INTERNATIONAL LAW OF THE SEA TRIBUNAL

No experience has been gathered so far in the practice of the Tribunal of requests for advisory opinions to the Seabed Disputes Chamber under articles 159, paragraph 10, and 191 of the Convention. Some questions have been envisaged, nonetheless, in Section H of Part III of the Rules of the Tribunal (entitled "Advisory Proceedings") while, at the same time, further questions arise from some provisions in that section.

The opening provision (article 130, paragraph 1) of section H quoted above, while stating that the procedural rules applicable to advisory proceedings are those set out in that section, also states that the Chamber shall "be guided, to the extent to which it recognizes them to be applicable, by the provisions of the Statute and of these Rules applicable in contentious cases." This provision is clearly derived from article 68 of the Statute of the ICJ and article 102, paragraph 2, of the Rules of the Court. An analysis of the provisions applicable to contentious cases is required to determine those that may be used as guidance in advisory cases. This exercise is particularly complicated because Section F of Part III of the Rules, entitled "Proceedings in Contentious Cases Before the Seabed Disputes Chamber," sets out a number of such provisions applicable to contentious cases that are not exclusively between States Parties and between States Parties and the Authority. Article 115 states in general terms that proceedings in contentious cases shall be "governed by the Rules applicable in contentious cases before the Tribunal." Therefore, it becomes necessary to determine whether or not rules concerning contentious cases before the full bench can be recognized as applicable to advisory proceedings before the Seabed Disputes Chamber.

Some interesting questions emerge in this exercise of considering the various steps in the advisory proceedings, taking as a basis the provisions of Section H mentioned above.

The Request for an Advisory Opinion

Article 131, paragraph 1, of the Rules provides that:

> A request for an advisory opinion on a legal question arising within the scope of the activities of the Assembly or the Council of the Authority shall contain a precise statement of the question. It shall be accompanied by all documents likely to throw light upon the question.

In light of the provisions concerning contentious cases, which may be recognized to be applicable (under article 130, para. 1), are there other elements that must be included in the request for an advisory opinion beyond "a precise statement of the question"?

The request for the advisory opinion institutes advisory proceedings and institutes them unilaterally. It seems, therefore, reasonable to look for further elements to be included in the provisions concerning contentious cases that deal with institution of proceedings by means of application.

In light of the provision of article 54, paragraph 1, of the Rules ("the application shall indicate the party making it") and of paragraph 2 of the same article ("the application shall specify as far as possible the legal grounds upon which the jurisdiction of the Tribunal is said to be based; it shall also specify the precise nature of the claim . . ."), it would seem reasonable to suggest that the following further elements should be contained in the request:

1. An indication clarifying whether the request is made by the Assembly, or by the Council. This is "the party" making the request.

2. An indication as to the way in which the question has arisen "within the scope" of the activities of the requesting organ of the Authority (this has to do with the "jurisdiction" of the Chamber to hold the advisory proceedings under article 190 of the Convention).

Moreover, when possible, it could be useful to include indications—by way of a summary and/or by reference to relevant documents annexed—as to the different views held during the discussions within the Assembly (or the Council) regarding the need to answer the question, the answer to be given to it, and the consequences different answers may have on the activities of the Assembly (or of the Council).

In light of paragraph 3 of article 54 and of article 56, paragraph 1, of the Rules, it would seem necessary that the request is signed by the organ representing the Assembly or the Council (presumably their presidents) or by the agent they have designated. Such an agent could, and in all likelihood would, be the Secretary-General of the Authority. If this is the case, one may wonder whether the requirement that when the request is signed by the agent, its signature must be authenticated by the diplomatic representative or the competent governmental authority, should be "recognized as applicable." In other words, is it really necessary that the Secretary-General's signature be authenticated by the President of the Assembly or of the Council?

Written Proceedings

Paragraph 3 of article 133 of the Rules states:

States Parties and the organizations referred to in paragraph 2 shall be invited to present written statements on the question within a time-limit fixed by the Chamber or its President if the Chamber is not sitting. Such statements shall be communicated to States Parties and organizations which have made written statements. The Chamber, or its President if the Chamber is not sitting, may fix a further time-limit within which such States Parties and organizations may present written statements on the statements made.

Thus, the written proceedings consist in the presentation of "written statements" and may be completed by further "written statements on the statements made."

Participation in the first round of written statements is open to all States Parties (and to those international organizations "which are likely to furnish information on the question" previously identified by the Chamber). Participation to the second round is open only to those States parties and international organizations that have participated in the first.

The provisions on "written proceedings" in contentious cases (articles 59ff. of the Rules) should be considered in order to determine whether they, or some of them, may be recognized as applicable.

Of particular interest seems to be the possibility of seeking guidance in advisory proceedings in article 59, which concerns, *inter alia*, procedural decisions, including those on time-limits, to be taken by the President in light of the views expressed by the parties. Two questions arise. The first is whether the President is, in advisory proceedings, supposed to consult about the procedure in application of this article and of article 45 of the Rules. And if he is, with whom is he supposed to consult? It would seem that unless certain States Parties have indicated their intention to submit written statements, there are in practice no identified interlocutors for the President to consult. Once such intention has been manifested, and in any case after the written statements have been submitted, the interlocutors for the consultations of the President are identified and may be consulted.

The second question is whether the six-month maximum time-limit set out in article 59, paragraph 1, is applicable to the filing of the written statements under article 133, paragraph 3. It would seem that as the six-months time-limit is a maximum, and as flexibility is provided in article 59, that time-limit could be taken as an indication to be followed also in advisory proceedings. However, as we shall see below, all advisory proceedings are "urgent" under the Convention and the Rules. The consequence should be that the time-limits fixed in practice should remain much below the maximum.

Initial Deliberations

It may be asked whether article 68 of the Rules (deliberations after the closure of written proceedings and prior to the opening of the oral proceedings) applies also to advisory proceedings. The preferable answer seems to be in the affirmative, provided there are oral proceedings. The deliberations mentioned in article 68 of the Rules seems to be as useful in advisory as in contentious cases. It may be added that article 12 of the Resolution on internal judicial practice of the Tribunal (whose article 3 considers in detail the deliberations mentioned in article 68 of the Rules) provides that its provisions apply "whether the proceedings before the Tribunal are contentious or advisory."

Oral Proceedings

According to paragraph 3 of article 133:

> The Chamber, or its President if the Chamber is not sitting, shall decide whether oral proceedings shall be held and, if so, fix the date for the opening of such proceedings. States Parties and the organizations referred to in paragraph 2 shall be invited to make oral statements at the proceedings.

The oral proceedings are not necessary. The Seabed Disputes Chamber decides whether they should be held or not.

It must be noted that invitations to participate in the oral proceedings shall be extended to "States Parties and the organizations mentioned in paragraph 2." This concerns all States Parties, not only those that have participated in the written proceedings. Although written proceedings may serve the purpose of permitting replies to arguments made in written statements, it would seem that they are a possible forum for States to present their views on the question submitted to the Chamber independently of whether they have made statements in the written proceedings.

It would seem, as a consequence, that the moment in time in which the decision as to whether to hold oral proceedings is taken is independent from that of the fixing of the time-limit for the written statements and from the fact that the written proceedings have or have not been completed. This interpretation makes the advisory proceedings before the Seabed Disputes Chamber much more similar to those before the ICJ than it would seem upon a first perusal of the relevant rules.[1]

The applicability *mutatis mutandis* to advisory proceedings of the provisions on oral proceedings in contentious cases (article 69ff. of the Rules) do not seem to present very difficult problems. Some remarks must, however, be made as regards article 69, which concerns the fixing of the date for the oral proceedings.

While, as regards the six-months rule, the same considerations made as regards article 59 of the Rules seem to apply, it must be stressed that in the consideration of the elements listed in paragraph 2 of article 69 in order to fix the date for the oral proceedings, some adaptation is made necessary because unavoidably the Chamber has to work in coordination with the Tribunal as a whole. So the priority required by article 90 for provisional measures proceedings may concern requests for such provisional measures submitted to the Tribunal as a whole and not only to the Chamber. The "special circumstances, including the urgency of the case or other cases on the List of cases," mentioned in paragraph 2 (c), must be read as regarding special circumstances and urgency not only of other cases before the Chamber, but also of other cases before the Tribunal. While the decision belongs to the Chamber or, if it is not sitting, to its President, it is obvious that the President of the Chamber must consult the President of the

Tribunal so as to proceed, or permit the Chamber to proceed, on the basis of full information as to the timetable for the Tribunal as a whole.

The Question of Urgency

Article 194 of the Convention, the general rule concerning advisory opinions of the Seabed Disputes Chamber, provides that: "Such opinions shall be given as a matter of urgency." In light of this general rule, all requests for advisory opinions are to be considered as urgent by the Seabed Disputes Chamber.

What is the relationship between this "urgency" and the urgency of a request for provisional measures, or of a request for prompt release of vessels, which according to articles 90 and 112 of the Rules have "priority over all other proceedings before the Tribunal"?

The problem arises when a request for an advisory opinion is submitted to the Chamber while it is engaged in a contentious case and a request for provisional measures has been made. It arises also when such request, or an application for prompt release, has been submitted to the Tribunal as a whole. The fact that the Chamber includes eleven judges of the Tribunal makes it impossible to deal with the two requests at the same time.

The provisions of articles 90 and 112 of the Rules are very precisely drafted. This could be held to have as a consequence that a request for provisional measures, or an application for prompt release, should, in principle, have priority over the proceedings for an advisory opinion, notwithstanding their "urgency" under article 194 of the Convention. While it is true that a provision of the Rules should not prevail over a provision of the Convention, article 90 is linked to article 290 of the Convention and urgency is inherent to provisional measures, as it is to prompt release under article 292 of the Convention.

It would seem, however, that the Chamber (or its President) has considerable discretion in this matter. Consultations with the President of the Tribunal would, in any case, be necessary in order to decide on the priority of either request in light of the overall schedule of work of the Tribunal, the Chamber, and of other considerations, such as the comparative importance of the questions. From the latter viewpoint, possible implications for human life, human rights, or the preservation of the environment might tilt the balance in favor of prompt release or provisional measures proceedings.

Article 132 of the Rules provides:

> If the request for an advisory opinion states that the question necessitates an urgent answer the Chamber shall take all appropriate measures to accelerate the procedure.

This provision indicates that an express statement in the request may make the consideration of the request more "urgent" that it would be under the general urgency clause of article 194 of the Convention. It would seem likely that such specific request for an urgent answer will concern (in particular, and not necessarily exclusively) cases envisaged in article 159, paragraph 10, of the Convention, namely those in which the request is made by the Assembly in order to determine the conformity with the Convention of a proposal before it. In such a case the Assembly "shall defer voting on that proposal pending receipt of the advisory opinion by the Chamber." Considering that sessions of the Assembly may be short and separated by rather long intervals, immediate response may be very useful.

It would seem that the very fact that the Assembly has decided to submit the request means in most cases that the question of the conformity to the Convention of a proposal pending before the Assembly has been hotly debated within it and that it is legally difficult and not devoid of political implications. If this is the case, "urgency" notwithstanding, it may not be possible, or opportune, to render the advisory opinion before the adjournment of the session of the Assembly. This possibility has been envisaged in the last sentence of article 159, paragraph 10, stating that:

> If the advisory opinion is not received before the final week of the session in which it is requested, the Assembly

shall decide when it will meet to vote upon the deferred proposal.

"Appropriate measures" mentioned in article 132 of the Rules may include: priority over provisional measures proceedings, the immediate calling to Hamburg of the members of the Chamber, the fixing of very short time-limits for the presentation of written statements under article 133 of the Rules, and a decision not to allow "written statements on the statements made" or oral statement. Of course, such "appropriate measures" should not go to the detriment of justice and of a full consideration of the issues. A delicate assessment of the comparative merits of proceeding very expeditiously and of the importance and difficulty of the question submitted for an advisory opinion will be necessary on the part of the Chamber or its President.

II: ADVISORY PROCEEDINGS BEFORE THE FULL TRIBUNAL UNDER ARTICLE 138 OF THE RULES

Article 138 of the Rules of the Tribunal provides, in paragraph 1, that the Tribunal (in its full bench) may give an advisory opinion "on a legal question if an international agreement related to the purposes of the Convention specifically provides for the submission to the Tribunal of a request for such opinion." This provision prepares the Tribunal to cope with possible requests for advisory opinions in case such competence were to be entrusted to it by future agreements.

The conditions to be satisfied are quite strict. Firstly, the agreement must be "related to the purposes of the Convention." This repeats article 288, paragraph 2, stating that the courts and tribunals referred to in article 287 have compulsory jurisdiction over any dispute "concerning the interpretation or application of an international agreement related to the purposes of this Convention, which is submitted to it in accordance with the agreement." Second, the possibility of a request for an advisory opinion must be "specifically" provided in the agreement. Vague or general formulations would not be sufficient. Lastly, as indicated in paragraph 2 of article 138, the request must be transmitted "by whatever body is authorized by or in accordance with the agreement to make the request." This last condition, although in an oblique way, introduces as a requirement that the advisory opinion should be requested by "a body." This seems in conformity with the basic concept, set out in article 96 of the Charter, and consistent with the provisions on advisory opinions by the Seabed Disputes Chamber, that advisory opinions are an instrument at the disposal of international organizations (although the word "body" suggests a rather broad approach to this concept) and not of States.

Whether article 138 is compatible with the Convention might perhaps be debated. Assuming that it is, one might also discuss whether conditions less strict than those prescribed could have been indicated in the Rules. It would seem that in article 138 of the Rules, the Tribunal tried to confine the innovation it introduced to what is consistent with the traditional functions of advisory opinions. To permit requests for advisory opinions not specifically authorized under the relevant agreement, or to accept that States could by agreement authorize themselves to request such opinions on their own would have been to tread on much unsafer ground.

Notes

¹ Article 66 of the Statute of the Court:

2. The Registrar shall also, by means of a special and direct communication, notify states entitled to appear before the Court or international organizations considered by the Court, or, should it not be sitting, by the President, as likely to be able to furnish information on the question, that the Court will be prepared to receive, within a time limit to be fixed by the President, written statements, or to hear, at a public sitting to be held for the purpose, oral statements relating to the question.

PROVISIONAL MEASURES BEFORE THE INTERNATIONAL TRIBUNAL FOR THE LAW OF THE SEA

Tafsir Malick Ndiaye[*]

In the various legal systems, the road that leads to jurisdictional settlement can be a true obstacle course before the final decision of a jurisdiction is reached. That decision may not only take time but may be emptied of its content when one party to a dispute adopts a unilateral and arbitrary attitude. The role of provisional measures is to prevent those unfortunate consequences, to ensure the effectiveness of the decision-making process, and to help maintain the status quo with regard to situations contested *pendente lite.*

In its order of August 17, 1972, in the *Fisheries Jurisdiction Case* (Federal Republic of Germany *v.* Iceland), the International Court of Justice set out the purpose of provisional measures. It said:

> Whereas the right of the Court to indicate provisional measures as provided for in Article 41 of the Statute has as its object to preserve the respective rights of the parties pending the decision of the Court, and presupposes that irreparable prejudice should not be caused to rights which are the subject of dispute in judicial proceedings and that the Court's judgment should not be anticipated by reason of any initiative regarding the measures which are in issue [§ 22].

Thus, the Court identified three elements:

a) Preserving the rights of each party;
b) Preventing irreparable prejudice; and
c) Not anticipating the decision of the Court.

---

[*] Judge, International Tribunal for the Law of the Sea.

M.H. Nordquist and J.N. Moore (eds.),
Current Marine Environmental Issues and the International Tribunal for the Law of the Sea, 95–101.
© 2001 *Kluwer Law International. Printed in the Netherlands.*

We shall briefly discuss the legal basis for the prescription of provisional measures by ITLOS (I); the conditions under which provisional measures may be prescribed by the Tribunal (II); and, finally, the effects of the provisional measures prescribed (III).

I. LEGAL BASIS

The United Nations Convention on the Law of the Sea (the Convention) confers upon ITLOS jurisdiction to prescribe, modify, or revoke provisional measures following a *prima facie* consideration of the jurisdiction of the arbitral tribunal to be established and an assessment of the urgency of the situation (article 290 § 5).

One may see this as concurrent jurisdiction in the sense that the Tribunal that prescribes the provisional measures will not be the forum that will deal with the merits, as is the case at the ICJ. From this perspective, the character of the incidental proceedings becomes doubtful. This is a point worth discussing.

Articles 89 to 95 of the Rules of the Tribunal, adopted on October 28, 1997, contain the provisions concerning procedures for submission of requests; the timing thereof; the measures requested and the grounds upon which the request is based; the possible consequences of rejection of the request for preservation of the respective rights of the parties; the grounds upon which the arbitral tribunal to be constituted would have jurisdiction; the urgency of the situation; the possibility of making a fresh request following rejection; and other procedural safeguards, such as the possibility afforded to the parties to present observations.

These provisions also provide for notification of the measures prescribed, modified, or revoked not only to the parties but also to other States Parties if the Tribunal considers it appropriate. Moreover, each party must inform the Tribunal as soon as possible as to its compliance with any provisional measures the Tribunal has prescribed. In particular, each party must submit an initial report upon the steps it has taken or proposes to take in order to ensure prompt compliance with the measures prescribed. Finally, the Tribunal may request further information from the parties on any matter connected with the implementation of any provisional measures it has prescribed.

II. Requirements

With regard to the requirements that must be satisfied for the prescription of provisional measures, the Tribunal must find that the parties have failed to reach agreement within two weeks following the date of the request. It is then that the Tribunal may prescribe measures if it considers that, *prima facie*, the arbitral tribunal to be constituted would have jurisdiction and that it is warranted by the urgency of the situation.

Jurisdiction of the Tribunal

To do so, however, the Tribunal must first satisfy itself as to its own jurisdiction to entertain the application before it. This task is relatively straightforward, since the Tribunal derives its authority to prescribe provisional measures from the Convention itself (article 290 §5) and from the Statute (article 25 §1), not from the request submitted by a party to the dispute.

Prima Facie Jurisdiction of the Tribunal

By contrast, the jurisdiction of the arbitral tribunal to entertain the merits of the case must be clearly established before the prescription of provisional measures; such jurisdiction arises only if it is reasonably probable that the arbitral tribunal would have jurisdiction on the merits. This review, even *prima facie*, is mandatory.

The determination of the law applicable to the dispute makes it possible to do so. Thus, ITLOS took the view that the provisions of Part XV, section 2, of the Convention were *prima facie* applicable to the dispute concerning Southern Bluefin Tuna (Australia and New Zealand *v.* Japan). Consequently, it should exercise the jurisdiction conferred on it by article 290 §5 of the Convention by prescribing provisional measures for the parties.

Urgency

Provisional measures, as we know, are essentially intended to preserve the rights of the parties and to prevent irreparable harm. The harm must be probable and imminent.

Preservation of the rights of the parties pending constitution of the arbitral tribunal is an embodiment of the principle of the equality of States and the equality of parties before the tribunal from a procedural perspective. The rights to be preserved are those that are capable of adjudication on the merits. From this requirement there arises a need to establish a link between rights requiring protection and those that are capable of being adjudicated as to the merits, without anticipating the final decision. With regard to irreparable harm, it is well-established practice that measures should not be prescribed unless the irreparable harm is imminent.

This establishes a close link between the harm and the urgency: if the irreparable harm is not imminent, there is no urgency.

Urgency was defined by the ICJ in the *Case concerning Passage through the Great Belt* as follows:

> Whereas provisional measures under Article 41 of the Statute are indicated "pending the final decision" of the Court on the merits of the case, and are therefore only justified if there is urgency in the sense that action prejudicial to the rights of either party is likely to be taken before such final decision is given [Order of 29 July 1991, ICJ Reports 1991, 9].

Urgency encompasses procedural and substantive aspects. Thus, article 90 of the Rules provides that a request for provisional measures has priority over all other proceedings before the Tribunal. And the President fixes the date of the hearing as soon as possible.

Urgency also means that the request before the Tribunal must be rapidly and appropriately dealt with. In that sense, urgency is an essential criterion of the request for provisional measures without which the measures cannot be prescribed within the meaning of the Convention. It constitutes, together with irreparable harm, the two fundamental elements for the prescription of provisional measures.

III. EFFECTS OF PROVISIONAL MEASURES PRESCRIBED BY ITLOS

I now come to the effects of provisional measures prescribed by the Tribunal, a matter of some difficulty.

Luis Delbez said that "the only thorny issue of law presented by provisional measures is that of their authority" [L. Delbez, *Les principes généraux du contentieux international* (Paris, 1962), 118].

In other words, what are the effects of provisional measures? Are such measures binding upon the parties and the Tribunal? The question is highly controversial but, despite appearances, remains unsettled. It might appear at first blush that such measures are binding inasmuch as it is the legal rule that prescribes, prohibits, or permits.

If one refers to the ICJ, one must note from the outset that the text of its statute leans more in favor of treating provisional measures as non-binding. The same is true of the preparatory work, which indicates clearly that provisional measures were to be non-binding. [See Jersez Sztucki, *Interim Measures in the Hague Court* (Kluwer, 1983).] The Rules are of little help. Moreover, practice is not conclusive and the different interpretations have developed in the doctrine, which remains split. [See H. Thirlway, "The Indication of Provisional Measures by the International Court of Justice in Interim Measures Indicated by International Courts," R. Bernhardt, ed., *Publications of Max Planck* (Berlin: Springer Verlag, 1994), 152, specifically 26 *et seq.*]

The problem is linked to the formulation of the texts but also to the nature of the orders. The preparatory work shows that the framers of the Statute of the Court preferred the verb "indicate" to "order." The United Nations Convention on the Law of the Sea, for its part, uses the word "prescribe." This, as we shall shortly see, does not settle the matter.

Advocates of the binding nature of provisional measures argue from a general principle of law pursuant to which States parties to an international dispute are under an obligation to refrain from any act that could nullify the decision of the jurisdiction. Thus, the measures prescribed would simply be the practical application of that principle. [See J. B. Elkind, *Interim Protection: A Functional Approach* (Nijhoff, 1981), 162.]

States, in becoming parties to an international dispute, have expressed their consent to be judged by a competent jurisdiction. This means that the provisional measures are binding if the treaty provisions between the parties so provide. The attendant effect is that violation of the measures prescribed amounts to a violation of an international obligation. But is there under international law an obligation to refrain from any act that nullifies the final decision? And can one seek reparation in the event of violation of such an obligation? In truth, the general principle outlined by Professor Elkind comes closer to a "moral obligation" arising from a logical necessity.

One may observe that the non-performance of measures prescribed does not actually hamper the course of procedure or benefit one party in subsequent stages. Nor does it affect the substance of the final decision of the arbitral tribunal.

Therein lies the crux of the matter. Provisional measures emerge as a phase in the decision-making process in which the tribunal notes the existence of rights to be protected but does not declare them. The measures freeze the rights pending a future decision.

The interlocutory and, therefore, provisional character of such orders deprives them of being *res judicata* because the measures can be modified or revoked. In other words, they can never be binding in the same sense as, for example, a declaratory judgment. Nor are they capable of being invoked as against third parties.

Employing a common legal nomenclature, we might say that provisional measures arise from acts *negotium*, in other words from the process by which the legal rule concerning expression of will emerges, whereas the final decision arises from the legal rule laid down. And it is only the latter that is binding and opposable.

Consideration of the content of measures prescribed leaves one even more skeptical. In the Saiga 2 case, for example, the Tribunal prescribed that one party should refrain from taking or carrying out any judicial or administrative action against the *Saiga*. It "recommended that the two parties endeavour to find an arrangement . . . pending the final decision . . ." [Operative paragraphs 1 and 2].

In the Southern Bluefin Tuna case, the Tribunal prescribed that the parties "ensure that no action is taken which might aggravate or extend the disputes"; and that the two parties "should resume negotiations without delay with a view to reaching agreement on measures for the conservation and management of southern bluefin tuna."

The foregoing excerpts show that the measures recommend and admonish the parties to do or not to do. But is there in international law a power to prescribe that is recommendatory or hortatory?

Another problem to be distinguished from that of the binding effect of provisional measures is that of their implementation. Article 95 of the Rules of the Tribunal sets out the applicable rules, but we believe that it is not up to the Tribunal to oversee the application of its judicial decisions because it affects the extra-procedural relations of the litigants.

IMPLEMENTATION OF DECISIONS OF INTERNATIONAL COURTS

Rüdiger Wolfrum[*]

I. INTRODUCTION

The implementation and enforcement of judgments and other mandatory decisions of international courts is one of the decisive factors for an effective peaceful settlement of international disputes, although literature thereon—at least compared to the literature on jurisdictional issues—is minimal.[1]

In addressing compliance with judgments and mandatory decisions of international courts, it is necessary to distinguish between compliance with incidental and interlocutory decisions and compliance with final decisions. The failure of a party to a dispute may lead to the imposition of a sanction of a procedural nature by the respective international court.[2] The situation is different in respect of decisions indicating, as under the Statute of the International Court of Justice,[3] or prescribing, as under article 290, paragraph 1, of the Convention on the Law of the Sea (the Convention),[4] provisional measures.

The problem of how to ensure compliance with final decisions of international courts, in particular, judgments, is more complex. As Rosenne[5] has pointed out, much depends upon the content of such decisions. Judgments may be of a declaratory nature and, accordingly, may not require direct execution, such as, for example a judgment stating that the conduct of a party was not in conformity with international law. For such judgments, the question of compliance does not arise directly. This is different for judgments that prescribe a certain conduct of a party to a legal dispute or oblige it to achieve a certain result. In the latter case the judgment debtor has a wide discretion; in the former such discretion may be more limited. The statutes of the various

---

[*] Judge, International Tribunal for the Law of the Sea.

M.H. Nordquist and J.N. Moore (eds.),
Current Marine Environmental Issues and the International Tribunal for the Law of the Sea, 103–112.
© 2001 *Kluwer Law International. Printed in the Netherlands.*

international courts provide for different approaches in this respect.

It is the attempt of this paper to first outline these various approaches of the existing systems concerning compliance with final decisions of international courts and, thereafter, to offer some consideration for improving existing systems with the view of improving their effectiveness. These considerations will be of a tentative nature only.

II. EXISTING APPROACHES CONCERNING COMPLIANCE WITH FINAL DECISIONS OF INTERNATIONAL COURTS

It is possible to identify different systems of how to ensure compliance with final decisions of international courts, namely decisions not taken in the traditional dispute between States but involving other entities such as individuals or juridical persons. In this respect, reference is to be made to legal disputes between the International Seabed Authority and an operator, including a State. In this case, enforcement powers were decentralized by vesting them into the respective organs of States responsible for the execution of judgments.

Another system was developed for the settlement of legal disputes within the world trade law system. Here, too, a decentralized system was established namely by leaving it to the State concerned to enforce the decision taken in its favor.

The third system is the one ensuring compliance with final decisions of the International Court of Justice. Under this system, a role is given to the United Nations, in particular, the Security Council, to give effect to judgments of the International Court of Justice. This system, accordingly, may be qualified as having a centralized means of enforcement.

Finally, reference is to be made to all the systems that satisfy themselves, like the one under Part V, section 3, of the Convention, in which it is only stated that ". . . any decision rendered by a court or a tribunal having jurisdiction shall be final and shall be complied with by all the parties to the dispute."[6]

Pursuant to article 39, Annex VI, of the Convention, decisions of the Seabed Disputes Chamber are to be considered and treated—as far as their enforcement is concerned—like decisions of highest courts of that State in which enforcement actions are to take place. This provision has to be read together with the other provisions of the Convention on the Law of the Sea concerning the obligation of States Parties to comply with any decision rendered by any court or tribunal having jurisdiction under the Convention (article 296, para. 1). However, it was felt that decisions of the Seabed Disputes Chamber were of a different nature. Since they may have to be enforced vis-à-vis individuals, private entities, or States acting on the same level as individuals, it was felt necessary to provide for the enforcement of such decisions on the national level.[7]

Article 39, Annex VI, of the Convention, by referring to decisions of the Seabed Disputes Chamber, embraces all binding decisions of the Seabed Disputes Chamber and, by virtue of article 15, paragraph 5, of the Convention, any ad hoc chamber of the Seabed Disputes Chamber.[8] The effect of article 39, Annex VI, of the Convention, is that the organs of a State responsible for enforcing national judgments are mandated and, in fact, obliged to enforce final decisions of the Seabed Disputes Chamber. That is why this system may be qualified as being based upon a decentralized form of enforcement.

This system has one advantage, but also one disadvantage, compared to the systems on enforcing compliance still to be discussed. It has the merit of having an effective enforcement system, since all States dispose of mechanisms to effectively enforce judgments of their national courts. Article 39, Annex III, of the Convention, does not open the possibility for the organs of the State concerned to scrutinize final decisions of the Seabed Disputes Chamber to establish, for example, whether the national order public induces non-execution. The disadvantage of that system derives from the fact that national systems on the enforcement of judgments may differ. However, States are under scrutiny in this respect since a non-enforcement or an ineffective enforcement of final decisions of the Seabed Disputes Chamber constitutes a violation of Part XI of the Convention on the Law of the Sea upon which the Seabed Disputes Chamber would have compulsory jurisdiction under article 187 of the Convention.

The second system referred to is the world trade law system. According to that system, dispute settlement procedures do not come to an end with the adoption of panel or appellate body reports. They continue until the issue is finally resolved. During the post adjudication stage—the implementation stage—the Dispute Settlement Body is in charge of surveying the proper implementation of recommendations and rulings. It also has, if necessary, to guide retaliatory measures.

A special procedure[9] is provided for in the case of disagreement about due compliance with recommendations and rulings. Such disputes shall be decided through recourse to the dispute settlement procedures, including, wherever possible, by resort to the original panel. If recommendations or rulings are not implemented within a reasonable period of time, article 22 DSU (Dispute Settlement Understanding) provides for compensation and suspension of concessions or other obligations. They are considered temporary measures while full implementation is preferred.

In a first step, upon request, the responsible party shall enter into negotiations with parties having invoked the dispute settlement procedure with a view to develop a mutually acceptable compensation. Such compensation is voluntary and—if granted—shall be consistent with covered agreements. If no agreement is achieved, any party having invoked the dispute settlement may request authorization from the Dispute Settlement Body to suspend vis-à-vis the Member concerned the application of concessions or other obligations under the covered agreements. Subject and extent of such retaliatory suspension are ruled upon by article 22.3 and 4 DSU. In order to take such measures, the respective Member has to request authorization from the Dispute Settlement Body. When such request includes measures under article 22.3 lit. b and c, the reasons therefore have to be stated. The Dispute Settlement Body shall authorize the proposed suspensions within a specified time limit, unless it is rejected by consensus or suspension is prohibited in the covered agreement. If the Member concerned objects to the level or subject of suspension, the matter shall be referred to arbitration according to article 22.6 and 7 DSU.

Given the temporary character of suspensions and their objective to achieve implementation, they may be applied until the measures found to be inconsistent have been removed, a solution to the nullification or impairment has been provided, or a mutually satisfactory solution has been reached. The surveillance of the DSU remains until the rulings and recommendations have been finally implemented.[10]

The third system referred to is the one concerning the enforcement of compliance with final decisions of the International Court of Justice. Due to the traditional separation of the adjudication from the post-adjudication phase in international law, the provisions concerning the enforcement of final decisions of the International Court of Justice found its place not in the Statute of the International Court of Justice but in the Charter of the United Nations (the Charter).[11] It is an open question whether this separation of the adjudication and the post-adjudication phase and, in particular, whether their attribution to different organs is mandatory.[12]

According to article 94, paragraph 2, of the Charter, if a party to a dispute fails to perform the obligations incumbent upon it under a judgment rendered, the other party may have recourse to the Security Council. The Security Council, if it deems necessary, may make recommendations or decide upon measures to be taken to give effect to the judgment. The words "if it deems necessary" underline the political nature—compared to the judicial nature of the final decision of the International Court of Justice—of the enforcement measure the Security Council might take. Referring to the discretion of the Security Council in this respect does not mean that the latter has the right to annul the final decision. This would be contrary to article 60 of the Statute of the ICJ, which states that a judgment is final and without appeal. Within this limit the Security Council is free to decide which kind of recommendations it should make and what kind of measures it should apply.[13]

Article 94, paragraph 2, of the Charter, has been invoked twice by Nicaragua following the Judgment of the International Court of Justice in the Military and Paramilitary Activities In and Against Nicaragua case.[14] On each occasion, the negative vote of the United States prevented the adoption of any resolution of the Security Council.[15] This and the lack of further practice concerning article 94, paragraph 2, of the Charter, proves that the attempt to vest the power to enforce final decisions of the International Court of Justice into the Security Council does not constitute a viable means. The Security Council once was, however, involved in the implementation of a judgment of the ICJ, for example, in the Territorial Dispute case (Chad/Libya). The parties concluded an agreement concerning the practical modalities for the implementation of that judgment, in particular, the withdrawal of the Libyan administration under the supervision of a team of Chad and Libyan officers and United Nations Observers.

In resolution 915 (1994), 4 May 1994, the Security Council established the United Nations Aouzou Strip Observer Group (UNASOG), while indicating that this was to assist the parties in implementing the judgment of the International Court of Justice. The resolution did not—and could not—refer to article 94, paragraph 2, of the Charter. Instead the Security Council emphasized that the establishment of such Observer Group helped promote peaceful relations between the parties in accordance with the principles and purposes of the United Nations.

According to article 296 of the Convention—the fourth system referred to—the parties to a dispute have to comply with any decision rendered by a court or tribunal having jurisdiction under Part XV, Section of the Convention on the Law of the Sea. This provision states the evident. There exists a general principle of international law according to which, when States agree to submit their legal disputes to an international tribunal, they assume the obligation to comply with the decision of that tribunal.[16]

In this respect, the Convention on the Law of the Sea merely reflects and reconfirms such principles as does article 94, paragraph 1, of the Charter.[17] Article 296 of the Convention, however, does not indicate whether and to what extent any court or tribunal—which includes the International Court of Justice, the International Tribunal for the Law of the Sea, and any Arbitral Tribunal—would have a role in monitoring the implementation of its decisions. If they do not have such function or at least some function to that extent, the enforcement of a final decision of an international court is left to the respective party to the conflict concerned. It may have recourse to countermeasures as provided by international law. This is unsatisfactory or even counterproductive since a legal conflict continues to exist amongst the States concerned, albeit in a different form.

III. CONCLUSION

As indicated earlier, I wonder whether it is really axiomatic that adjudication and the post-adjudication phase are to be separated and that the international courts concerned have no role to play in the post-adjudication phase. The WTO system proves that other approaches are possible. Further precedents exist to prove this point.

In the Special Agreement by which the Burkina Faso *v.* Mali case was brought before an ad hoc Chamber of the ICJ, the Chamber was required to nominate in its judgment three experts to assist the parties in the demarcation of the border. The International Court of Justice considered that as part of the implementation of the judgment it had delivered.[18] This may have been an exceptional case but nothing can prevent States from following such procedure where suitable and developing it into a general rule.

There is one further set of precedents worth reporting. When issuing provisional measures, the International Court of Justice requests the parties to a legal dispute "to inform the court of all measures which it has taken in implementation of this Order."[19] This is done so, in spite of the question of whether provisional measures indicated by the ICJ are binding. The International Tribunal for the Law of the Sea follows this practice. In respect of it, there is no doubt about the binding nature of its provisional measures. The Tribunal stated in the Southern Bluefin Tuna

Cases[20]—while referring to article 95, paragraph 1, of the Rules—that the parties to the disputes were under an obligation to report on their compliance with any provisional measure. The President of the Tribunal was even entrusted to request such further reports and information considered appropriate. Neither the Order nor the Rules of the Tribunal give any indication as to how the Tribunal might act if it found the parties to be in non-compliance. Certainly the powers of the Tribunal are limited in this respect. Nevertheless, the obligation to report itself exercises some pressure upon the parties to the conflict to implement the provisional measure. This pressure may be enforced if the matter of non-compliance would be discussed in the international court of the tribunal concerned.

It is of interest to note that such request for information on compliance has not been included in the operative part of a judgment. It would be worth considering whether such a request would be a legitimate step towards a more active role by international courts as far as compliance with their final decisions is concerned.

Notes

[1] E. Hambro, L'Exécution des sentences internationales (1936); C. Vulcan, "L'Exécution des décisions de La Cour Internationale de Justice d'après la Charte des Nations Unies," 51 *RGDIP* (1947): 187; O. Schachter, "The Enforcement of International Judicial and Arbitral Decisions," 53 *AJIL* (1960): 1; and M. Reisman, *Nullity and Revision: The Review and Enforcement of International Judgments and Awards* (1971).

[2] S. Rosenne, *The Law and Practice of the International Court, 1920-1996*, 3d ed. (1997), 214 et seq.

[3] Article 41, ICJ Statute. See E. Szabó, "Provisional Measures in the World Court: Binding or Bound to be Ineffective?," 10 *Leiden Journal of International Law* (1997): 475-489.

[4] For further details, see R. Wolfrum, "Provisional Measures of the International Tribunal for the Law of the Sea," 37 *IJIL* (1997): 420-434.

[5] Note 2, 216.

[6] Article 296, para. 1, Convention on the Law of the Sea.

[7] *United Nations Convention on the Law of the Sea, 1982: A Commentary*, Vol. V (1989), 414.

[8] Ibid.

[9] Article 21.5, Dispute Settlement Understanding (DSU), <http://www.wto.org/english/tratop-e/dispu-e/dsu-e.htm>.

[10] For further details, see P. T. Stoll, "World Trade, Dispute Settlement," *Encyclopedia of Public International Law*, Vol. IV (2000), 1520-1529, with further references.

[11] Rosenne (note 2), 249, considers that to be relevant. See also H. Mosler, "Article 94," B. Simma, ed., *The Charter of the United Nations: A Commentary* (1994), para. 7 et seq.

[12] This view seems to have been taken by Rosenne (note 2), 249.

[13] Mosler (note 11), para. 11.

[14] ICJ Reports 1986, 14 et seq.

[15] 41 SCOR Sup. July, August, September 1986 (S/18230), 50; ibid., Sup. October, November, December 1986 (S/18415), 27; A. Tanzi, "Problems of Enforcement of Decisions of the International Court of Justice and the Law of the United Nations," *European Journal of International Law* (1995): 539.

[16] H. Kelsen, *Principles of International Law*, 2d ed., by R. W. Tucker (1966), 543.

[17] In fact, the International Court of Justice in its judgment in the Haya de la Torre case (ICJ Reports 1951, 71) only referred to the general obligation rather than the specific one under the Charter when it discussed the obligation of compliance with the earlier decision in the Asylum case (ICJ Reports 1950, 266). See Rosenne (note), 219.

[18] ICJ Reports 1986, 554 (650), Order of 9 April 1987, ICJ Reports 1987, 718.

[19] LaGrand Case (Germany *v.* United States of America), Request for the Indication for Provisional Measures, Order of 3 March 1999, ICJ Reports 1999, 16.

[20] Request for Provisional Measures, Order of 27 August 1999.

ITLOS PROCEDURES AND PRACTICES: BONDS

Edward Arthur Laing[*]

I propose to focus on two aspects of the Tribunal's evolving practice in the area of the prompt release procedure: bonds and the appreciation of evidence. Before doing this, let me remind you that the Convention's provisions on prompt release contemplate the use of bonds in two contexts. Firstly, the bond may be set at the domestic level by the judicial or other authorities of a detaining State as a condition for release of a vessel or its crew from detention. Secondly, at the international level it might be concluded that the bond set by the detaining State is not reasonable. In that case, a fresh bond may be required as the condition for release ordered at the international level. At that level, release is likely to be ordered by the international adjudicating body that is authorized to evaluate the reasonableness of bonds set at the domestic level or that orders bonds at the international level. The body in question is likely to be ITLOS.

I

First, I want to examine a largely textual issue relating to the reasonableness of the bond or bonds that might be ordered in the domestic or the international context. Let us recall that in the first (domestic) context, reasonableness is almost invariably required by what we may call the "allegation provisions," viz articles 73, 220, and 226. These, *inter alia*, authorize detention in connection with situations or incidents relating to exploration, exploitation, conservation and management of the living resources of the exclusive economic zone, or relating to protection from pollution of the marine environment, including cases where vessels have violated generally accepted international rules and standards. Article 292 authorizes the adjudicating body to scrutinize the

---

[*] Judge, International Tribunal for the Law of the Sea.

M.H. Nordquist and J.N. Moore (eds.),
Current Marine Environmental Issues and the International Tribunal for the Law of the Sea, 113–123.
© 2001 *Kluwer Law International. Printed in the Netherlands.*

reasonableness of any bond set in this first context. The one possible exception to the requirement of reasonableness might come from the authentic French text rendition of the adjective in article 73 qualifying "bond or other security." The word used there is *suffisante*, which may be translated as "sufficient." I agree with the position that has been advanced that the French word has or must be presumed to have the same meaning as "reasonable" and that it adds nothing to the phrase in which it appears. At first sight, then, we might appear to have crossed the Rubicon on this issue.

As already noted, the second context in which bonds may be required is where, having concluded that the bond set by the domestic bond-setting judge or other authority is not reasonable or where it finds that none was set at all, the Tribunal decides to order prompt release upon the posting of a bond or other financial security. Although article 292, paragraph 4, makes no mention of a requirement of reasonableness, it is obvious that any bond that is determined by the Tribunal is presumptively reasonable.

So far, the Tribunal has not articulated a necessary and proper distinction regarding the criterion of reasonableness. That distinction is between qualitative reasonableness and quantitative reasonableness. Although the Tribunal's judgments imply recognition of this dichotomy, those judgments largely focus on quantitative reasonableness. The French word *suffisante* seems to advert to the quantitative aspects, while the English word "reasonable" embraces both the quantitative and qualitative aspects. On that basis, the French word does have viability and adds a useful shade of meaning to the English text. However, sufficiency in the French version, or quantitative reasonableness, cannot have been intended to stand alone without its qualitative partner.

II

Turning to more substantive aspects of bonds, firstly I will touch on **qualitative aspects of reasonableness**. I suggest that in the task of articulating this aspect of reasonableness, the Tribunal will have to identify broad parameters and increasingly more specific criteria. Whatever selections are made, however, the concept of qualitative reasonableness must certainly be contextual and circumstantial. This will obviously involve a substantial measure of variability over time; even a significant measure of fluidity. However, the Tribunal will have to be vigilant in resisting the temptation experienced by all parties to handle the concept in an excessively malleable or an unduly subjective manner.

The Tribunal has not yet substantially laid out specific criteria or parameters. Though the Tribunal has made it clear that its function is an international one, it still needs to squarely address the question of the relevance of or weight to be given to the law of the detaining State. In the *Monte Confurco* case, the Tribunal talked about balancing or reconciling the interests of the detaining State and the flag State. I think that this approach is useful, but it is subject to a possible limitation. That limitation is the potential of this approach to over-emphasize the domestic law, especially the law of the detaining State. The approach might, in particular cases, overlook the very specific international parameters and touchstones in Parts V and XII of the Convention referenced in the "allegation provisions" of the Convention to which I have referred: articles 73, 220, and 226, which explicitly invoke "international rules and standards" and "laws and regulations adopted . . . in conformity with the Convention."

The foregoing is not intended to deny that the Tribunal is required to deal with, or "apply," the domestic law, treating that law as a "fact," to use the expression of some of the jurisprudence. This does not mean, however, that the Tribunal should pay undue attention to the enforcement jurisdictional trends of the detaining State, whether these be of national judicial decisions or patterns of actions by its executive branch or law enforcement authorities.

Provisionally, there might be some role to be played by norms and practice evolving within the framework of a formal regional organization that has functions closely relevant to the circumstances in which the vessel was detained. However, this will require much thought.

In addition to what I have called the broad parameters of qualitative reasonableness, it is evident that relevant secondary criteria should include such characteristics of reasonableness as consistency, proportionality, balance, fairness, moderateness, suitability, and tolerableness. These are broad notions. They are also extremely variable, as is the concept of reasonableness itself. Yet they may strengthen the arms of prudent adjudicators.

III

I turn to the **quantitative aspects of reasonableness.** As I have already mentioned, the Tribunal has emphasized these. This has largely been in connection with its task of setting the bond at the second or international stage after the Tribunal has determined that the bond set by the domestic authorities is not reasonable (in the qualitative or the quantitative sense, or both senses). In the *Camouco* case, the "factors that are relevant in an assessment of the reasonableness of bonds or other financial security" were stated to include:

> The gravity of the alleged offenses, the penalties imposed or imposable under the laws of the detaining State, the value of the detained vessel and of the cargo seized, the amount of the bond imposed by the detaining State and its form.

There are, therefore, at least six factors:

(1) The gravity of the offenses alleged to have been committed;
(2) The penalties imposed or imposable under the law of the detaining State;
(3) The value of the detained vessel;
(4) The value of the cargo seized;
(5) The amount of the bond imposed by the detaining State; and
(6) The form of the bond.

Most of these factors are of a quantitative nature. Like the Tribunal in the recent *Monte Confurco* case, I shall focus on the first four of the six factors.

The Tribunal's handling of these issues is evidently undergoing development. It seems relatively clear, however, that although the language from the *Camouco* that I quoted appears to apply to both the domestic and the international stages of bond-setting, the Tribunal's practice seems to suggest that in the Tribunal's discussions of quantitative issues it has been mainly preoccupied with the second or international context.

As far as the first factor of *the gravity of the offenses alleged to have been committed* is concerned, this is the only one of the four factors where the Tribunal's analytical approach seems concretely to encompass qualitative issues. For instance, in the *Monte Confurco* case, the Tribunal's discussion focuses on the arguments of the parties and a guarded statement of its own positive perceptions about whether the vessel's acts constituted what might be called the necessary juridical facts or, in criminal cases, *actus reus*. There has not been much discussion of quantitative issues. Probably this is because this factor seems to overlap somewhat with the second, more quantitative factor of the penalty that may be imposed. Perhaps, however, the Tribunal might consider under this rubric the range of potential penalties, as opposed to focusing exclusively on the quantum of the actual penalty that the detaining State proposes to impose. This could be juxtaposed against the background of Parts V and XII of the Convention and even, perhaps in the future, the relevant regional trends mentioned earlier.

As for *the penalties imposed or imposable*, this factor has not yet been emphasized by the Tribunal, but its quantitative nature is evident. It might be useful in the future to assess the detaining State's laws, also against the background of Parts V and XII of the Convention.

Turning to *the value of the vessel*, it should be noted that article 111, paragraph 2(b), of the Tribunal's Rules does not require the invariable provision of information on or assessment of this value.[1] Such information is required only where it is "appropriate." We therefore have to ask whether in each case where the Applicant leads evidence on value, the Tribunal should assess the question of appropriateness. Should the parties routinely supply such information? What would be the potential impact of such action? If the value is low, should that point the Tribunal in the direction of setting a ceiling or a floor for the bond? If the Tribunal gets bogged down in the minutia of the value of the vessel, as opposed to other assessment factors, can this have a boomerang effect? For example, might it help to catapult the detaining State into confiscating the vessel? Even if the parties supply data on the vessel's value, is the Tribunal really required to make a determination of value? To what end? In the *Monte Confurco* case, the parties debated at some length the question of the vessel's value, and the Tribunal eventually accepted the lowest of some four values that had been proposed. This amounted to some two percent of the security set by the Tribunal. Eventually the vessel was placed under a confiscation order, which was timed to precede the anticipated release.

One last question: any exercise in determination of value of a vessel involves some notoriously difficult methodological questions. Therefore, given the abbreviated nature of prompt release proceedings and even granting that the parties may supply information, is the Tribunal really *required* to make a determination of value?

As far as concerns the factor of *the value of the cargo*, such information is not required by the Rules. Let us assume that this information is logically relevant to article 73. Should the Tribunal expect the parties to supply information on this, even though the Rules contemplate only information about cargo *capacity* as a method of identifying the value of the vessel? Can the same be true for articles 220 and 226, where the cargo is often likely to be petroleum? In the *Monte Confurco* case, the Tribunal stated that the cargo of catch of fish on board as well as the fishing gear were relevant in the assessment of the reasonableness of the bond. At any rate, in the Rules, information on cargo capacity is not mandatory, and it is probably arguable that there are several cases where the cargo or cargo capacity is not relevant at all.

118

Furthermore it must be asked whether there might not be some cases in which even mention of the value of the cargo by the Tribunal would be imprudent.

In relation to all of these assessment factors, let us assume that they have a general or theoretical relevance, at least in connection with the bond set by the Tribunal. Let us further assume that evidence is led or the Tribunal obtains information pertinent to these factors. Should the Tribunal feel compelled invariably to spell out in the judgment its detailed assessment of such quantitative data? I should think not, and I am sure that the Tribunal would agree that prudence suggests that even when we are dragged to the well, we need not drink.

IV

I will now address the **identification of the nature, form, and content of the bonds** being determined by the Tribunal. This is a matter that the Tribunal is currently studying, possibly with a view to identifying some desiderata, since it may be that if the parties are left to their own devices, the sort of difficulties[2] experienced in connection with the efforts of the parties to devise a bond after the *Saiga* judgment will continue.

This touches slightly on the issue of characterization. In the *Saiga* case, the Tribunal held that it possesses authority to make the necessary characterization of the apparent actions and incidents that give rise to the allegation trigger under any of the three relevant articles of the Convention and that this could trump any characterization by the detaining State authorities. Although this decision was criticized in some quarters, I believe that the Tribunal was quite correct if, in fact, the international bond-setting and, indeed, prompt release proceedings are a truly autonomous and independent institution. Furthermore, it cannot be beyond imagination that the detaining State could make a characterization that is either inaccurate or, frankly, distorted. Besides, when the flag State has to prepare and present its Application, under considerable humanitarian pressure it might not have full access to the facts and to the detaining State's laws. Hence, in proper cases the Tribunal must make the characterization whether the apparent actions of the vessel and its Master might constitute an administrative infraction, involve civil or quasi-civil responsibility, might be criminal or perhaps even hyper-criminal, might seem to involve (under the detaining State's law) a measure of deterrence, and so on.

The question here is whether it should be for the Tribunal or the parties to determine whether the instrument to be used should be of a particular, generally known type used in a field of law that is hypothetically or deemed to be applicable or that is actually applicable or whether, for example, it should be a composite type of instrument. So far, in ordering security, the Tribunal has opted for in-kind security and for bank guarantees, actually indicating texts for inclusion. Interestingly, it has not acceded to the suggestions of flag States that it should require that the guaranty be "first class." Whatever the Tribunal does, it will be useful for us to note the substantial variety of types of bonds used in shipping and general practice. These include bank guarantees, instruments establishing suretyship relations, letters of guarantee or undertaking by P & I Clubs, and even letters of credit. I believe that it will be worthwhile in the future to explore a fair range of types of instruments. Perhaps, also, even if the parties are permitted to make the choice, a default type of instrument could be devised. At some time, the Tribunal might consider undertaking the function of determining the role, if any, that it might be able to play; that is, by developing practice under articles 113 and 114 of the Rules, relating to possible functions by the Tribunal as a depositary of bonds or as an agency for otherwise assisting the parties.

V

I finally turn to the standard for the appreciation of evidence. You will probably recall that in the *Saiga* case, the Tribunal adopted the standard of "arguable" or "sufficiently plausible" in relation to whether an allegation of non-compliance with article 73's requirement of a release against a reasonable bond had been made out. In this connection, it needs to also be recalled that prompt release is a special type of very expedited proceeding. This partly justifies the standard of appreciation. Also, it has been noted that in several other key provisions, the Convention envisages a "bare allegation" (not full proof, I must stress) as the standard of appreciation. This has some general similarities to the standard for provisional measures. I would go further and suggest that it is worth considering whether the standard should apply not only to the issue of whether the allegation has been made out but also to many aspects of prompt release cases, in relation to reasonableness, or even assessments of the conduct of the vessel or its crew and the actions of the detaining State.

On the other hand, I disagree with another suggestion that has been made that another "appreciation" standard should apply in prompt release cases. That standard is the "free" or "considerable" margin of appreciation standard used by European human rights adjudicators in evaluating domestic measures and decisions. I believe that this European doctrine has a limited geographical, cultural, societal, and transactional ambit. If that standard is one of garden variety international human rights law, I contend that it is not a standard that can be grafted onto the sphere of prompt release where the Tribunal is trying to assess, in a completely different context, the reasonableness of the domestic bond or the compliance of domestic authorities with unprecedented autonomous international notions with multifarious components. Clearly, the two institutions are not *in pari materiae*, even though I readily concede that prompt release has a distinct human rights dimension.

On the other hand, if the objective of the considerable or free margin of appreciation standard is to supply a rebuttable presumption, that standard could not work in many prompt release situations, on account of the novelty and variety of the patterns of facts and of the potential international legal considerations in such cases. This may be compared with the generally routine nature of the human rights cases and the familiarity and sophistication of many domestic European courts with universal humanitarian trends.

Finally, if the standard falls under adjectival law, it is quite unlikely that if its essence is the considerable or free appreciation of judicial, executive, legislative, and other *governmental acts*, it covers the same ground as does a diminutive standard for the appreciation of the allegation-based *evidence* produced by the parties, even if that standard is claimed to be permissive.

Notes

[1] Paragraph 2(b) anticipates that the Application can include information concerning the vessel's "tonnage, cargo capacity and data relative to the determination of its value . . . ."

[2] Mainly about language, such as the word "consideration." Some of these were apparently attributable to the variety of languages spoken by several of the players from differing domestic legal cultures.

PANEL III

ITLOS and Practitioners

THE CASE-LAW OF ITLOS (1997-2001): AN OVERVIEW

Shabtai Rosenne[*]

In the ten to fifteen minutes at my disposal, I am not going to discuss the substance of the jurisprudence of the International Tribunal for the Law of the Sea (ITLOS). ITLOS was established and became operational on October 1, 1996, a little less than five years ago. That is not a long period in which to evaluate the work of a new international tribunal. It received its first case in 1997. The Tribunal's General List already has eight entries, a large number of cases for the first quinquennial of a new international Tribunal. However, those statistics can be misleading, since entry in the List is a technical and administrative matter for the Tribunal.

The Tribunal has had to deal with six separate maritime incidents involving the United Nations Convention on the Law of the Sea (UNCLOS): the *M/V Saiga* between Saint Vincent and the Grenadines and Guinea (1997-1999), two cases arising out of a single incident involving one ship;[1] the *Southern Bluefin Tuna* cases, Australia and New Zealand against Japan (1999), formally two cases against a single respondent but joined as a single case;[2] the *Camouco* case (Panama v. France) (2000);[3] the *Monte Confurco* case (Seychelles v. France) (2000);[4] the *Conservation and Sustainable Exploitation of Swordfish Stocks in the South-Eastern Pacific Ocean* case (Chile and the European Union) (2000) to have been determined by an *ad hoc* Chamber of the Tribunal, but at present suspended by the parties while further negotiations are in progress;[5] and the *Grand Prince* case (Belize v. France).[6]

A striking thing about these cases is that all of them except *Saiga* related to fishery management matters. *Saiga* also indirectly related to fisheries management, in the sense that the incident arose in the exclusive economic zone (EEZ) of the respondent

---

[*] General Editor, *United Nations Convention on the Law of the Sea 1982: A Commentary.*

M.H. Nordquist and J.N. Moore (eds.),
Current Marine Environmental Issues and the International Tribunal for the Law of the Sea, 127–140.
© 2001 *Kluwer Law International. Printed in the Netherlands.*

State alleging violation of its customs regulations applicable in that zone. *Saiga*, *Camouco*, *Monte Confurco*, and *Grand Prince* were initially requests for the prompt release of vessels detained by the coastal State for violation of its fisheries legislation, brought under article 292 of the Convention and articles 110 and following of the Rules. *Saiga* was off the West African coast in the Atlantic, and the other three, *Camouco* fishing for Patagonian Toothfish in the EEZ of France's Southern and Antarctic Territories (Reunion and the Kerguelen Islands), the *Monte Confurco* and *Grand Prince* fishing for the same fish in the same French EEZ. The swordfish case (which appears to have some similarities to the recent Spain *v.* Canada case in the International Court of Justice[7]), however, relates to Chilean fisheries management measures outside the EEZ. Swordfish are a highly migratory species according to Annex I of UNCLOS.[8] Toothfish is a straddling stock. It fetches a high price on the Japanese market.

In four cases, *Saiga*, *Camouco*, *Monte Confurco*, and *Grand Prince*, the applications were filed on behalf of the flag States, in each instance a flag of convenience. Only *Saiga* has produced a judgment on the merits, and it contains a number of important interpretations of the Convention, especially as regards flags of convenience and hot pursuit, as well as of general international law, especially as regards the espousal of claims relating to crew members not of the nationality of the applicant State, and the calculation of pecuniary damages.[9] *Grand Prince* is the first case in ITLOS in which the Tribunal, by a narrow majority and over a strong joint dissent, found that it had no jurisdiction under article 292 to entertain the application. The Tribunal's reasons, however, were based on contentions that had not been argued by either of the parties in the preceding written and oral phases. The Tribunal justified this unusual action by saying that:

> According to the settled jurisprudence in international adjudication, a tribunal must at all times be satisfied that it has jurisdiction to entertain the case submitted to it. For this purpose it has the power to examine *proprio motu* the basis of its jurisdiction (Judgment, para. 77).

That does not mean that it should not give the parties an opportunity to present their arguments on the issue as seen by the Tribunal, especially as article 76 of the Rules of the Tribunal (corresponding to article 61 of the Rules of Court of the ICJ) lays down detailed provisions regarding the Tribunal's indication to the parties of any points or issues that it would like the parties to address specifically.

The *Saiga, Camouco, Monte Confurco,* and *Grand Prince* cases led to judgments on prompt release. *Saiga (No. 2)* and *Southern Bluefin Tuna*[10] led to Orders prescribing provisional measures of protection. It is satisfactory to be able to report that those judgments and orders were complied with, as is required by articles 200 and 292 of the Convention.[11] In the prompt release judgments against France, where the Tribunal fixed the bond and ordered the release, the competent Court in Reunion held that since France had ratified the Convention, by virtue of article 55 of the French Constitution the Convention takes precedence over national laws and is binding on France and its courts. Consequently, the French court was obliged to fix the bond for release at the sum determined by the Tribunal, in lieu of its own original sum.[12] That is an interesting example of an internal court following a decision of a competent international court.

In *Saiga*, the prompt release proceedings were held before the applicant decided to institute substantive proceedings. Those proceedings, alleging violation by the coastal State of the rights of other States in the EEZ, commenced in the form of an Annex VII arbitration under article 287 of the Convention, since neither of the parties had agreed on a single settlement procedure. It took that step later, on December 22, 1997, during provisional measures proceedings. While those proceedings were in progress on the basis that the merits of the case would come before an Annex VII arbitral tribunal, the parties agreed to transfer the merits of the case to the Tribunal. That agreement formed the basis for the remainder of that case.[13] *SBT* was the first phase in a case that was later settled by arbitration under Annex VII of the Convention, the first instance of this. To prescribe provisional measures, ITLOS had to satisfy itself that the matter was urgent and that the proposed arbitration tribunal *prima facie* would have jurisdiction to determine the case. This, as the experience of the International Court of Justice shows, is a low threshold.[14] After much more substantial pleading, the arbitration tribunal found that it was without jurisdiction over the merits.[15] Mr Morgan discusses the ITLOS phase elsewhere in this volume.[16]

In view of academic expressions of concern at the multiplication of international tribunals with possibly overlapping jurisdiction, I think that it is safe to say that given the state of acceptances of the compulsory jurisdiction of the International Court of Justice, only the *SBT* case could *possibly* have been sent to that Court unilaterally, but its jurisdiction would have been challenged by virtue of reservations in the different acceptances of the compulsory jurisdiction of the three countries involved, and possibly also on other grounds.[17] Moreover, since there was some urgency in that case, while the ICJ could have issued an order indicating provisional measures of protection with reasonable speed, indeed possibly as quickly as ITLOS, any decision on the merits would have required several years. As a practical matter, ITLOS, coupled with the Annex VII arbitration, was the only international dispute settlement procedure that was in a position to render a binding decision on those cases with all the necessary speed.[18]

In all the cases so far before ITLOS, three judges *ad hoc* have been appointed. In the *SBT* case, Australia and New Zealand jointly appointed Professor I. Shearer of the University of Sidney to that position to balance the Japanese member of the Tribunal, Judge Yamamoto. In the *Grand Prince* case, France appointed Professor J. P. Cot to balance Judge Laing.[19] One member of the *ad hoc* Chamber for the Chile/EU dispute is a national of one of the member States of the EU, Judge Wolfrum, and Chile has appointed Professor Orrego Vicuña as Judge *ad hoc*.[20]

In all the cases heard so far by ITLOS, witnesses and witness-experts have been called. On the whole, their examination proceeded in what is now commonplace in international tribunals, following the common law model of examination in chief, cross-examination and re-examination. Occasional difficulties have been caused when attorneys not familiar with this system of examining witnesses have been handling the case, and the President has had to rule on the admissibility of a question, even on cross-examination. In one case an expert witness was examined on the voir dire. That is a very exceptional common law procedure to test the qualifications of an expert/witness or, more frequently, the absence of possible bias in a juror. It has been used once in the International Court of Justice.[21] It causes difficulties because questions to test the qualification of the expert-witness can easily become questions on the substance that really belong to the cross-examination phase. I believe that for an international court, cross-examination is probably the more effective way of discrediting an expert/witness.

The Tribunal has had an interesting experience regarding language, and we must take note of it. In the *Saiga (No. 2)* proceedings on the merits, one witness gave his evidence in Wolof, the language spoken in the region of the Niger and Congo. One of the members of the Tribunal understood Wolof and could control the interpretation when necessary.[22] That is the first occasion, so far as I know, in which an international tribunal has heard a witness giving evidence in one of the unwritten languages of Africa. In this instance, no particular difficulty seems to have been experienced. A competent interpreter from Wolof into French was employed, and his interpretations were further interpreted into English, the working language of most of the judges of the Tribunal. Double interpretation, of course, drags the proceedings out, but in international litigation, it cannot be avoided. The lesson of this case is that given the make-up of crews, especially on flag-of-convenience merchant vessels, we must expect the use of "rare" and possibly unwritten languages and even dialects to become a regular feature. It will undoubtedly impose a difficult administrative and logistical burden on the Tribunal, as well as costs. Moreover, it may not always be easy on short notice to find a competent interpreter to translate into one of the Tribunal's working languages.

The cases of prompt release and the requests for provisional measures have each brought out another aspect, which, as far as I know, is a peculiarity of ITLOS and for which there is no guidance from any other international tribunal. Both article 290 of the Convention on provisional measures and article 292 on prompt release empower ITLOS to act on the request regardless of whether it is seised of the merits of the case. For provisional measures this is amplified in article 25 of Annex VI, the Tribunal's Statute. What is more, unlike the Statute of the ICJ and the controversy that it has produced, both article 290 (6) and article 292 (4) provide that the decision of ITLOS shall be complied with. In the Rules of the Tribunal, rules regarding provisional measures and prompt release are found in Part III, on Procedure. Provisional measures constitute Part III, section C, Incidental Proceedings, articles 89 to 95. Rules regarding prompt release proceedings are Part III, section E, articles 110 to 114. Furthermore, Rule 112 (4) requires the decision of the Tribunal on prompt release to be in the form of a judgment.[23] Strictly speaking, as such, under article 296 of the Convention as well as Annex VI, article 33, in the case of ITLOS, the *decision* has no binding force except between the parties *and in respect of that particular case.*

In the *Saiga (No. 2)* case, questions relating to the prompt release were the principal object of the claim. The Judgment (para. 180) recognizes that the *(No. 2)* case "is distinct from the prompt release proceedings and the Judgment of 4 December 1997 [prompt release] is not in issue in the present case." At the same time, in dealing with the nationality of the ship, the Tribunal based itself partly on the 1997 proceedings and judgment (paras. 69-72). The arrangement that the Tribunal has adopted has the consequence that prompt release proceedings are not placed in the category of "incidental proceedings." They appear as "proceedings" pure and simple.

The *Saiga (No. 2)* case alone throws doubt on this approach. The circumstances of the vessel's initial arrest and the delay in releasing the crew and vessel after the prompt release judgment were elements in the merits phase and formed subjects of the request in the second case for the prescription of provisional measures. One of the claims in the instrument instituting the proceedings in what the Tribunal entitled the *Saiga (No. 2)* case was precisely the release of the vessel and crew in accordance with the 1997 Judgment. Not surprisingly, the chief provisional measure requested was the release of the vessel and its crew. They were released while those proceedings were in progress, in fact making those proceedings moot.[24] In that case it is difficult to say that the prompt release proceedings were not, or, perhaps more accurately, did not become, incidental proceedings, although incidental to what is another matter.

The fact that ITLOS can have a residual jurisdiction for those two procedures when it does not have jurisdiction over the mainline case itself means that, in fact, there are two types of provisional measures proceedings and two types of prompt release proceedings, namely in each respect, one where ITLOS does have mainline jurisdiction, and the other where it does not. The Statute recognizes this for provisional measures.

The conditions required before ITLOS can prescribe provisional measures are different for the two types of case. By article 290 (1), where ITLOS is seised of the dispute, it may prescribe provisional measures that it considers appropriate under the circumstances to preserve the respective rights of the parties to the dispute or to prevent serious harm to the marine environment, pending the final decision, if it considers that *prima facie* it has jurisdiction under Part XI (in the case of the Seabed Disputes Chamber) or Part XV of the Convention. This is, as I have mentioned, a very low threshold, and, in fact, the jurisdiction can be exercised in a pending case for the purpose of prescribing provisional measures so long as the absence of jurisdiction is not manifest, a very rare occurrence.

Where ITLOS does not have mainline jurisdiction, however, it has a residual jurisdiction to prescribe, modify, or revoke provisional measures "if it considers that *prima facie* the tribunal which is to be constituted would have jurisdiction and that the urgency of the situation so requires." Here again the *prima facie* jurisdiction of the tribunal to be constituted is a very low threshold, since ultimately that tribunal's jurisdiction will depend on the agreement by which the parties proceed to arbitration. Here the residuary jurisdiction of ITLOS rests on pure guesswork.

The only substantive condition that article 290 (5) of the Convention imposes is that of urgency. That may have been the one element that was missing in the provisional measures phase of the *SBT* case. That notwithstanding, and I hope Mr Morgan will forgive me, I consider that ITLOS had little choice but to prescribe provisional measures, especially as it did not follow the applicants and issue a one-sided Order but instead followed the usual practice of the International Court of Justice in making the provisional measures reciprocal and applicable to both parties.

Just how hypothetical *prima facie* jurisdiction, sufficient for provisional measures, can be is illustrated by two cases, one in the International Court of Justice and the other in ITLOS.

The ICJ case is *Anglo-Iranian Oil Co.* (Provisional Measures) case. Here the Court first held that it did have *prima facie* jurisdiction over the merits and proceeded to indicate provisional measures of protection. However, a year later, after full argument on the issue, the Court decided that it did not have jurisdiction to deal with the merits of the case.[25] In *SBT*, ITLOS likewise decided that the arbitral tribunal that would be constituted would have *prima facie* jurisdiction over the merits. What ITLOS did not foresee, and indeed could not have foreseen, is that when the parties got down to organizing the arbitration under Annex VII, they would not only agree that there was an issue of jurisdiction outstanding between them, but also that this issue would be decided first as a preliminary objection. Even less, of course, could ITLOS foresee that the arbitral tribunal would find that it did not have jurisdiction to determine that dispute.

It is, perhaps, also surprising that given the hypothetical nature of the jurisdictional issue in the provisional measures proceeding, ITLOS did not include the usual statement that the ICJ includes in such cases, to the effect that its decision in no way prejudged the question of the jurisdiction of the arbitral tribunal to deal with the case, although it did include such a statement in its provisional measures order in the *Saiga (No. 2)* case (para. 46).

In *Anglo-Iranian*, the ICJ, although declaring that it had no jurisdiction, at the same time declared that the order indicating provisional measures ceased to be operative upon the delivery of the judgment declining jurisdiction. That ruling was followed by the arbitral tribunal in the *SBT* case, with, however, an important and carefully crafted rider, to the effect that the revocation of the Order "does not mean that the Parties may disregard the effects of that Order or their own decisions made in conformity with it" (paras. 66 and 67). That is the consequence of the obligation that the Law of the Sea Convention imposes on the parties to comply with the provisional measures order. According to information that I have received, that arbitral award, including those remarks about the provisional measures, has had the effect of unblocking the diplomatic *impasse* between the parties and has opened the way to a more rational arrangement for the management of stock of southern bluefin tuna. This is a good example of the judicial process in the settlement of disputes. Statements of disappointment in academic writings that the arbitration did not go into the merits completely fail to appreciate that the function of the courts is to settle disputes, and nothing else.

I would like to say one other thing about that incident. In academic circles, one hears criticism that five distinguished international lawyers overruled what had been decided by the court composed of twenty-two distinguished experts on the Law of the Sea, all well versed in the Convention. Nothing could be further from the truth. What ITLOS had to decide was whether the arbitral tribunal to be constituted would have jurisdiction, and, of course, it is very rare for an arbitral tribunal to be faced with preliminary objections to its jurisdiction. But this was not a traditional arbitral tribunal. Recourse to arbitration was compulsory. The arbitration took place under Annex VII of the Convention, which envisages that in such circumstances there can be a challenge to the jurisdiction of the arbitral tribunal (article 288 (4)). There is a major difference between a decision that a future tribunal (or even the same tribunal) has *prima facie* jurisdiction over the merits, reached after summary argument, and a decision reached after full argument that the court in question does not have jurisdiction to go into the merits. The International Court of Justice did not overrule itself in 1952 when it decided that it could not deal with the *Anglo-*

Iranian Co. case. By the same token, the arbitral tribunal did not overrule ITLOS in the *SBT* case.

There is another aspect of these cases warranting notice. Of the six maritime incidents that have come before the Tribunal, three of them, *Camouco*, *Monte Confurco*, and *Grand Prince*, concerned alleged fishing violations by vessels flying flags of convenience, each one fishing for the same fish in the same EEZ. Each case concerned alleged violations of the fisheries regulations of the coastal State, France. More than that, although in each case the vessels were flying a flag of convenience, it appears that the beneficial owners of the vessel or its charterers were all from Spain. It is a matter of common knowledge that Spain, a traditional distant water fishing State, has been badly hit by the establishment of exclusive economic zones in parts of the oceans in which its fisherfolk had traditionally fished, notably off Georges Bank in the northwest Atlantic area.

The isolated treatment by ITLOS of individual incidents obscures the broader overall picture and conveys an impression of a tendency for the Tribunal to give preference to the shipowner over the coastal State in prompt release cases, and not to take into consideration the general fisheries management problems of the coastal State. In *Monte Confurco*, Judge Anderson in his dissenting opinion made some very pertinent, if discreet, allusions to this. He mentioned the relevance of balancing the respective interests of France, the coastal State, and what he termed the "applicant." In that context, "applicant" presumably does not refer to the flag State as the nominal applicant in inter-State litigation but to the representative of the vessel authorized by the flag State to bring the proceedings in its name under article 292 (2) of the Convention. Under that provision, the application for release may be made only by *or on behalf of* the flag State of the vessel. In all the prompt release cases to date, the application was made not by the flag State but on its behalf.

Article 110 (3) of the Rules of the Tribunal provides that an application on behalf of the flag State should be accompanied by an authorization from the competent authority of the flag State, as well as by documents stating that the person submitting the application is the person named in the authorization. It shall also contain a certification that a copy of the application and all supporting documents have been addressed to the flag State. The effect of this is to place the authorities of the flag State in a passive position in flag of convenience cases.

In the *Grand Prince* case, the Tribunal considered that some of the documents furnished by the applicant contained "an element of fiction" (para. 65). Judge *ad hoc* Cot made some critical remarks about advocates appearing before the Tribunal in Part II of his declaration. Judge Anderson, in his separate opinion, went further. "The Agent appointed by Belize is not well placed, as a non-Belizean lawyer in private practice in Spain, to explain to the Tribunal the seeming inconsistencies in the statements of different government departments and agencies in Belize." Judge Treves in his separate opinion also adverted to this aspect in more general terms. This is a serious matter that warrants closer attention by the Tribunal.

While ITLOS is thus consolidating itself in the consciousness of the distant water fishing community, we should not overlook that the ICJ also has some major sea-law cases on it docket. It has just delivered its judgment in the long, drawn out *Maritime Delimitation and Territorial Questions between Qatar and Bahrain* case.[26] That Judgment contains important pronouncements on maritime delimitation matters, both as regards territorial sea and as regards EEZ and continental shelf.

The Court has pending the *Land and Maritime Boundary between Cameroon and Nigeria*, with Equatorial Africa intervening in the maritime part of the case, the *Pilau Ligitan and Pulau Sipadan* case between Indonesia and Malaya with the Philippines applying for permission to intervene,[27] and the *Maritime Delimitation between Nicaragua and Honduras in the Caribbean Sea* case.

There may be other cases pending, perhaps for arbitration if they are not settled through diplomatic means. So you see, maritime disputes are prominent in current international disputes, and I do not see any serious competition between the different dispute settlement processes at work on these cases.

Notes

[1] The *M/V Saiga* case (Prompt Release), 1 ITLOS Reports (1997), 16; The *M/V Saiga (No. 2)* case (Provisional Measures), 117 ILR 111; (Merits), 38 ILM 1323 (1999). For the decision of the Court of Appeal of Conakry, Chambre Corectionnelle, upholding the initial detention of the vessel, see the decision of 3 February 1998, Judgment No. 12, Ministère public c. Alexandrovich (the captain of the *Saiga*). Manuscript of decision in the author's archives. Judgements, etc., of the International Court of Justice and of ITLOS not yet available in printed form are taken from their respective website: <www.icj-cij.org> and <www.un.org/Depts/los/>.

[2] The *Southern Bluefin Tuna* cases (Provisional Measures) (1999), 117 ILR 148.

[3] The *Camouco* case (Prompt Release) (2000), 29 ILM 666 (2000). For the decision of the Court of Appeal of Saint Denis complying with the ITLOS prompt release judgment, see Judgment No. 266/2000, PG:99/02715, *Sobrido et al v. Etat français* of 21 March 2000. Copy kindly supplied by the ITLOS Librarian, Ms. E. Schaffer.

[4] The *Monte Confurco* case (Prompt Release), Judgment of 18 December 2000. For the decision of the competent French court complying with that Judgment, see Tribunal d'Instance de St Paul, Ordonnance de référés No. 12-00-000951, 12 January 2001, *Perez et al. v. Etat français*. Text kindly supplied by Ms. Schaffer.

[5] The *Conservation and Sustainable Exploitation of Swordfish Stocks in the South-eastern Pacific Ocean* case (Constitution of Chamber), Order of 20 December 2000, new time limits, Order of 16 March 2001.

[6] Judgment of 20 April 2001.

[7] ICJ Reports 1998, 432. This was the first case heard under the revised Rules of the Tribunal—the revision of March 15, 2001, slightly extending time-limits in prompt release proceedings. For those amendments, see Press Release ITLOS/Press 44, 21 March 2001. The Tribunal decided that those amendments would enter into force forthwith. It is unusual for an international tribunal to bring amendments to its Rules into force before they have been circulated to States.

[8] It is possible that the list of highly migratory species in Annex I of the 1982 Law of the Sea Convention is incomplete. Article 1 (*f*) of the Honolulu Convention on the Conservation and Management of Highly Migratory Fish Stocks in the Western and Central Pacific Ocean of September 5, 2000, defines "highly migratory fish stocks," for the purpose of that instrument, not only by reference to that Annex I, but also adds "and such other species of fish as the Commission [for the Conservation and Management of Highly Migratory Fish Stocks in the Western and Central Pacific Ocean, established by the Convention] may determine."

[9] For my observations on that case, see Sh. Rosenne, "The International Tribunal for the Law of the Sea: Survey for 1999," 15 *International Journal of Marine and Coastal Law* (2000): 443, 449.

[10] For my observations on that phase of the case, see ibid., 464.

[11] There were difficulties over the compliance with the prompt release judgment in *Saiga*, and those difficulties led to the second set of proceedings. However, during those second proceedings the prompt release judgment was implemented. In its judgment in *Saiga (No. 2)*, the Tribunal rejected claims by St. Vincent regarding allegations that Guinea had not complied fully with the prompt release Judgment. Judgment of 1 July 1999, para. 183 (10) and (11). For my observations on that phase, see my article cited in supra note 9, 449.

[12] See note 3 above.

[13] *Saiga (No. 2)* case, Order of 20 February 1998 accepting the submission of the case. In its Judgment of 1 July 1999, ITLOS, *inter alia*, awarded to Saint Vincent the sum of $2,123,357.00 with interest. Guinea had difficulties in meeting that judgment debt, and the matter was finally resolved through the good offices of the Secretary-General, Mr. Kofi Annan.

[14] Sh. Rosenne, "Provisional Measures and *Prima Facie* Jurisdiction Revisited," *Essays in honour of Shigeru Oda* (in the press).

[15] For the award of August 4, 2000, see the website of the International Center for the Settlement of Investment Disputes of the World Bank (ICSID), that body having supplied Registry facilities for the arbitration: <www.worldbank.org/icsid>; 39 *ILM* 1359 (2000). On May 29, 2001, the Australian Foreign Minister Mr. Downer, after a meeting with his Japanese counterpart Ms. Tanaka, issued a press release announcing the end of the dispute with Japan and the immediate lifting of the bans on Japanese fishing vessels visiting Australian ports. Details of the settlement are contained in Media Release AFFA01/42TU of the Minister for Forestry and Conservation of the same date. This shows how a judicial decision declining jurisdiction may be as much a contribution to settling a bitter dispute as a decision on the merits, and perhaps even more so.

[16] See pp. 173-213.

[17] I would like to take this opportunity to clear up a possible misunderstanding regarding a passage in volume V of the Virginia *Commentary* regarding the place of the *compulsory* jurisdiction under Article 36 (2) of the Statute of the International Court of Justice in relation to Part XV of UNCLOS. Referring to the words "or otherwise" in the first phrase of article 282, paragraph 282.3, of that *Commentary* states that those words were "meant to include, in particular, the acceptances of the jurisdiction" of the Court by declarations made under Article 36 (2) of the Statute. The mere acceptances do not, of course, constitute any agreement as between States forcing them to refer a given dispute to that Court. The declarations express a willingness to accept the jurisdiction if another State having made a declaration institutes proceedings. That was clearly the intention behind those words.

[18] Prompt release can also be a matter for diplomatic settlement even if international litigation about the matter is in progress. In the International Court of Justice, see the *Fisheries Jurisdiction* (Spain v. Canada) case, ICJ Reports 1998 (para. 22), 432 and 446.

[19] It appears from paragraph 18 of the Judgment of April 20, 2001, that Belize furnished the Tribunal with observations on the appointment of Professor Cot as Judge *ad hoc*. The Tribunal considered those observations and found no objection to the choice. No further information is vouchsafed in that Judgment, which does not indicate the majority by which that decision was reached.

[20] Annex VI, article 17, regulates the appointment by parties to a dispute of judges *ad hoc*. I understand that the Tribunal takes the view that the European Union (EU), as a party to a dispute, is not entitled to appoint a judge *ad hoc*. That position may not be compatible with Annex IX, article 7, paragraph 2, of the Convention, providing that Part XV applies mutatis mutandis to any dispute between Parties to the Convention, one or more of which is an international intergovernmental organization. In the present case, the issue was side-stepped by the inclusion in the *ad hoc* Chamber of a judge having the nationality of one of the member States of the EU. The EU is, so far, the only international organization entitled to become a party to the Convention, and several of the judges are of the nationality of member States. But other organizations may, in due course, become eligible to participate in the Convention or in one of the international agreements adopting Part XV of the Convention for dispute settlement. Accordingly, one can envisage a dispute involving such an organization, when none of the members of the Tribunal have the nationality of any of its member States. Article 31 of the Honolulu Convention (supra note 8) indirectly introduces Part XV of UNCLOS as its dispute settlement procedure, and article 35, on accession, envisages "regional economic integration organizations" as being able to accede to the Convention.

[21] Sh. Rosenne, III *The Law and Practice of the International Court of Justice 1920-1996*, 1358.

[22] For an example, see ITLOS/PV.99/5, 20.

[23] This is a major change made by the Tribunal from the draft rules prepared by Special Commission 4 of the Preparatory Commission. In its Final Draft Rules of ITLOS (LOS/PCN/SCN.4/WP.16/Add.1), the rules for prompt release were in section D, Incidental Proceedings, subsection 2, articles 89 to 93, and assumed that the decision would be embodied in an order. The Tribunal has vouchsafed no explanation of why it made this fundamental change in the nature of prompt release proceedings.

[24] That was the immediate object of the request. And see the Order of 11 March 1998, paras. 21, 35, and 36.

[25] ICJ Reports 1951, 89; 1952, 93.

[26] Judgment of 16 March 2001.

[27] ICJ Press Communiqué 2001/7, 15 March 2001.

ITLOS: An International Lawyer's Perspective

*Philippe Sands**

May I begin by thanking the organizers of the Twenty-fifth Annual Conference of the Center for Oceans Law and Policy, and the International Tribunal for the Law of the Sea, for allowing me the opportunity to participate in this timely Conference. The subject is an important one, and I feel especially privileged to participate with such distinguished company on a panel that provides litigators with an opportunity to comment on the Tribunal's performance thus far. This is all the more so where the audience includes so many distinguished members of the Tribunal.

I would like to use the limited time available to explain how an academic barrister, with a little experience before this and other international tribunals, assesses the state of things after five years. In so doing I will touch upon what strikes me as the central issue, namely the relationship between a court and its "clients," a subject that Judge Rosalyn Higgins has also addressed in her contribution to the most recent issue of the *International and Comparative Law Quarterly*. The title of her article—"Respecting Sovereign States and Running a Tight Courtroom"[1]—neatly encapsulates concerns that compete but are not inherently incompatible.

It is a notable feature of the early twenty-first century that the international legal landscape is now dotted with the presence of a growing number of permanent international courts and tribunals. A century ago, there were no international courts. There also were no international practitioners before such courts prior to the arrival of the Central American Court of Justice in 1907 and the Permanent

---

* Professor of International Law, University of London; Global Professor of Law, New York University Law School; Director, Project on International Courts and Tribunals (www.pict-pcti.org); and Barrister, Matrix Chambers, London (www.matrixlaw.co.uk). The views expressed in this contribution are personal.

M.H. Nordquist and J.N. Moore (eds.),
Current Marine Environmental Issues and the International Tribunal for the Law of the Sea, 141–158.
© 2001 *Kluwer Law International. Printed in the Netherlands.*

Court of International Justice fifteen or so years later. Even half a century ago the number of standing, permanent courts was minimal, with the International Court of Justice standing in glorious isolation. As Judge Higgins has put it, "from 1922 to 1960 the International Court of Justice at The Hague stood alone as the forum for the resolution of international disputes."[2] But today the situation is much changed.[3] Beyond the ICJ, there are regional human rights courts in Europe, the Americas, and Africa; economic courts in Europe and various parts of Africa; the World Trade Organization's Dispute Settlement Understanding, panels, and Appellate Body; and international criminal tribunals for the former Yugoslavia and for Rwanda, and the soon to be established International Criminal Court in The Hague, whose Statute was adopted in Rome in 1998. There are also standing arbitration institutions, such as ICSID, Inspection Panels at various multilateral development banks, and administrative tribunals. And, of course, since 1996, there is also the International Tribunal for the Law of the Sea, our reason for being here today.

These bodies do not exist on paper alone. Almost without exception they have a growing case load, and they present international litigators with a range of potential fora before which to litigate international disputes. Indeed, it is a curious feature of the early twenty-first century that forum shopping is now possible. I consider this development to be entirely positive, not least because it creates a competitive environment in which the various tribunals begin, in effect, to compete for business and consequently modernize their working practices. Another feature of many of these bodies is that they are not all state-centered. Individuals, NGO's, corporations, and international organizations are now actively involved in cases before some of these bodies. In some cases, these new actors are formally involved. This can be as a party—for example in the presently suspended proceedings between Chile and the EU before this Tribunal—or as an intervenor. And in other cases, even if they are not formally involved, these new actors are present behind the scenes, exerting their influence in numerous ways.

This new world of international litigation before international bodies provides the context for the emergence of an international bar. A practitioner's perspective on ITLOS can be a comparative perspective, in which it is possible not only to *describe* the manner in which proceedings are conducted but, additionally, to *assess* such conduct by reference to proceedings before other international bodies.

This is the context for my comments. I have been privileged to be involved in two ITLOS cases, first as Counsel for St. Vincent and the Grenadines in the provisional measures phase of the *Saiga* case, and in drafting the Memorial for the main application. And then in the back row, "devilling" for my colleague James Crawford who was acting for Australia and New Zealand, in the provisional measures phase of the *Southern Bluefin Tuna* cases. Moreover, my perspective on the Tribunal is a comparative one, since I have been fortunate to have the opportunity to be involved in other international procedures, including those of the ICJ, the WTO procedures, and ICSID. Each of these bodies has its own unique purposes and character, and rightly functions according to the particular practices and procedures designed to achieve those purposes and reflect that character. It should also be said that my practitioner's perspective is that of an English barrister, with all that implies for a particular—and some would say peculiar—view as to how courts should function and how we, as counsel, should relate to them.

In relation to institutional and procedural aspects, on the one hand, and substantive aspects, on the other, I have been generally impressed with the efficient and productive way that the Tribunal has operated thus far. It is no simple task to establish as fully operational a new judicial institution with its own registry and a bench of twenty-one judges (and occasionally more), and no less so when it is on a subject as vast and complex as the law of the sea, which necessarily forms a part of the general international legal order. As our distinguished moderator, Professor Rosenne, has indicated in his paper, there have been no less than seven cases filed with the Tribunal in its first five years. This figure compares favorably with other international courts and tribunals in their infant years.

I begin with one aspect of the Tribunal's institutional character, namely its composition. Beyond the substantive merits of a litigator's case, one factor will always be to the forefront of a practitioner's mind, and that is the identity of his or her bench. The composition of this Tribunal is of interest, reflecting the institution's character as a post-colonial, post-independence body. In some ways, the composition of this Tribunal may be thought by some to be more representative of the principal legal and political interests in the world today than other bodies. In gender balance, of course, it is not, but one could hardly address that complaint to the judges themselves.

When I appeared before the Tribunal, I was struck by two elements in particular. The first element was that a majority of the judges—twelve out of twenty-one—are from the developing world, and just six are from OECD members. This compares with the situation at the International Court of Justice, with seven out of fifteen from the developing world, and six from OECD countries. One should not make too much of this aspect, of course, but it is not without its significance for the preparation of a case and perhaps also for its outcome, a point that I will return to later.

A second, and related, factor is that whereas at the International Court of Justice, for example, all five permanent members of the United Nations Security Council have a national on the bench (notwithstanding the fact that four out of five—the United Kingdom is the notable exception—do not in general accept the compulsory jurisdiction of the Court), by contrast, at ITLOS there is no judge of French nationality (although there is a judge nominated by France). There is also no American judge, because the United States is not a party to UNCLOS and no American national has, thus far at least, been nominated. The absence has an impact on various aspects of a Tribunal's work, including language, the consequences of which should not be underestimated for the development by the institution of its working practices.

The courtroom "feel" of the Tribunal is accordingly different from that of the International Court. It cannot escape the attention of the practitioner before The Hague Court that he (or, very occasionally, she) is appearing before a body whose composition is not unreflective of that of the Security Council. That feeling has not been present for me at this Tribunal. In a curious way, it feels a lot more like a domestic court in England in the sense that the degree of attention to the nationality or background of the judges is somewhat diminished. In making this point, I want to be absolutely clear that I am not intending to cast aspersions on the independence of the International Court or of any of its judges. Indeed, it is perhaps inevitable that the United Nation's "principal judicial organ," which has been actively involved in resolving international disputes for more than fifty years—many of them dealing with highly sensitive and overtly political issues—will have accumulated a collection of "baggage" that necessarily informs the way it functions. And this, of course, informs the manner in which a practitioner will prepare the case. With ITLOS, there is, as yet, no such baggage, and the *tabula rasa* means perhaps that the focus is necessarily rather more on the nuts and bolts of the facts and law of the case than on the character of the institution or the identity (or nationality and background) of the judges.

That does not, of course, mean that the practitioner before this Tribunal will pay no regard to the identity or nationality of the judge. In the *Saiga* case, counsel certainly will have considered the national provenance of the judges, by reference to a number of factors, including whether they came from a coastal State with an exclusive economic zone, or from a state with a large shipping registry engaged in distant, international oil bunkering and fisheries activities. And similar considerations informed the preparation of the provisional measures phase of the *Southern Bluefin Tuna* cases. But in both cases, it does not appear that national provenance played any real role in informing a judge's view on the legal merits.

In this regard, it is also worth noting that members of the Tribunal have shown restraint in preparing statements or separate and dissenting opinions, or, where they have been produced, limiting their content and lengths to proportions that are manageable and easily digestible. I have long considered that one of the reasons for the institutional success of the European Court of Justice has been the outright bar on such statements and opinions. This has tended to promote a sense of community and collegiality that has strengthened the institution, even if it means that losing counsel does not obtain the benefit of knowing that his or her views were positively received by at least some members of the bench.

Closely related to the composition of the bench are the working procedures adopted by the international court. In contrast to the situation pertaining to national courts, the judges of an international court are in a remarkable position to influence the development of working procedures and practices. In this regard also, the Tribunal has, in my view, made a positive start. In my experience, this Tribunal has operated with far more of the cut and thrust that characterizes a national court in England than some of its international counterparts elsewhere. I do not have time this afternoon to address all of the innovations introduced by the Tribunal, but two practice developments concerning the management of cases—one formal, the other informal—strike me as reflective of a general approach.

The first concerns the procedure this Tribunal has adopted of directing the parties to those issues that it would like to have addressed. This springs, presumably, from paragraph 14 of the 1997 Guidelines Concerning the Preparation and Presentation of Cases before the Tribunal, which provides:

> Each party should submit to the Tribunal, prior to the opening of the oral proceedings, (a) a brief note on the points which in its opinion constitute the issues that still divide the parties; (b) a brief outline of the arguments that it wishes to make in its oral statement; and (c) a list of authorities, including, where appropriate, relevant extracts from such authorities, proposed to be relied upon in its oral

statement. None of these materials will be treated as documents or parts of the pleadings.[4]

The approach will be familiar to counsel appearing at the Royal Courts of Justice in the Strand, required as they are to produce "skeleton" arguments summarizing the key points in issue and their views upon them. It has the merit of narrowing down the issues in dispute, which will, of course, save time, a precious resource for any court. The approach of the Tribunal is noteworthy because it reflects a more active role played by the institution in defining the key issues, rather than simply leaving the parties to use their time in the oral phase to determine for themselves what they wish to address. That more active role in itself reflects a changing conception of the role of the body: is it merely a servant of the parties before it (the more "traditional" approach), or does it have a broader responsibility under UNCLOS and in the interests of international justice to assist in the definition and presentation of the case (the "modern" approach)? In those phases of the *Saiga* and *Southern Bluefin Tuna* proceedings to which I was privy, shortly before the opening of the oral phase, the President of the Tribunal met with representatives of the parties to discuss the key issues that the Tribunal, on the basis of a deliberation, wished the parties to address. A list of issues, even some questions, was presented to the parties. With an ICJ background, it came as something of a surprise to be presented, in the *Saiga* case, with such a list. But it had the positive effect of concentrating counsel's mind on the salient issues, and assisting us in not wasting time on issues that the Tribunal did not wish to have addressed. In my view, it is an approach that other international courts and tribunals might usefully consider, not least because it would provide a means of reducing time in the courtroom.

The second feature worthy of mention concerns the manner in which the Tribunal has conducted itself during the oral phase. The public international litigator versed in the practice of more established bodies expects to present an oral statement on the basis of a prepared text, with no interruption or exchange with the court. To the extent that there are questions, they will often come at the end of the oral phase, and the parties will be given time—two weeks or more—to respond to the questions in writing. Consistent with its more active management of cases, this Tribunal has, in my experience, adopted a more modern and interventionist approach. This is reflected, for example, in the response of the Tribunal to an objection raised by St. Vincent and the Grenadines when counsel for Guinea raised for the first time, in his concluding statement during the oral phase, the question of non-exhaustion of local remedies before the courts of Guinea.[5] The fact that such an objection could be raised, and that it could be disposed of on the spot by the President of the Tribunal, was unusual. Similarly, in the provisional measures phase of the *Southern Bluefin Tuna* case, the Tribunal's President intervened during the conduct of a *voir dire* on no less than three occasions. The President's first intervention was prompted by an objection from Counsel for Australia and New Zealand.[6] His second intervention, however, occurred *proprio motu*.[7] The President's third intervention sent a clear message:[8]

> Mr Slater, I do not think the expert should answer these questions at this time. We are not talking about whether the work was done expertly. We are talking about whether the expert is an independent expert, and I would suggest that we keep them separate.

Counsel for Japan took the hint, reserved his remaining questions for later, and was excused by the President.[9] In an English (or American) court, such an exchange would perhaps not be remarkable. By comparison with some other international tribunals, however—although probably not the international criminal tribunals for the former Yugoslavia and Rwanda—it reflects the "hands-on" managerial approach that has characterized the Tribunal's first years.

For many domestic practitioners, these two examples would not be notable. At the international level, however, it reflects a concrete example of the Tribunal's commitment to modernization, an attempt to alter what Judge Higgins has called "the culture of excessive deference to State sovereignty in a range of procedural issues."[10] Given its youth, the approach is noteworthy and in my view commendable, and can only enhance the attractions of the Tribunal from the perspective of the practitioner.

SUBSTANCE

Practitioners are interested in procedure, but they are also interested in substance, and I should say something about the Tribunal's contribution thus far. Procedure and substance are closely related, of course, and the issues of composition, language, and working practices and procedures inevitably will have an impact on the substantive outcome of a case. Professor Rosenne has comprehensively and eloquently described the Tribunal's case law thus far, and I am not sure that I can—or need to—add a great deal in the limited time available. It is noteworthy that the Tribunal has already faced a broad range of substantive issues. Generally, it has handed down judgments that are clear, reasonably decisive, prepared and delivered expeditiously, and have generally attracted sufficient majorities to endow them with appropriate authority.[11] And it is a particular feature of the decisions adopted thus far that they do not give the reader the impression that they are tempered by any "culture of excessive deference to State sovereignty." Indeed, some powerful states have found themselves on the receiving end of the Tribunal's application of the law.

This provides, perhaps, a moment to say something more concrete about substance.[12] Since two other participants on this panel have chosen to address aspects of the *Southern Bluefin Tuna* case, it is appropriate to consider the Tribunal's approach in the provisional measures phase, given the decisive Order prescribed by the Tribunal. I entirely endorse Professor Rosenne's view that the Tribunal was right to prescribe provisional measures and that it was "the only international tribunal that was in a position to render a binding decision on those cases with all the necessary speed."[13] I would add my own sense, for what it is worth, that I cannot easily imagine many other international courts adopting such far-reaching provisional measures on a matter relating to conservation measures. The provisional measures brought an early end to Japanese bluefin tuna fishing in the waters governed by the 1993 Convention. Moreover, the respect shown by Japan to the Order in the form of its full implementation is commendable.

On the merits phase of the case, however, I probably do differ from Professor Rosenne. Although it is entirely speculation, I have my doubts as to whether this Tribunal would have declined jurisdiction in the *Southern Bluefin Tuna* cases, as the Arbitral Tribunal did. This is not to say that I am convinced that the Tribunal would have found for Australia and New Zealand on the merits. But this Tribunal, judging from the approach it has taken thus far to jurisdictional issues, and its rather "modern" approach to international law and international legal process, including its conception of the judicial function (and, in particular, the relationship between the Tribunal or court and the parties in proceedings before it) would, I think, have found that it had jurisdiction. Indeed, I express a hope that it would have done so. In my opinion, the Judgement of the Arbitral Tribunal is an unfortunate one that looks to the past, is out of touch with the underlying principles of the UNCLOS system, and is unpersuasive in the logic of its reasoning.

The Tribunal found for Australia and New Zealand on most of the issues that were relied on by Japan. In particular, it ruled that:

(a) There was a legal dispute between the parties, not merely a scientific dispute.

(b) That dispute involved the interpretation and application *both* of the 1993 Convention and of UNCLOS.

(c) The dispute was not moot.

(d) UNCLOS standards continued to govern the legal relations of the parties.

(e) All the procedural prerequisites for submission of the dispute to Part XI settlement were satisfied.

But it found against Australia and New Zealand on the basis that by agreeing to article 16 of the 1993 Convention, Australia and New Zealand had agreed by implication that no dispute would ever be submitted to compulsory procedures under Part XI (unless it involved egregious conduct or bad faith). That approach is premised upon two propositions, one involving the interpretation of article 16 of the 1993 Convention, and the other involving the interpretation of article 281(1) of UNCLOS.

The first proposition is that article 16 fell to be read as if it involved the exclusion of compulsory jurisdiction under other conventions in relation to disputes arising under those conventions. There is no evidence from the *travaux* or other circumstances that the parties intended this. A bystander at the negotiations for the 1993 Convention who pointed out that article 16 excluded Part XV would have been greeted with the response—we are only dealing with the 1993 Convention, not with UNCLOS. Moreover reliance on the Antarctic Treaty is wholly unpersuasive. It is extremely curious that an Arbitral Tribunal construing a 1993 Convention in the year 2000 should do so by reference to a 1959 Treaty that dealt with a different subject matter, had different parties, and was adopted in an era of Great Power conflict where the avoidance of compulsory adjudication was a high priority. Unlike the Antarctic, the context provided by UNCLOS was not an ideological disagreement, an unresolved sovereignty dispute, and a refusal to submit disputes to third party adjudication. On the contrary, Part XV of UNCLOS was the result of an expressed determination to submit a major area of state activity to "compulsory procedures entailing binding decisions." Confronted with this intention, the presumption must be that other jurisdictional clauses under other conventions do not exclude the application of Part XV of UNCLOS in relation to disputes relating to UNCLOS. And since the Arbitral Tribunal had expressly found that there was a dispute between the parties under UNCLOS,[14] it is difficult to see how, on any logical basis, jurisdiction could be declined. In my view, if the parties to one treaty (with a facultative dispute settlement clause) wish to exclude compulsory jurisdiction under another treaty (providing for compulsory jurisdiction over the matters governed by that treaty), they should be required to say so in clear terms. Article 16 does not directly address disputes under UNCLOS.

The second proposition that the Arbitral Tribunal relied upon is that the words "does not exclude any further procedure" in article 281(1) of UNCLOS apply to a facultative dispute settlement clause. The Tribunal interprets these words as if they read, "does not allow for any further procedure without the consent of all the parties." This seems an obvious misreading of the article when it is read systematically in the context of Part XV. The Arbitral Tribunal treats section 2 ("Compulsory procedures entailing binding disputes") as if it was irrelevant to the interpretation of chapter 1. Read in its context, article 281 is intended to deal with the situation where the parties to UNCLOS have agreed to settle some UNCLOS dispute in some other way, that is, some way that would produce finality at least in the sense of excluding any further procedure for the settlement of the dispute. It is obvious that article 16 taken alone could not and did not do this. What further procedure did it exclude? What dispute did it settle?

The ancillary reasons given by the Tribunal in support of its decision are no more persuasive. To rely on the exclusions in article 297 of UNCLOS in support of the proposition that Part XV is not intended to be an effective and general dispute settlement provision is bizarre. Those exclusions (which did not apply here) only make sense *if* Part XV is seen as a compulsory system of dispute settlement. And perhaps most troubling of all is the Tribunal's "reintroduction" of Part XV in respect of "egregious breaches" and cases involving lack of good faith. The relevant passage appears to assume these are coterminous, but, of course, they are not. Proof of subjective bad faith is a difficult matter, and a breach of conservation or pollution provisions might be egregious without actual bad faith being shown (for example, in case of gross negligence in taking necessary precautions). But the basic point is that there is absolutely no textual basis for reading articles 16 or 281 (1) as if they excluded only some further procedures and not others. This is pure invention, a rewriting of Part XI, and not an interpretation.

The Award of the Arbitral Tribunal reflects a traditional deference to the sovereign in approaching the subject of jurisdiction. It is difficult not to conclude that if the drafting of the

Award had been in the hands of a person or persons not imbued with a culture of sovereign deference, or perhaps concerned about the "fragmentation" of international judicial control, then the Award on Jurisdiction and Admissibility may have taken another path. I conclude by expressing the hope that as and when this Tribunal has the opportunity to address the issue, it will remain true to the spirit that has imbued its approach over the first five years of its life.

Notes

---

[1] 50 *ICLQ* 121 (2001).

[2] Ibid., 121.

[3] See generally P. Sands, R. Mackenzie, and Y. Shany, *Manual of International Courts and Tribunals* (Butterworths, 1999).

[4] ITLOS/9, 28 October 1997. By comparison, it is worth noting the ICJ's most recent statement, in 1998, on the subject of oral presentations:

> E. The Court draws the attention of parties to the fact that, according to Article 60, paragraph 1, of the Rules of Court:
>
> > 1. The oral statements made on behalf of each party shall be as succinct as possible within the limits of what is requisite for the adequate presentation of that party's contentions at the hearing. Accordingly, they shall be directed to the issues that still divide the parties, and shall not go over the whole ground covered by the pleadings, or merely repeat the facts and arguments these contain.
>
> These provisions must of course be complied with, especially when objections of lack of jurisdiction or of inadmissibility are being considered. In those latter events, pleadings must *inter alia* be limited to a statement of the objections and exhibit the requisite degree of brevity (Note Annexed to Press Communiqué 98/14, 6 April 1998).

[5] ITLOS/PV.98/3, Verbatim Record, 24 February 1998:

> MR. von BREVERN: The request of St. Vincent and the Grenadines to the arbitral tribunal transferred, now to you, was made on 22 December, and this was well before the national remedies had been exhausted. This also applies of course to the proceedings about which we are speaking here, about the application for provisional measures. This was done before everything had been exhausted in Guinea. I think this is an important point and I would like to read something about that in your judgment. I think the measures taken by St. Vincent and the Grenadines were too early.
>
> THE PRESIDENT: Mr. Sands?
>
> MR. SANDS: I apologize for interrupting, Mr. President. This is the first time that we have heard this argument in these proceedings. In two rounds of written proceedings and the first round of oral arguments we have heard nothing about this argument. Our understanding was that at

this reply stage the parties are limited to matters which have been previously raised in the proceedings yesterday or in the written proceedings. This is the first time that this point has been raised.

THE PRESIDENT: Thank you very much. Mr. von Brevern?

MR. von BREVERN: Mr. President, I thought that Article 295—and I think I should read it out—

THE PRESIDENT: Mr. von Brevern, Mr. Sand's objection is that this argument, which of course is a very important argument, has not been raised at all up to this stage. As I said at the beginning, it is not permitted for new matters, matters which have not been brought to the attention of either the Tribunal or the other parties, to be introduced. That was the objection. I thought you were going to respond that they [sic] there has been a previous reference to this.

MR. von BREVERN: Mr. President, again that is something that divides English lawyers from other lawyers. In my opinion these are facts. The facts are known to you. Why do I have to introduce these obvious facts? If you look into your files, you know them precisely. The Tribunal of the first instance was on—whatever. The Supreme Court judgment was on 3 February, and that is known to all of you. It is also known to all of you that the request was previously and you also know Article 295. The consequence is what I say now. But, even if I had not worked on it, I think it would have been up to you to decide according to 295.

THE PRESIDENT: Very well, then. Now that you have made a point in response to the objection, I suggest that you proceed with your next point.

[6] ITLOS/PV.99/20, 18 August 1999.

MR CRAWFORD: Mr President, I do not see how that question is relevant to the qualifications of this witness. What CCAMLR has done has absolutely nothing to do with the qualifications of this witness. He can ask it in cross-examination as much as he likes. The question is whether he is qualified to give his testimony.

THE PRESIDENT: I was going to say, Mr Slater, that you will, of course, have an opportunity to cross-examine. I understand that the purpose of the present proceeding is to enable you to put in context something connected with the suitability or expertise of the witness. I suggest that you restrict it to that. You will still have an opportunity to cross-examine him on the substance.

MR SLATER: I very much appreciate that. I think it is important that the Court should have the opportunity to understand the distinctions between how this assignment that has been handled by this witness and how he has handled his professional assignments in the past and to understand in full context whether or to what degree this witness is being presented as an independent scientist and whether his opinion should be accepted on that basis, which is what has been presented to the Court so far.

THE PRESIDENT: As I said, you are permitted, by agreement between the parties, to lead questions to that effect. The point that I am making, and the point that Professor Crawford made, is that when it comes to whether the expert is capable of providing the scientific evidence, that is part of the evidence itself. If there is something to suggest that the expert is not a suitable, independent person, that is the purpose of your questioning at this stage. I think you should try to draw a distinction between the two, the independence, and therefore suitability, as a witness, and I think that the question of capacity and expertise belongs to the second part.

MR SLATER: I will certainly try to focus on the question of independence, and that was really the question that I was asking, which was this witness's recognition that the Commission has selected independent experts itself in the past.

MR CRAWFORD: Mr President, the behaviour of the Commission has nothing to do with the qualifications of Professor Beddington. The question of whether Professor Beddington is qualified to give the evidence is given. What the Commission has done is a completely different question and can be asked about in cross-examination.

MR SLATER: The Commission has identified for itself, that is Australia, New Zealand and Japan have collectively by consensus identified a number of independent scientific experts who, they have agreed, could present independent evidence and advice to the Commission. I think it is important that the Tribunal should have an opportunity to understand the difference between those independent experts, those independent scientists, who have themselves made a statement to this Court, and this witness who is being offered on behalf of a party.

THE PRESIDENT: Mr Slater, I do not think that the fact that somebody, is not selected by a commission as an independent expert rules that person out as an independent expert. It is quite plain that there are always a limited number of experts who can be chosen. There is also the question of whether they are aware of the person's abilities and interests. Therefore, I do not think we can accept that merely because the Commission has chosen some independent experts, one could draw the conclusion that therefore anybody who is not on that list qualifies *ipso facto* not to be independent.

MR SLATER: I appreciate that, Mr President, and I will try to ask some different questions of this witness if you do not wish to have those on this occasion.

[7] THE PRESIDENT: Mr Slater, once again I believe that these are matters which you could deal with in cross-examination. We are dealing here not with the basis on which the documentation was produced, I think we are dealing here with the question of whether this expert can be accepted as an independent expert. If he is an independent expert, the fact that he had material sent to him by the parties would not be either extraordinary or improper.

MR SLATER: The question is what range of materials was sent to him, and I just have a few questions on that subject. By way of example, I did not see any reference to the Protocol for the Pilot Experimental Fishing Programme that was conducted in 1998. Did you review that?

[8] *Ibid.*

[9] *Ibid.*

[10] Supra note 2, 131.

[11] *Saiga (No. 1)* (Prompt release, 4 December 1997): unanimous (x1), 12-9 (x4); *Saiga (No. 2)* (Provisional measures, 11 March 1998): unanimous (x4); *Saiga (No. 2)* (Merits, 1 July 1999): unanimous (x2), 18-2 (x9), 17-3 (x1), 13-7 (costs); *Southern Bluefin Tuna* (Provisional measures, 27 August 1999): 21-1 (x3), 20-2 (x4), 18-4 (x1); *Camouco* case (Prompt release, 7 February 2000): unanimous (x1), 19-2 (x3), 15-6 (x1); and *Monte Confurco* (Prompt release): unanimous (x4), 19-1 (x2), 17-3 (x1), 18-2 (x1).

[12] In preparing this part of the paper, I have benefited from receiving the views of Professor James Crawford. Nevertheless the views expressed are personal to the author.

[13] See chapter by Shabtai Rosenne, "The Case-Law of ITLOS (1997-2001): An Overview," 130.

[14] "[T]he Tribunal concludes that the dispute between Australia and New Zealand, on the one hand, and Japan, on the other, . . . while centred in the 1993 Convention, also arises under the United Nations Convention on the Law of the Sea" (para. 52).

ITLOS—A Practitioner's Perspective

Nick Howe[*]

Two years ago I gave my final speech on behalf of St. Vincent and the Grenadines in the oral phase of the hearings in the M/V Saiga (No. 2) case. It is therefore an opportune time to look back at the history of the Saiga cases and I particularly welcome the opportunity to do so from a practitioner's perspective in the short time that I have today.

My background is in the practice of commercial maritime law. Those experienced in this field will know that London considers itself to be the world's center of private international dispute resolution. It seeks to attract clients from all over the world by offering them a neutral forum with adjudicators of the highest caliber. Judges with many years of practice in this field sit in the Commercial and Admiralty Courts of the High Court of Justice. Highly specialist barristers regularly appear before them or the multitude of specialist commercial arbitration panels also based in London. More than a dozen firms of solicitors are renowned for their expertise in this area—either as specialist firms or as specialist departments within larger firms. In my career, I have worked in three of these firms and worked with, or against, most of the others. Although I now practice on my own, I continue to work very closely with this community.

I know that regret has been expressed by some practitioners in London that the International Tribunal for the Law of the Sea (the Tribunal) was not to have its base there.[1] There are many obvious ways that the work of the Tribunal could complement that of the existing practitioners in London. Moreover, while the Tribunal's closest parallel bodies may be public international forums such as the International Court of Justice, there is no doubt that it also

---

[*] Solicitor, Howe & Co.

M.H. Nordquist and J.N. Moore (eds.),
Current Marine Environmental Issues and the International Tribunal for the Law of the Sea, 159–171.
© 2001 Kluwer Law International. Printed in the Netherlands.

strives to attract a wider range of users including the international business community.[2]

It is as a member of that community that I comment on my experiences in the M/V Saiga cases today. Before doing so, I stress that what I say below is my own personal view and should not in any way be attributed to St. Vincent and the Grenadines or any of the other parties associated with the M/V Saiga cases. Bearing in mind the short time available, I confine my comments to three specific areas: access, efficacy, and enforcement.

ACCESS

One commentary said: "[T]he most significant aspect of the case of the Saiga is, of course, that the case was brought at all."[3] Whether or not this is precisely what the author of that comment meant, I have seen very few commentaries that even touch upon the numerous practical hurdles that have to be overcome to bring such a case.[4] From a commercial practitioner's perspective, one of the first questions that arises about the Saiga case is, indeed, how did it come to be brought at all?

Those who know the work of the Tribunal will be familiar with the basic factual circumstances that brought the Saiga cases before it. In the early hours of October 28, 1997, the vessel was detained by Guinean patrol boats before being escorted back to Conakry. A few days later, the Master was obliged to discharge her cargo of gas-oil. He was subsequently prosecuted in Guinea and ultimately fined sums in the order of U.S. $15 million for alleged customs offenses.[5]

Those familiar with commercial maritime disputes will be able to imagine what was happening during this time. To put this in context, I start by outlining the fundamental basis upon which most commercial shipping activity is conducted. Most vessels are owned by a one-ship company incorporated in a convenient jurisdiction and registered in the same, or another, appropriate jurisdiction. Managers responsible for a number of vessels will often manage them. The managers will employ the crew on behalf of the Owners. The vessel is likely to be chartered. She may be bareboat chartered, in which case the Charterers will take over management of the vessel. She may be time chartered, most likely for a period between a month and two years. Whether time chartered or not, she may be voyage chartered for a specific voyage or voyages from named port to port or ports. Subject to the precise terms of the relevant charterparty or charterparties, any of these parties may contract with others for the vessel to carry goods on their behalf.

Each of the relevant interests mentioned above will take out one or more policies of insurance to reduce their overall risk of exposure. At the very minimum, Owners will have Hull and Machinery insurance in respect of the vessel herself as well as Protection and Indemnity insurance to cover third party liabilities. Owners or managers may have separate policies in relation to the crew and other persons on board the vessel. Charterers will have Charterers' liability insurance to cover their liabilities, both to other interests in the vessel and to third parties. Cargo interests will all arrange cover to protect them in the event of loss or damage to their cargo or matters such as General Average.

Thankfully, in the case of the Saiga the position was fairly simple. The owning company was incorporated in Cyprus and the vessel was, of course, registered in St. Vincent and the Grenadines. The managers were based in Scotland. There was only one relevant charterparty, a time charterparty. One company owned her entire cargo that, albeit a separate legal entity, operated in the same Swiss-based group as the time Charterers. This made for two very separate groups of "primary" interests, Owners and Charterers/cargo. It also made for a series of very separate groups of "underlying" insurance interests: four in particular being Owners' Hull and Machinery, Owners' P&I, Charterers' Liability, and Cargo.

The way matters developed between those parties following the detention would be familiar to any practitioner that has ever dealt with an unwanted detention of a commercial vessel, whether due to the acts of local authorities or other parties, or physical circumstances such as breakdown or collision. Within a very short time, obvious formalities are dealt with; for example, Charterers will declare the vessel off-hire. Moreover, each of the primary parties will send communications putting each and every one of the others on notice that they hold them fully responsible for any and all losses, while at the same time reserving all of their rights. Details will be sent to all of the underlying insurers. Most of the interested parties will pass their resulting files to one of the firms of London solicitors that I previously mentioned, seeking that they review and advise on the best way to preserve their respective clients' position. At the same time, teams of representatives or "experts" will fly to the location of the vessel in an effort to resolve the situation. Sometimes they are successful and other times they are not. In either case their subsequent reports can be adduced as evidence in support of their clients' position in any subsequent litigation.

In the case of the Saiga, many representatives from the different interests involved tried very hard to find a satisfactory solution to the problem in Conakry in the days following her arrival. The main hurdles that they encountered included the lack of consistency of position between the various Guinean officials they spoke to and the fact that a number of those officials were insisting that a crime be admitted and a resulting fine paid before the vessel could be released. Guinea quoted the provisions of article 251 of the Guinean Customs Code to the Tribunal in their final submissions at the Prompt Release stage: "The Customs authority shall be authorised to negotiate settlements with the persons proceeded against for customs offences. Settlement may be made before or after the final Judgment."[6] However, it is noteworthy that in the days immediately following the detention, none of the Guinean officials involved were able to tell any of the attending representatives what offenses they believed had been committed.

As developments unfolded on a daily basis, the differences of perspective between the interests in the Saiga became clearer. Owners and their underlying interests had the most to lose by virtue of the vessel's continuing detention, because they were losing money on a daily basis while not earning hire. They said that it was a problem of the Charterers' making for ordering the vessel to this area and insisted that the Charterers are, therefore, responsible for this. They further maintained that Charterers should do whatever it took to secure the early release of the vessel.

Charterers and their underlying interests denied any such responsibility. Charterers are regularly involved in bunkering activities off the West African coast. Any sort of acceptance that they might have acted illegally on this occasion would have much wider ramifications in respect of their activities to the extent that such a course could threaten their very business. Cargo and their underlying interests initially wanted the cargo preserved on the vessel. However, once it is discharged, they wanted to preserve their rights to seek recovery of it or its value, whether from the party taking the cargo or even from Owners who they say allowed this to happen. Again, any sort of acceptance that they had been involved in illegal acts has potentially wide ramifications, including not only prejudicing their chances of obtaining any recovery, but it also risks voiding their insurance cover because of the warrantee of legality contained therein.

The general feeling of resulting frustration is summed up in the following extract from a contemporaneous message of Owners:

> We presume that your legal advisors were relying upon the comfort and security of a London office when they suggest that "the Master allowed to be discharged [from] the vessel" as grounds for seeking damages from Owners for loss of cargo. Looking down the business end of an automatic weapon in the hands of Guinean Military and threatened with incarceration in a Guinean gaol fairly concentrates the mind. . . .

The expression "flag of convenience" is used a lot in the Saiga cases. While I know in general terms what is meant by this expression, I fear that I would be hard pressed to accord it some form of legal definition. Moreover, I am concerned that some observers less familiar with the industry may somehow have formed a negative view of the ramifications of the use of the registries intended by this expression and associate these with poor standards and avoidance of responsibilities. As a practitioner in the commercial maritime community, I know that the use of such registries is the backbone of the modern shipping industry. This is not to say that there cannot be room for improvement in some instances, but by and large the course of international commerce has benefited greatly from the extensive use of the flags of states such as St. Vincent and the Grenadines.

In my experience, such registries are usually extremely efficient and well-run organizations. Far from tolerating poor standards and enabling Owners to avoid their responsibilities, they are extremely vigilant in ensuring that vessels registered under their flag have undertaken all necessary safety and other matters to ensure compliance with international standards. Provided that the formalities are complied with, however, it is obviously not the job of the registry to monitor the specific business dealings of each and every one of the vessels on its registry. The Commission of Maritime Affairs of St. Vincent and the Grenadines would not be expected to have been aware that the Saiga had been operating as a bunkering vessel on the high seas prior to her detention. Bearing this in mind, the Commissioner at the time, the late Mr. Dabinovic, cannot be praised too highly for the role taken by St. Vincent and the Grenadines in defending the interests in the vessel once they had become appraised of the situation.[7]

The extreme nature of the attack (wounding four crew members, two very seriously) and the subsequent detention of the vessel and crew in Conakry was considered unacceptable by representatives of each of the main players involved. In these circumstances, the obvious course of "paying a fine" in the hope of securing her release became increasingly unattractive as time passed on. The interests behind the Saiga therefore considered using the Tribunal as an alternative way forward to resolve the deadlock that had arisen, not only with the Guinean officials, but also between themselves.

The parties' decision to put the differences between them "on hold" while an application was made to the Tribunal was not an easy one to make. A number of important issues had to be considered. One of the most important of these issues was that of costs. As a commercial practitioner, I know that about the only thing that is common to all clients is their desire to keep legal costs down! The most frequently asked questions before and during litigation are "how much?" and "how long?" One of the most frustrating parts of my job has always been to try to explain to clients that since law is not an exact science, it is simply not possible to give firm and fast answers to these questions. The most one can ever do is give "best estimates" based on the information then available, which remain subject to review. This process is always difficult with one client in litigation before a familiar forum. How much more difficult it was with the various conflicting interests in the Saiga in a potential venture before a previously unused forum.

Balanced against the potential costs concerns was an increasing perception of difficulties within the various departments in Guinea. The general feeling was that a course of action that would force Guinea to explain itself to a high profile international Tribunal might of itself achieve the primary objective if it could help convince Guinea that its interests would best be served by releasing the vessel before the application had to be heard.

Even if the application did have to be made before the Tribunal, the "Prompt Release" procedure was perceived as providing a short "in and out" solution to the problem, rather than starting a potentially lengthy and costly battle that could easily get out of hand. With the benefit of hindsight, it may be true that an application might better have been made under article 290 of the Convention.[8] However, such a process would have required the parties to agree first that St. Vincent and the Grenadines should submit a full claim against Guinea to an arbitral tribunal and contemplate all the ramifications of that. In practical terms, such a course was inconceivable in November 1997 in the circumstances detailed above.

In this manner, an application for the Prompt Release of the Saiga under article 292 of the Convention was first presented to the Tribunal on November 13, 1997, and came for its first hearing just over a week later on November 21.

As I have sought to outline above, the process of getting it there was an extremely difficult one and, frankly, one that is only likely to be repeated in the foreseeable future in cases where there is similarly no viable alternative.[9] If the Tribunal wishes to receive more applications in respect of vessels with underlying commercial interests, it will have to find a way to make it easier for those parties to have access to it. I understand that a suggestion to expressly grant private parties, such as the Owner or Charterer of a vessel, a right to submit the question of prompt release to the Tribunal was not accepted during the deliberations of the Third UN Conference on the Law of the Sea.[10] However, article 110 of the Rules of the Tribunal provides: "An application for the release of a vessel or its crew from detention may be made in accordance with article 292 of the Convention by *or on behalf of* the flag state of the vessel" [emphasis added]. The extent to which commercial parties might, in the future, be generally authorized to make applications "on behalf of" a flag state, for example, as a benefit of registration under a certain flag, is unclear to me. What does seem clear is that the present position creates such significant practical difficulties to the flag state and the commercial interests behind it to make an application that it can hardly be said to maintain a fair balance between protecting the interests of the detaining state and those of the flag state.

EFFICACY

Potential future users of the Tribunal will consider its decisions and the speed with which they are made with interest to determine the extent to which justice is seen to be done. In the Saiga cases, the facts speak for themselves in that both parties were sufficiently content with the Judgment of the majority at the "Prompt Release" stage to transfer substantive jurisdiction for the merits stage from an arbitral tribunal to the Tribunal itself.

From a practitioner's perspective, it seems to me that there is a conflict of approach within the Tribunal between, on the one hand, the members who appear to adopt a conservative "public international law" approach to its decisions, and, on the other, those who appear to adopt a more "commercial" approach. The most striking example of this in the Judgments of the Tribunal to date was with its first decision in the case of the M/V Saiga at the Prompt Release stage where the application succeeded by the narrow majority of 12-9.

This fundamental conflict next arose in such an obvious manner on the question of payment of costs in the Saiga (No. 2) case. This time the balance tipped the other way in that the Tribunal decided by a majority of 13-7 that each party should bear its own costs. This was notwithstanding that both parties had requested the Tribunal to award costs to the successful party. Given all of the circumstances of the case, I must confess that I have some difficulty in understanding the rationale of the majority of the Tribunal on this issue, which they do not explain.[11] However, I end this section by emphasizing that while I do not, of course, agree with everything that has been said throughout the Saiga proceedings, this is the only real issue upon which I, as a commercial practitioner, fundamentally disagree with the approach of the majority of the Tribunal in what turned out to be a fairly complex piece of litigation encompassing two detailed Judgments and a third Order.

ENFORCEMENT

Article 296 of the Convention provides an express statement about the binding nature of the Tribunal's Judgments. It is implicit from section 2 that such Judgments should be enforceable in the national courts of the states that have taken a dispute to the Tribunal. Beyond this, no obvious mechanisms are provided to enforce a Judgment of the Tribunal.

I had the privilege of attending a day of talks at the new ITLOS building on September 23 last year when Mr. (formerly Judge) Warioba spoke about Enforcement of the Tribunal's decisions. The thrust of his thesis, drawing significantly on the experience of the African countries and the ICJ, was that international law is compliance based, not enforcement based. I understood him to be saying by this that states comply with Judgments of international courts because they can see the sense of doing so, not because they are forced to do so. With my limited knowledge of other areas of public international law, I can see how this was the only proper way for the ICJ to have developed and why this remains today the proper approach for other public international bodies. Indeed, I have no doubt that such an approach is also perfectly proper with regard to the enforcement of the "public international law" points that are likely to arise before the Tribunal.

However, I regret that such an approach has little attraction to a commercial practitioner. The idea that the only forum available to enforce the Tribunal's Orders should be the courts of the unsuccessful state is very unattractive. It borders on farcical to suggest that such orders could only be enforced through the very courts that the Tribunal has had to expressly overrule to make its Order (as happened in the M/V Saiga [No. 2] case). If this was really the only way to enforce the Tribunal's Judgments, there would be little prospect that a commercial practitioner would ever recommend his paying clients incur substantial sums by way of legal costs to obtain such a Judgment again!

It is not the job of the Tribunal itself to ensure compliance with its own Judgments any more than it would be of any other dispute resolution forum. In England, the High Court has procedures available to help enforce Judgments of numerous courts and arbitration bodies operating in England and in other countries where relevant treaties apply. Similar procedures exist in most domestic forums, but there is no parallel mechanism for enforcement of international Judgments.

Enforcement of the Tribunal's Judgments ultimately rests with the international community that brought the Tribunal into existence. There are many ways in which it could act within its existing structures to help in this process. By way of example, UN bodies, such as the World Bank and the IMF, could be made aware of instances where states have failed to honor the Tribunal's Judgments as a matter of routine. This could, then, be a factor to be taken into account in future dealings. Conversely, failure to take any action in such circumstances would run the risk of being interpreted as the international community condoning the debtor state's conduct.

A number of avenues of enforcement of the Judgment in the M/V Saiga (No. 2) case were considered by the interests that I represent while it remained unsatisfied. None of these avenues were perceived to be without risk. Moreover, all parties obviously wanted to resolve the matters by agreement with Guinea if possible. In this context, a number of steps were taken by senior representatives of St. Vincent and the Grenadines over recent months to obtain voluntary satisfaction of the Judgment by Guinea. One of the most public of these steps being when the Ambassador and Permanent Representative to the United Nations of St. Vincent and the Grenadines raised the issue at the Fifty-fifth United Nations General Assembly in New York on October 26, 2000.

Following these steps, Guinea mandated a delegation to discuss settlement of the outstanding amounts. Together with my colleague Maitre Thiam, whom I worked with throughout the Saiga cases, I have had the privilege of meeting with that delegation over the last few days. The delegation made it clear to us that Guinea is now prepared to make substantial efforts to comply with the Tribunal's Judgment, notwithstanding the many serious difficulties that presently exist in their country. I was happy to help the parties conclude an agreement that included a timetable for payment of the amounts awarded.

CONCLUSION

From my perspective as a commercial practitioner, the Tribunal has already demonstrated in its first few cases an ability to respond quickly and deal sensibly with fundamentally commercial disputes. The case of the Saiga is already a success story for the simple reason that the Tribunal helped secure her release without having to pay a "fine."

Whether the Tribunal may develop to be a widely used body for determination of fundamentally commercial disputes in the future may depend to a large extent on whether its Judgments are perceived to be enforceable. This is really a decision for the international community that will be judged by the efforts that it is prepared to make to monitor compliance with the Tribunal's Judgments. Provided that Guinea makes full payment under the recently concluded agreement, the M/V Saiga (No. 2) case can only serve to help demonstrate the potential in this regard.

I can certainly see an opportunity for the work of the Tribunal to overlap with, and find a place in, the world of private international dispute resolution. This would be not only with my community in London, but also with the parallel commercial maritime dispute resolution communities throughout the world. I wish it every success in this process.

Notes

[1] For example, see article appearing in *The Lawyer* (July 1999).

[2] For example, see the handout: "Settlement of Law of the Sea Disputes and the Insurance Industry" issued on the occasion of the opening of the Headquarters Building of the Tribunal, July 3, 2000.

[3] Vaughan Lowe, "The M/V Saiga: The First Case of the International Tribunal for the Law of the Sea," 48 *ICLQ* 187 (January 1999): 195.

[4] But see comment about persuading the vessel's flag state to make an application written by another commercial practitioner from London: David Pitlarge, 2 *Int. M. L.* 35 (1998): 38.

[5] Tribunal de 1ere Instance De Conakry, Judgment No. 4821, 17 December 1997.

[6] Verbatim Record, 24, lines 5-9.

[7] See "International Law of the Sea Tribunal Hears First Case," in 10 *International Ship Registry Review* 7 (April 1998).

[8] See Dissenting Opinion of Vice-President Wolfrum and Judge Yamamoto in the case of the *M/V Saiga*, para. 19.

[9] Note the high level of fines sought to be imposed by the authorities of Reunion in the *Camouco* case and the *Monte Confurco* case.

[10] See generally Rainer Lagoni, "The Prompt Release of Vessels and Crews before the International Tribunal for the Law of the Sea: A Preparatory Report," 11 *IJMCL* 2:147.

[11] See Joint Declaration by Judges Caminos, Yankov, Aki, Anderson, Vukas, Treves, and Eiriksson on the Question of Costs in the *Saiga (No. 2)* case.

A Practitioner's Critique of the Order Granting Provisional Measures in the *Southern Bluefin Tuna* Cases

Donald L. Morgan[*]

Introduction

I appreciate the opportunity to discuss from a practitioner's viewpoint the Order of August 27, 1999, of the International Tribunal for the Law of the Sea (ITLOS or the Tribunal) imposing Provisional Measures upon the Parties in the *Southern Bluefin Tuna* cases. I will also discuss the proceedings that led to the Order. My law firm and I had the honor of assisting Japan in those cases. I wish to make it clear, however, that the views I express are not offered on behalf of Japan, rather they are solely my own in response to an invitation from the sponsors of this symposium.

My central thesis is as follows: The Order did not address a number of important factual and legal issues that the Parties presented or additional important issues that the Provisional Measures themselves raised. Clear resolution of those issues would have been of substantial value not only to the Parties, but also to the public at large and future litigants concerned about what the United Nations Convention on the Law of the Sea (UNCLOS or the Convention) requires and how it will be interpreted and applied in future adjudications before the Tribunal. The Tribunal unduly truncated the proceedings, reducing the time for Parties to assist it by thoroughly preparing and effectively presenting their proofs and arguments and reducing the time for the Judges to review and consider the materials the Parties presented and to explain the bases of their rulings.

---

[*] Partner, Cleary, Gottlieb, Steen & Hamilton.

M.H. Nordquist and J.N. Moore (eds.),
Current Marine Environmental Issues and the International Tribunal for the Law of the Sea, 173–213.
© 2001 *Kluwer Law International. Printed in the Netherlands.*

BACKGROUND

I shall start with a brief review of the events leading to the adjudication that Australia and New Zealand brought to the Tribunal on July 30, 1999, when each filed its Request for the Prescription of Provisional Measures. Except as otherwise noted, all of the following background was presented to the Tribunal and was not disputed there.[1] A more detailed statement of background facts, not all of which was available to ITLOS, is set forth in the Appendix to this paper.

The only known spawning ground for Southern Bluefin Tuna is south of Java, Indonesia, and off northwest Australia. Juveniles migrate southward along the west coast of Australia and stay in the coastal waters of southwest, south, and southeast Australia. As the tuna grow, they extend their distribution into southern portions of the Pacific, Indian, and Atlantic Oceans. They mature physically at age 8, and some live to be more than 40.

Japan, a nation singularly dependent upon the oceans for food, began fishing for the species in the 1950s. The tuna proved to be very popular among consumers in Japan. By 1961, the Japanese catch reached its historic high of about 78,000 metric tons (mt). This catch declined gradually and leveled in a range of 20,000 to 30,000 mt from the mid-1970s until 1985. The areas fished initially included the spawning grounds, but in 1971, the tuna industry voluntarily restricted fishing areas and seasons in order to avoid catching small fish and fish in the spawning grounds.

Australian fishing for the tuna also began in coastal waters in the 1950s, starting with small-scale trolling and gradually shifting to pole/line and purse seine (net) fisheries. The catch increased in the 1960s as the purse seine industry targeted one and two year olds for canning. In 1972, this catch reached its historic high of 21,500 mt, about 2,370,000 fish, only about a quarter of the tonnage but almost double in number of the approximately 1,216,000 fish caught by Japan in 1961.[2]

Due to concerns about this quick increase of juvenile catch and declines in the catch rate of Japanese long-line vessels, Australia, New Zealand, and Japan established an informal SBT management arrangement in 1982. Their scientists agreed that although the parental stock had declined by 1980 to about one-third of its 1960 level, the recruitment level of new fish had not dropped substantially and the 1980 level was sufficient to replicate the next generation. The Parties agreed on a goal of maintaining the level of the parental stock at approximately the 1980 level. When they realized that the recent high catches of juveniles would in due course lead to a drop in the parental stock below the 1980 level, the Parties agreed on the goal of restoring the stock to the 1980 level by 2020. The first step was to limit the Australian catch to 21,000 mt in 1983 and 14,500 mt in 1984. For 1985, the three nations agreed on a total allowable catch (TAC) of 38,650 mt, of which 23,150 were allocated to Japan, 14,500 to Australia, and 1,000 to New Zealand. TACs and allocations were thereafter set for each succeeding year, with TAC declining to 11,750 mt in 1989, of which 6,065 were allocated to Japan, 5,265 to Australia, and 420 to New Zealand, reductions from 1985 of seventy-four, sixty-three, and fifty-eight percent respectively.

At Australia's request in 1986 and again in 1990, the Japanese tuna industry made funds available to purchase significant portions of Australia's allocations. In the early 1990s, the Japanese tuna industry also assisted Australia by contributing knowledge about fish farming and long line fishing to encourage a shift to older and fattier fish that would result in taking fewer fish and improve profitability by serving the Tokyo market for sashimi.

The three nations continued to confer at least annually on SBT matters and agreed year by year on TAC and allocations of that catch among themselves, keeping them at the 1989 quantities. In 1993, they formalized their cooperation by entry into the first species-specific treaty in furtherance of UNCLOS' general directive to cooperate in that manner, the Convention for the Conservation of Southern Bluefin Tuna. This "Tuna Treaty" went into effect in 1994 and, like UNCLOS, had twin goals of conservation and optimum utilization. Toward that end, the treaty established a Commission to set TAC and allocate quotas on a year-by-year basis. The Commission could act only by unanimity of its three members. Unanimity became increasingly difficult to attain, however, as Japan saw signs of recovery of the stock beginning several years after the reductions in TAC in the 1980s, and advocated an increase in TAC. Australia and New Zealand refused to agree to an increase. For a few years, Japan reluctantly agreed to the previous year's TAC and allocations, because Australia threatened to exclude Japanese vessels from its waters and ports if Japan did not agree. Starting in 1997, however, the Commission failed to agree on a TAC, and Australia carried out its threat of exclusion. New Zealand did likewise in 1998 when Japan proceeded with the pilot stage of its Experimental Fishing Program (EFP).

From 1997 on, there was no Tuna Convention limit on anyone's catch. Australia, which was to complain later about the unilateral aspect of Japan's decisions to conduct scientific research, unilaterally decided it would continue to catch the tuna and would limit itself to its last allocation from the Commission. New Zealand took similar unilateral action, as did Japan, each on a year-by-year basis. Non-parties to the Tuna Convention increased their catches substantially during the 1990s.

The two sides disagreed within the Commission on how the stock was faring, by starting with different perceptions about the density of fish in areas and seasons fished before the catch reductions of the 1980s, but no longer fished. Japan put high weight on the assumption that the density was the same as in areas and seasons still fished. New Zealand's most favored assumption was that there were no fish in areas and seasons no longer fished, while Australia's views were similar, though less extreme. The only feasible means of narrowing or resolving the difference in the stock assessments in the near term was to compare catch rates in areas and seasons still commercially fished with catch rates in areas and seasons no longer commercially fished. In the mid-1990s, Japan proposed a joint EFP to collect comparative catch rate data in a systematic way. All three nations agreed through the Commission that such a program "can be an effective tool for reducing uncertainty in stock assessment, resulting in more responsive and appropriate management," and adopted principles for an EFP and a timetable for work on an EFP.[3] Shortly thereafter in late May 1996, Japan tabled a detailed proposal for a joint EFP. Australia and New Zealand raised various procedural objections to consideration of the proposal and offered critiques of it. Japan repeatedly made adjustments to its proposal to accommodate comments from Australian and New Zealand scientists and offered to reduce its future commercial catches if the EFP were to impair recovery of the stock.

At Australia's insistence, the Commission also invited panels of external fisheries experts to advise on its scientific processes and the proposed EFP. Those scientists concluded the EFP was reasonable and necessary to help resolve the differences between the two sides. In 1998, Japan conducted a pilot program for a three year EFP to begin in 1999. Consideration of an EFP within the Commission intensified. Four EFP workshops took place in the first half of 1999, and the two sides came close to agreement both as to study design and quantity, with Australia and New Zealand contemplating an EFP of 1,200 to 1,500 tons, not far from Japan's plan for 2,000 tons. Shortly before Japan's long announced June target to begin the EFP, however, Australia proposed a substantially different EFP that would take many years to produce any results that would meaningfully reduce existing levels of uncertainty. Japan then undertook the EFP alone. Japan had invited Australia and New Zealand to provide observers on the vessels conducting the EFP, but the invitation was not accepted. Observers from other countries did participate.

Australia and New Zealand (ANZ) threatened litigation to stop the EFP. Japan offered mediation and also arbitration pursuant to the dispute resolution provisions of the Tuna Convention. These offers were rejected unless Japan immediately stopped the EFP, which would have conceded the issue in dispute. On July 15, 1999, ANZ served notices of claim on Japan for arbitration pursuant to the dispute resolution provisions of UNCLOS, with requests for provisional measures, and lodged copies with the Registrar of the

Tribunal.[4] On July 30, they each filed Requests for Provisional Measures with the Tribunal.

How the Tribunal's Order Dealt With Issues of Jurisdiction

The threshold issue there was jurisdictional. Japan contended that the entire dispute arose within the context of and was covered by the Tuna Treaty and that its dispute resolution provisions should govern.[5] These provisions did not encompass resort to UNCLOS arbitration in the absence of the consent of all the Parties, and Japan did not consent to that. ANZ, on the other hand, took the position that they could proceed under the dispute resolution provisions of either the Tuna Treaty or UNCLOS. They argued, but in only very general terms, that the EFP violated one or more of UNCLOS' articles 64 and 116-119, and the Tribunal focused on those contentions. Neither ANZ, nor later the ITLOS Order, however, identified any aspect of the dispute that arose under UNCLOS but not also under the Tuna Treaty. Paragraph 55 of the Order nevertheless announced in only conclusory terms that the Tuna Treaty did not preclude arbitration under UNCLOS.

As was shown later before the arbitral tribunal, there are scores of treaties that relate to some matters that are also potentially subject to UNCLOS arbitration, but that have dispute resolution provisions that do not require compulsory and binding third-party settlement.[6] It seems to be an eminently fair inference that at least some parties negotiating such treaties expect that disputes arising under them could be resolved only in accordance with them. Arguments have nonetheless been made in favor of compulsory UNCLOS jurisdiction. Future controversy may abound in this area, despite the subsequent ruling in the *Southern Bluefin Tuna* cases by an arbitral tribunal that the dispute was to be resolved pursuant to the Tuna Treaty. It would have been helpful to future litigants and practitioners alike if the Order had set forth reasons why it had at least *prima facie* jurisdiction.[7] Did that depend on the particular text of the Tuna Treaty's dispute resolution provisions? Did it matter what that text said? Are States parties to UNCLOS powerless to negotiate treaties on Law of the Sea matters that

provide that disputes arising under them will be resolved only by
negotiation and consent? Was the issue controlled by the text of
UNCLOS, and if so, by which provisions? One can hope that
future cases will shed light on these jurisdictional issues.

How the Tribunal's Order Dealt With Japan's Factual
Defenses to the Requests for Provisional Measures

Perhaps of less importance, but still important, is how the
Tribunal (having found *prima facie* jurisdiction), acted on the
Requests for Provisional Measures. The Requests filed on July 30,
1999, were similar but not identical to the July 15 Requests.[8] The
Annexes to the Australian Request included its July 15 Statement
of Claims and Grounds on which it is based, comprising thirty
pages of legal argument, and a supporting scientific paper of
twenty-seven text pages prepared by its scientists Polacheck and
Preece for purposes of the adjudication. This would be
supplemented on August 11 by a twenty-two-page commentary on
the Polacheck and Preece paper by a retained expert,
Professor John Beddington.

On the very same day the Registrar received the Requests, he
distributed copies to Japan with a notice requiring it to file its
Response by August 6.[9] On August 3 the President of the Tribunal
set the oral hearing for the week of August 16. While quite
possibly ANZ would argue that the urgency of the situation
required such abbreviated response times, the Tribunal's
scheduling decisions were made before any substantive response
on urgency or any other issue had been made by Japan. The
Tribunal also decided that each side would have only four hours to
present its case in chief, and one and a half for rebuttal.[10]

These constraints posed a number of tactical problems for
Japan, including how to deal as a factual matter with fisheries
science issues relating to the desirability of the EFP, issues that
were complex and to which a large volume of documents prepared
in the context of the Tuna Treaty Commission and the Parties'

earlier informal cooperative efforts was relevant. Japan submitted a Response of fifty-five pages and annexed approximately 1,250 pages of prior communications among the Parties. There was wholly inadequate time at the hearing to present a scientific case through questioning witnesses. Japan thus decided to rely upon the fact that the Commission's own panels of independent, expert scientists, who had devoted much time and effort in 1998 and 1999 to the opposing contentions of the Parties and thus were particularly knowledgeable about the matters in dispute, had concluded that the EFP was a reasonable one. Japan asked those Commission-selected scientists to provide their advice directly to the Tribunal, and they did so on August 4.[11] They saw "a strong need to gather additional information on the [fishing] grounds," and they regarded the EFP as "satisfactory in terms of statistical design and practical considerations." In general they were supportive of the EFP.

Japan also relied heavily upon the fact that it had offered "Pay Back," that is, to reduce its future commercial catch to compensate for any harm to the recovery of the stock by 2020 that might be shown to have been caused by the EFP. Pay Back was a well established concept that the Parties themselves had utilized: a reduction in a future commercial catch would compensate for a prior year's over catch in terms of recovery of the stock. Indeed, Pay Back was what ANZ sought in their Requests for Provisional Measures: make Japan reduce its commercial catches to compensate for the fish caught in the 1998 pilot program and in the 1999 EFP. Indeed, Pay Back was what the Tribunal ordered, although limited to the 1999 EFP catch.

True, ANZ argued at the hearing that Pay Back would not work if, but only if, the species were on the verge of extinction and the EFP somehow caused it to collapse.[12] As Judge Vukas' Separate Opinion notes in paragraph 5, however, ANZ's intent to continue their commercial catches was difficult to reconcile with any belief on their part that the EFP presented an urgent concern for the state of the stock, let alone a belief that the stock was on the verge of extinction.

As a legal matter, Japan was entitled to expect that as a sovereign its decisions were entitled to some deference and that it was more than sufficient that the EFP was objectively reasonable and included an offer of Pay Back.

How then does the Tribunal's Order deal with Japan's principal factual defense, that the EFP was reasonable and Pay Back was available? By ignoring it. The Separate Opinions likewise ignore it.[13]

How the Tribunal's Order Dealt With Other Important Issues

The Order also ignored a number of legal issues. One involved the standard for granting Provisional Measures.[14] Japan argued for traditional international law criteria, such as risk of irreparable harm imminently threatened to occur before a decision on the merits or, in these cases, before constitution of an arbitral tribunal.[15] ANZ argued for a far lower standard, that it was sufficient if their scientific "concerns" were "reasonable," "worst case scenarios are not excluded,"[16] "the particular rights asserted by the Applicants . . . are not manifestly incapable of existing in law," the scientific material submitted by the Applicants "establishes the possibility of the right claimed and the possibility of the danger to which that right was exposed," the available information "does not exclude the possibility that damage . . . might be shown" that might be irreparable, or that "the rights asserted are not manifestly unfounded."[17] While apparently declining to apply traditional criteria, the Order sheds no light on what the new standard might be.

Another vigorously disputed legal issue not mentioned in the Order was whether the Precautionary Principle, or the Precautionary Approach, had attained the status of customary international law.[18]

I will come back to the Precautionary Approach but wish to note here some issues that arose from or became apparent only in the Order itself. The Provisional Measures it imposed differed from those requested by the Parties.[19] This, I submit, presents the question of what criteria or standards should guide the Tribunal in granting such different measures. The Order says only that the Tribunal's Rules (article 89, para. 5) provide that the Tribunal may grant different measures. Certainly future potential litigants would be interested in knowing whether there are *any* limits on what the Tribunal might or can do, and if there are any limits, how one could anticipate where they might be. The Order also did not explain how its grant of different measures, or its Rule, was consistent with the text of section 3 of UNCLOS, article 290, that "Provisional measures may be prescribed . . . only at the request of a party . . . and after the parties have been given an opportunity to be heard."[20]

A related question suggested by the Order is whether the power to prescribe additional measures can override specific provisions of UNCLOS. I have in mind the fact that the Tribunal restricted ANZ's catches after having ascertained that all of those catches were taken within their respective EEZs except for that of one Australian vessel.[21] The Order might, in this context, have addressed the provision of section 1, article 56, of UNCLOS, that a coastal State has "sovereign rights for . . . exploiting, conserving and managing" living natural resources within its EEZ. What about the specification in section 1, article 61, that "The coastal State shall determine the allowable catch" within its EEZ? What rights, if any, do coastal States waive by resorting to the Tribunal or by requesting provisional measures? What is the significance, if any, of the fact that the tuna are migratory, within and outside of the EEZs? Will uncertainty about the answers tend to discourage coastal States from resorting to the Tribunal?

Caution, Precaution, and the Precautionary Principle

There are also questions raised by the emphasis that the Order and some of the accompanying Separate Opinions placed on a cautionary approach to the tuna catch. Here it may be instructive to place UNCLOS, the Precautionary Principle, and what has come to be known as the Precautionary Approach to Fishing (PA2F) in historical perspective. According to Serge Garcia, a fisheries expert at the UN Food and Agriculture Organization, PA2F is a recent development, which did not find significant support until the early 1990s.[22] By that time, the Precautionary Principle had rather recently come into vogue for regulating and often preventing entry into the market of chemical products on the basis that lack of scientific certainty should not preclude rigorous protective measures. The Precautionary Principle was regarded as too extreme for fisheries, given the world's needs for food and the economic needs of those engaged in fishing, so a less Draconian precautionary "approach" was pursued within fisheries management organizations and treaty negotiations.

In contrast to those developments, Garcia and others he cites note that UNCLOS is particularly silent regarding uncertainty, precaution, risk, probabilities, and the need to take protective action in the absence of scientific certainty, all hallmarks of a precautionary approach. They explain that the silence is not "surprising considering that [the] scientific basis [of UNCLOS] was established . . . in the 1960s and 'frozen' by the difficult negotiation process in the early 1970s."[23] Proponents of PA2F regard as dangerous UNCLOS' specification of Maximum Sustainable Yield (MSY) as the target reference point for the desirable level of catch, since that implies that the catch will be greater than MSY fifty percent of the time (and lower the other fifty percent of the time).[24] A precautionary approach instead requires a limit reference point (which could be MSY) and a lower target reference point, which Garcia terms the Optimum Yield. There is a buffer zone between the two that may be invaded by the actual catch, but if the limit is being approached, corrective action should then be taken to assure that the limit itself is only rarely exceeded and to get back down to the Optimum Yield.[25]

Garcia notes that the UN Fish Stocks Agreement is PA2F friendly and provides flexibility to use MSY as the limit on catch.[26] While from a food-supply standpoint an MSY catch would be desirable and would have been so regarded in the 1960s, experience in the past few decades has proven that fisheries sciences suffers from many uncertainties that can lead to over fishing and subsequent inability to realize MSY and even threaten serious harm that can be reversed only in the long term. Thus, it now seems prudent to settle for a lesser but steadier catch.

Nevertheless, the contrast between UNCLOS, with its exclusive use of MSY as the only explicit reference point for development and management targets, and the PA2F is striking, at least to fisheries experts. This contrast appears repeatedly in UNCLOS. For example, sections 2 and 3 of article 61 obligate coastal States to maintain or restore "populations of harvested species at levels which can produce the maximum sustainable yield." Article 62 requires a coastal State to determine its capacity "to harvest the entire allowable catch" and where such capacity is absent, "to give other States access to the surplus."

The Order refers to UNCLOS as seeking both conservation and optimum utilization but does not appear to attribute any *significance* to optimum utilization or MSY. Have optimum utilization and maximum sustainable yield been read out of UNCLOS? If so, how?

Some of the Separate Opinions do discuss the Precautionary Principle and the Precautionary Approach[27] and recognize the difficulty of applying them in adjudication. I think Garcia's paper can again be instructive. He explains that for precautionary approach management to work, States must first agree on quantitative standards, or what he calls reference points, together with some quantification of acceptably low levels of risk that they might be exceeded.[28]

In order to answer the otherwise open-ended question of how much caution is enough, I submit that such reference points are also necessary in adjudication. Litigation is ill suited to creating such standards, considering the appropriateness of taking into account a wide variety of factors including economic and environmental factors for which there simply are no established decision rules.[29] The parties to the Tuna Treaty had agreed on some such reference points, that is, the level of parental biomass needed to sustain the stock and the time for recovery (until 2020).

Indeed, the Parties cast their arguments within the context of the Tuna Treaty in those terms and differed on what impact the EFP would have on achieving the desired 1980 parental biomass by 2020. Whether the Parties were in compliance with those standards could have been the subject of meaningful adjudication. The Parties would have known what evidence and argument would be relevant to a decision.

The Tribunal instead chose as the factual basis for the Order what it found to be agreement among the Parties that "the stock . . . is seriously depleted and is at its historically *lowest* levels" and that this is a cause for "serious biological concern."[30] The apparent basis for these statements was minutes of meetings of the Scientific Committee of the Tuna Commission some years earlier and reference to them by Counsel for ANZ in the morning session of August 18. Whether there was agreement depends on what those minutes, drafted in English by ANZ, meant to the Parties when made, and whether what they meant when drafted continued to represent the Parties' views in August 1999. The quoted statements could not have meant that the stock was as low as it had ever been, that is, "lowest." Such a reading is inconsistent with use of the plural for "levels." This is not just a matter of semantics. In fact, the minutes and Counsel's reference to them, speak of "historically *low* levels," not "*lowest*."[31] Moreover, the "historically low levels" language appears in the minutes as early as 1990,[32] and ANZ had not only continued their commercial catches but increased them over the subsequent decade. In any event, there was ample evidence that Japan was convinced by the mid-1990s that the stock was recovering and was progressing toward the 2020 goal of restoration to the 1980 level, and, thus, was necessarily higher than the lowest it had ever been.

The Parties disagreed about recovery, it is true. The point is that there was not an agreed position about the state of the stock. That difference seems masked by the erroneous quotation about *lowest* levels.[33] The other terms taken from the minutes are all non-quantitative and subject to a range of interpretations. They do not undermine Japan's position that: (1) the EFP was consistent with attaining two specific reference points on which the Parties had agreed for stock management purposes, reaching 1980 stock levels by 2020; and (2) that the EFP could, depending upon its results, serve the goal of conservation (if the stock were shown to be declining) or the goal of optimum utilization (if the stock were confirmed to be recovering).[34]

As the legal basis for the Order, the Tribunal cited first its own view, without reference to any specific authority, that "the parties should in the circumstances proceed with prudence and caution to ensure that effective conservation measures are taken to prevent serious harm to the stock." [35] Japan would say that Pay Back avoided serious harm. The Order also said there was urgency to preserve the rights of the Parties, presumably those of ANZ, and that there should be no increase in anyone's total catch over the last agreed catch. What right ANZ had to such a limit, particularly when they continued to harvest SBT, the Order did not say; the Tuna Treaty does not provide Australia or New Zealand a veto over Japan's actions, and neither does UNCLOS.

Consideration of Judicial Style and the Rule of Law

I appreciate that differences among the domestic legal systems represented on the Tribunal and in their style of rendering decisions may account for the absence of clearer explanations in the Order of how the Tribunal reached the result that it did. Some jurisdictions seem quite content with decisions that announce the result and provide little, if any, of the underlying reasoning.[36] In addition to differences in judicial style, some commentators have suggested that multinational tribunals at times may lack consensus as to reasoning and delete statements that may displease one group or another of the judges.[37]

Still, I submit that the purposes of UNCLOS would, for a number of reasons, be well served by fuller and clearer explanations of how the Tribunal resolved the arguments and issues that were presented to it or that the grant of different provisional measures raised. One is simple fairness to the Parties.

Second, there would be more guidance to those to whom UNCLOS is applicable respecting how to act in the future. Surely, informed voluntary compliance will be more effective than a series of unexplained case-by-case rulings, in instructing the extensive and growing regulated community of what must be done to comply with UNCLOS.

Third, future litigants are entitled to know what rules or principles of decision the Tribunal will apply, so that they will know what evidence and argument they should present to the Tribunal, to "have their day in court."[38] To make one's "day in court" meaningful, a party "must have some conception of the issues toward which his proofs and arguments are to be directed."[39]

Respect for the Tribunal and support for UNCLOS itself can be influenced by assurance that parties do obtain a meaningful opportunity to be heard. They should thus know what the Tribunal has thought about the arguments and proofs they have advanced in a particular case and should, over time, obtain increasing guidance as to what arguments and proofs would be deemed important in future cases.

In sum, the Order falls well short of what one would regard as the Optimum Yield in the *Southern Bluefin Tuna* cases, cases of first impression that presented a number of important issues regarding the proper interpretation of UNCLOS. While the Separate Opinions provide some of the authors' thinking, none deals with the full range of issues I have discussed, none is joined by a majority of the Tribunal, and they totally ignore some issues.

In support of the Order, some might say it was expeditiously issued,[40] and protective of the stock. This was not a ship seizure case, however. No vessel and cargo were impounded, and no crew were being denied liberty. Pay Back was a recognized safeguard against harm to the stock.

The only exception to the efficacy of Pay Back for which anyone argued involved the stock being on the verge of extinction, a condition belied by ANZ's continuation of their commercial catches. Suppose however that the possibility of extinction was real or that the Tribunal so concluded. Suppose further that there is wide latitude to prescribe Provisional Measures. What should be done? The answer came from the testimony to the Tribunal of ANZ's own expert witness, Professor John Beddington: Reduce the catch.[41]

What part of the catch, one may ask? How would continuation of commercial catches help avert extinction or promote conservation? Not at all. Those catches would only increase the risk of a collapse. On the other hand, the EFP *might* avert a collapse. If it were to show the stock in a drastic state of decline, not only the parties to the Tuna Convention but also other jurisdictions, which also and increasingly were catching the tuna, would feel compelled to greatly reduce, if not terminate, their catches.[42] Should not the prudence and caution found appropriate by the Tribunal have placed priority on the EFP?

APPENDIX A[43]

Efforts at Cooperation Among the Parties
Prior to the ITLOS Proceedings

Southern bluefin tuna (SBT) (*Thunnus maccoyii*) are a highly migratory species of pelagic fish listed in Annex I of UNCLOS. Their only known spawning ground is in the waters south of Java, Indonesia, and off northwest Australia. From the spawning ground, juvenile SBT migrate south along the Australian west coast to the south coast of Australia, from which they migrate on a seasonal basis to the middle of the Indian Ocean. SBT permanently abandon coastal waters beginning at age 5, after which they can be found throughout the southern portions of the Atlantic, Pacific, and Indian Oceans. Fishermen from Indonesia, Taiwan, the Republic of Korea, and some flag of convenience countries, as well as Japanese, Australian, and New Zealand fishermen catch and market SBT. Japan is the principal consumer of SBT and imports approximately ninety percent of the total.

Commercial fishing of the species developed from the early 1950s, reaching its highest level of 81,000 metric tons (mt) in 1961. The Japanese catch was 78,000 mt, approximately ninety-seven percent of the total. The Japanese fleet fished by longline methods, catching mainly large fish individually on hooks attached to long lines. Australian fishing utilized purse seine methods that involve catching fish in nets. Australia in general targeted younger, smaller fish, with the consequence that each ton of fish caught by Australian methods involved taking more fish than are taken per ton by Japanese methods. Per ton caught, Australian fishing has a greater adverse long-term effect upon the stock.

In 1971, the Japanese industry introduced voluntary conservation to restrict fishing areas/seasons in order to avoid catching small size fish as well as spawning stock.

In 1982, Japan, Australia, and New Zealand began informally to manage the SBT catch. Scientists of the three countries recommended that the goal of management should be to achieve the parental stock levels that existed in 1980 in order to secure future levels of recruitment (entry of new fish into the fishery). The three States agreed on a Total Allowable Catch (TAC) applicable to all three States in 1985. This was steadily reduced from 38,650 mt in 1985 to 11,750 mt in 1989, a reduction of approximately seventy percent in four years. Japan contributed to this reduction by reducing its quota by seventy-four percent, from 23,150 mt in 1985 to 6,065 mt in 1989. On several occasions during this period, the Japanese tuna industry provided Australian tuna fishermen with financial and/or technical assistance with a view to reducing their catch of juveniles.

In 1993, the conservation efforts of the three countries were institutionalized by the conclusion of the Convention for the Conservation of Southern Bluefin Tuna (Tuna Treaty). The objective of the Tuna Treaty is stated to be "to ensure, through appropriate management, the conservation and optimum utilization of SBT" (article 3). In article 5, the Parties agree to: take measures to ensure the enforcement of the Tuna Treaty; provide scientific information, fishing catch and effort statistics, and other data relevant to the conservation of SBT; cooperate in collection and exchange of fisheries data, biological samples, and other information relevant for scientific research on SBT; and to cooperate in the exchange of information regarding any fishing for SBT by nationals of any State or entity not a party to the Tuna Treaty.

The instrument for the furtherance of the ends of the Tuna Treaty is the Commission for the Conservation of SBT (the Commission). The Commission is to meet at least once a year. Each Party is to have one vote, and decisions of the Commission are to be taken by unanimous vote.

The specific functions of the Commission are to collect and accumulate relevant information and consider such matters as "the interpretation or implementation of the Tuna Treaty and the measures adopted pursuant to it," as well as "regulatory measures for conservation, management and optimum utilization of SBT." In addition, the Commission considers matters that will be reported by, or be entrusted to, the Scientific Committee (see below).

The Commission is expressly called upon:

> for the conservation, management and optimum utilization of SBT: . . . [to] decide upon a total allowable catch ("TAC") and its allocation among the Parties . . . (article 8[3][a]).

In deciding upon allocations, the Commission is required to consider a number of factors that include relevant scientific evidence, the need for orderly and sustainable development of SBT fisheries, the interests of the Parties through whose EEZ or fishery zone the SBT migrate, the interests of Parties whose vessels engage in fishing for SBT, the contribution of each Party to conservation and enhancement of, and scientific research on, SBT, together with any other factors that the Commission deems appropriate (articles 8[4][a-f]).

The Commission also has power to make recommendations to the Parties in order to further the attainment of the objectives of this Tuna Treaty (article 8[5]). The Commission is to take full account of the report and recommendations of the Scientific Committee (article 8[6]). Decisions of the Commission under article 8(3) are binding on the Parties (article 8[7]). The Commission is also to develop systems for monitoring all fishing activities related to SBT.

The Tuna Treaty established the Scientific Committee as an advisory body to the Commission (article 9[1]). Its functions are to: assess and analyze the status and trends of the population of SBT; to coordinate research and studies on SBT; to report to the Commission its findings or conclusions, including consensus, majority and minority views, on the status of SBT stock; and to make recommendations to the Commission on matters concerning conservation, management and optimum utilization of SBT (article 9[2]). Each Party has a representative on the Committee.

Additionally, there is provision for a Secretariat of the Commission and for a budget. The Parties also agreed to take measures in relation to non-Party States and other entities engaged in fishing for SBT by inviting them to participate in relevant meetings (article 14[1]) and by taking other steps foreseen in article 15.

Article 16 contains dispute settlement provisions similar to or virtually identical with those in: the Antarctic Treaty, 1959, article XI; the Convention for the Conservation of Antarctic Marine Living Resources (CCAMLR), 1980, article XXV; the Convention on the Conservation and Management of Pollock Resources in the Central Bering Sea, 1994, article XIII; and the Agreement on the Conservation of Cetaceans of Black Sea, Mediterranean Sea and Contiguous Atlantic Oceans, 1997, article XII. All of these Conventions, while foreseeing the possibility of recourse to the ICJ or to arbitration with the consent of the parties, clearly and deliberately exclude the possibility of compulsory judicial or arbitral settlement.

There are no agreed minutes of the *travaux préparatoires* of the Tuna Treaty signed by the Parties. It is possible, however, to trace the evolution of article 16 through a series of drafts exchanged by the Parties from as early as 1988. These drafts show that the question of dispute settlement was given due consideration by the Parties and that the decision to adopt the present text, which precludes non-consensual arbitration, was deliberately taken in preference to one that would have given compulsory jurisdiction to an arbitral tribunal. It is, moreover, evident that the Parties never contemplated that settlement of Tuna Treaty disputes would ever take place under UNCLOS dispute settlement procedures.

The first draft, dated April 7, 1988, was prepared by New Zealand and was tabled at a meeting of a Trilateral Working Group on Possible Institutional Arrangements for International Management of SBT, April 19-21, 1988. It contained a dispute settlement article virtually identical with article XXV of the CCAMLR.

At the same meeting, Australia tabled a draft with the dispute settlement provision more briefly expressed:

Article 8.1. If any dispute arises between any two or
more of the parties concerning the interpretation or
application of this Agreement, those parties shall consult
among themselves and with any other party whose interests
may be affected with a view to resolving the dispute
amicably as early as possible.

The second meeting of the Trilateral Working Group was held
on September 8-10, 1988, and had before it a Consolidated
Working Text dated August 26, 1988, prepared by Australia. This
contained no more than the first paragraph of the dispute
settlement provision of the CCAMLR, followed by a note that:

New Zealand favours the inclusion of a clause
specifically referring to the International Court of Justice
and other dispute settlement mechanisms.

The third meeting of the Trilateral Working Group (July 25-28,
1989) had before it a draft tabled by Japan. The dispute settlement
article was noted as being identical to the consolidated text on this
issue. That text was identical with the first paragraph of the
CCAMLR text. There was no discussion of the dispute settlement
article at the fourth meeting of the Trilateral Working Group on
September 13-16, 1989. As part of the Final Clauses, it was agreed
to leave this item to the Legal Drafting Group.

There then appears to have been an interval of over two years
before any further documents emerged. A draft from Japan,
marked January 30, 1992, reproduced the previous single
paragraph text based on the first paragraph of the CCAMLR. The
next document, headed "Australian input to Japan's 1992 draft
text," contains a slight alteration of the CCAMLR text, but still no
compulsory procedure.

This was echoed in another Japanese draft proposed on
February 10, 1992:

Article XIII [Dispute settlement]

If any dispute arises between two or more of the Contracting Parties concerning the interpretation or application [implementation] of this Convention, those Contracting Parties shall[, before requesting consideration by the Commission under Article V: paragraph 3(1),] consult among themselves with a view to having the dispute resolved by negotiation, enquiry, mediation, conciliation, arbitration, judicial settlement or other peaceful means of their own choice.

This manifestly did not create compulsory jurisdiction.

The next draft is headed "Consolidated Working Text, 13 February 1992." This contains two texts—the first is a repetition of the Japanese draft set out above; the second is a text that is attributed to New Zealand:

Article XV [Dispute Settlement]

1   If any dispute arises between two or more of the Parties concerning the interpretation or application of this Convention, those Parties shall consult among themselves with a view to having the dispute resolved by negotiation, inquiry, mediation, conciliation, arbitration, judicial settlement or other peaceful means of their own choice.

2   Any dispute of this character not so resolved shall, with the consent in each case of all Parties to the dispute be referred for settlement to the International Court of Justice or to arbitration; but failure to reach agreement on reference to the International Court or to arbitration shall not absolve the Parties to the dispute from the responsibility of continuing to seek to resolve it by any of the various peaceful means referred to in paragraph 1 above.

3   In cases where the dispute is not resolved it shall be
referred to arbitration in accordance with the Annex to this
Convention (NZ).

As can be seen, the first two paragraphs are identical with the
whole of article XI of the Antarctic Treaty 1959 and with the first
two paragraphs of article XXV of the CCAMLR. The third
paragraph, however, introduces the idea of compulsory arbitration
if the dispute is not otherwise resolved. It was proposed that there
should be an Annex dealing with arbitration.

Australia commented as follows:

Article XV: Dispute Settlement

Before making a decision on this provision we would
appreciate clarification from New Zealand on what
provisions are intended for inclusion in the proposed Annex
on arbitration. Prima facie, we believe that the paragraph
suggested by Japan coupled with the paragraph similar to
that in para 3 of the NZ proposal and an appropriate Annex
would be acceptable.

New Zealand's comments were as follows:

Article XV: Dispute Settlement

New Zealand does not accept Japan's argumentation for
deletion of the New Zealand proposal under this Article.
Australia has asked for an explanation by New Zealand of
the content of the proposed annex on arbitration. As
indicated during the February session in Wellington, New
Zealand believes that the Annex on Arbitration in
CCAMLR is a good model for the SBT convention.

This comment did not explain, however, why New Zealand, while regarding the CCAMLR as a "good model," had replaced the optional recourse to arbitration therein by a compulsory one.

The next draft eliminates the reference in paragraph 3 to compulsory arbitration. It appeared at the Sixth Working Group on Institutional Arrangements of CCSBT and is headed "Canberra, 14 August 1992." It was agreed by the delegates and is as follows:

Article 16 Dispute Settlement

1. If any dispute arises between two or more of the Parties concerning the interpretation or implementation of this Convention, those Parties shall consult among themselves with a view to having the dispute resolved by negotiation, inquiry, mediation, consultation, arbitration, judicial settlement or other peaceful means of their choice.

2. Any dispute of this character not so resolved shall, with the consent in each case of all Parties to the dispute, be referred for settlement to the International Court of Justice or to arbitration; but failure to reach agreement on reference to the International Court or to arbitration shall not absolve Parties to the dispute from the responsibility of continuing to seek to resolve it by any of the various peaceful means referred to in paragraph 1 above.

3. In cases where the dispute is referred to arbitration, the arbitral tribunal shall be constituted as provided in the Annex to this Convention.

After further consideration by each delegation, the Parties agreed on the draft in October 1992 at the Eleventh Trilateral Management Meeting with certain minor amendments, which are underlined in the text below:

Article 16 Dispute Settlement

1. If any dispute arises between two or more of the Parties concerning the interpretation or implementation of

this Convention, those Parties shall consult among themselves with a view to having the dispute resolved by negotiation, inquiry, mediation, <u>conciliation</u>, arbitration, judicial settlement or other peaceful means of their <u>own</u> choice.

2. Any dispute of this character not so resolved shall, with the consent in each case of all Parties to the dispute, be referred for settlement to the International Court of Justice or to arbitration; but failure to reach agreement on reference to the International Court <u>of Justice</u> or to arbitration shall not absolve Parties to the dispute from the responsibility of continuing to seek to resolve it by any of the various peaceful means referred to in paragraph 1 above.

3. In cases where the dispute is referred to arbitration, the arbitral tribunal shall be constituted as provided in the Annex to this Convention. <u>The Annex forms an integral part of this Convention</u>.

This series of drafts shows beyond doubt that the possibility of compulsory dispute settlement was considered and deliberately was not adopted. No suggestion was made that recourse to the dispute settlement provisions of UNCLOS could provide an alternative and compulsory method of achieving judicial or arbitral settlement of disputes under CCSBT.

Subsequent to the establishment of the CCSBT in 1993, the Parties pursued cooperation in relation to SBT entirely within the framework of the Convention. The Commission established as a management goal the recovery of the SBT parental stocks to 1980 levels with 2020 as the target year for achieving this objective.

From the first Commission meeting held in May 1994, Japan argued, on the basis of scientific advice, that the conservation measures taken in the 1980s were producing improvements in the stock and that the TAC should be increased. Australia and New Zealand (ANZ) argued that the TAC should be held steady or even decreased. The Commission was unable to reach unanimous agreement on the TAC and national allocations for the 1998 fishing season and thereafter. This was due to the Parties' widely divergent assessments of the condition of the SBT stock and the prospect of its recovery to 1980 levels. Those divergent assessments largely reflect the different weights assigned by different scientists to alternative assumptions in what was otherwise generally a common analytical framework.

Japan's continuing and continuous commitment to the work of the Commission was revealed in a number of facts. Even before the establishment of the Commission, Japan had repeatedly proposed the development of a joint Experimental Fishing Program (EFP). In 1991, Japan agreed to the establishment of a Real Time Monitoring Programme (RTMP) with the objective of securing data on a more timely basis and collecting information regarding fish density for areas and times historically fished but in which fishing had been curtailed as a result of quotas. But the RTMP was terminated in 1995—when Australia found itself unable to continue to allocate a portion of its national quota to the RTMP.

At the First Annual Meeting of the Commission in May 1994, Japan proposed for the first time the concept of an EFP conducted within the Commission framework to gather data in those areas where fishing had taken place in the past. Japan suggested that an additional plenary meeting of the Commission be held in September 1994 to consider the proposal. ANZ did not accept the suggestion. So when the RTMP ended in 1995, the Commission was left with no source of information with respect to fish density at times and in areas from which fishing activity had receded by reason of the Parties' earlier curtailment of their activities.

In the course of late 1995 and 1996, Japan made various proposals in the Commission for an increase of TAC and a jointly-conducted EFP. These proposals were based on scientific analyses showing that an increase in TAC would not harm the SBT stock and that an EFP would facilitate the collection of data enabling the Scientific Committee to come closer to agreement with respect to stock assessment. For the seventh successive fishing season,

however, the Commission in April-May 1996 held the TAC at
11,750 mt. Japan's agreement was once again secured by
Australia's renewed threat to exclude all Japanese fishing vessels
that were catching yellowfin and bigeye tuna as well as SBT from
Australia's exclusive economic zone and its ports.

Nonetheless, at the Second Special Meeting of the Commission
in 1996,

> the parties considered the issue of experimental fishing
> programme and came to a general agreement to work
> collaboratively on timely development and evaluation [of
> an] experimental fishing programme. The parties noted that
> EFP proposals, while carrying additional short term risk,
> can be an effective tool for reducing uncertainty in stock
> assessment, resulting in more responsive management.

In a document produced at that special meeting and entitled
"Objectives and principles for the design and implementation of an
EFP," the Commission acknowledged that "increasing removals
[catch] above the current TAC should provide an opportunity for
experimental fishing programme to proceed." The document states
that before proceeding with an EFP, the Commission would need
to agree both on the way in which the EFP would be conducted
and on the way in which results coming from the programme
would be incorporated into the stock assessment and the future
management decision-making for the fishery.

The Commission received a scientific report proposing a three
step process:

> (1) agreement on the range of uncertainty to be
> considered in evaluation of EFP proposals;
> (2) an initial evaluation of the effect of changed catch
> levels on the prospect of recovery; and
> (3) evaluation of how to use the information derived
> from the EFP.

The report indicated that there was nothing to prevent Step 3 from being conducted in parallel with Steps 1 and 2. The Commission then agreed on a timetable involving the completion of Steps 1 and 2 in late May 1996 so that it could consider specific EFP proposals at its September 1996 meeting and commence a pilot EFP before the end of 1996.

Late in May 1996, however, the implementation of the agreed timetable was frustrated by Australian scientists who then used the failure to meet the timetable as an excuse to block consideration of an EFP at that time.

When the matter was next proposed to be considered at the Second Meeting of the Scientific Committee from August 26 to September 5, 1996, a Japanese request for the Committee to allocate one half-day of the Committee's eleven-day meeting to consideration of its EFP proposal was rejected after almost three days of debate on the ground of lack of time. Accordingly, Japan presented its "Joint Pilot Plan" for an EFP to the Third Annual Meeting of the Commission itself in September 1996 and, in time for the resumption of the meeting in February 1997, circulated a revised version of the proposal incorporating comments received from ANZ. Once again, however, ANZ refused to discuss Japan's proposal, even for a jointly-conducted EFP, on the ground that Steps 1 and 2 of the framework mentioned above had not been completed. The meeting ended with the TAC for the 1997 fishing season remaining unchanged once again.

The Scientific Committee at its summer 1997 meeting could not complete Steps 1 and 2. The differences between the Parties about TAC surfaced again at the Fourth Annual Meeting of the Commission, which was held in three sessions: September 1997 and January and February 1998. New Zealand proposed a reduction of 3,000 mt, Australia proposed that no change be made, and Japan urged a 3,000 mt increase. Faced by an ANZ refusal to consider its specific pilot joint EFP proposals, Japan eventually announced at the third session that it would voluntarily adhere to its previous quota for commercial fishing and also commence a three-year EFP of 2,000 mt annually beginning in June 1998. (However, because negotiations lasted deep into July, the 1998

EFP was implemented as a pilot program starting on July 10, 1998, with an anticipated catch of 1,400 mt.)

Japan continued to explain its proposals and to negotiate with ANZ through May and June and into July 1998. Despite Japan's analysis showing that the pilot EFP would have a negligible effect on the probability of stock recovery, ANZ adhered to their view that the SBT parental biomass remained "at such a low level that it cannot withstand additional catches beyond the TAC previously agreed." But ANZ did concede "that a well-designed, implemented and monitored EFP has the potential to make substantial contributions towards improving stock assessments and management."

On July 8, 1998, New Zealand delivered an Aide Memoire to the Japanese Ambassador referring to Japan's announcement of its intention to start an EFP for SBT on July 10. New Zealand observed that Japan's action would be "contrary to the consensus decision-making process" of the Tuna Treaty and "without the agreement of the other parties" to the Tuna Treaty. New Zealand stated that it would need "to consider what action would best preserve its rights as a party" to the Tuna Treaty. It asked that "Japan make a strong commitment to cooperation in the conservation and management of SBT through the consensus decision-making process of the Commission . . . ."

On July 13, 1998, a media release from the New Zealand Acting Minister of Foreign Affairs and the Minister of Fisheries, announced that New Zealand had closed its ports to all Japanese vessels fishing for SBT. The Ministers said that "Japan's action was clearly contrary to the spirit of conservation and sustainable management laid out in the [Tuna Treaty]. . . ."

Finally, agreement could not be reached. Japan conducted the pilot EFP from July 10 to August 31, 1998.

The Parties then agreed to create an EFP Working Group, comprised of representatives of the Parties as well as independent scientists, to develop a joint EFP. The Commission asked this Working Group to use its best efforts to decide upon a joint EFP for submission to the Commission as soon "as practicable, ideally by mid-April 1999." Although the independent scientists within the Working Group were to play the same role as the scientists of the Parties, it was agreed that if a consensus could not be reached, "the Parties may invite the independent scientists to play an adjudicatory role in completing the Working Group's advice to the Commission."

At the first meeting of the EFP Working Group at the beginning of February 1999, Japan was again the only Party to submit a concrete EFP proposal for consideration—and this notwithstanding the express understanding of all the Parties to present specific proposals prior to this meeting. The third meeting of the EFP Working Group was held in late March 1999. It had been foreseen as the last in the series, intended to bring the plan for an EFP to finalization.

Japan tabled an amended proposal aimed at meeting concerns raised by ANZ at the second meeting. Australia introduced its first EFP proposal, which it had not circulated in advance of the meeting and which it refused to have included in the official records of the Working Group. Even so, some progress was made towards agreement on a joint EFP for 1999. In particular, the Working Group's Sub-Group on the Design and Specification of EFP, which concentrated on merging the Japanese and Australian proposals, agreed that an EFP could be conducted in the regions known as Area 7 in June 1999 and in Area 8 in July and August 1999. This decision was endorsed by the Working Group.

In April 1999 at the fourth meeting of the EFP Working Group, Japan presented a proposal amended to take into account points raised at the third meeting. In contrast, Australia presented a new EFP proposal, inconsistent with the agreement reached at the previous month's third EFP Working Group meeting, in that it would have excluded fishing in Area 7 and required a random distribution of vessels in Area 8 that was financially impractical. Australia became increasingly insistent upon developing "fisheries-independent" indices of stock abundance—a position that was even more financially impractical, if not impossible. ANZ together refused to endorse the "decision rules" prepared by the chairperson of the Working Group and its independent members and accepted by Japan. These proposed rules stated that it was important to be "as adaptive as possible" during the initial phase of the EFP and also that agreement upon certain areas upon which ANZ were insisting, such as assessment of EFP results and effect on stock, was "not needed to initiate an EFP." Consequently, the EFP Working Group could not finalize a recommendation to the Commission. Japan, therefore, expressed its willingness to have the independent scientists play an adjudicating role, as contemplated by the agreement of the Parties at the December 1998 negotiations under Article 16(1) when the EFP Working Group was established. ANZ refused to accept this proposal.

At an informal bilateral meeting between Australia and Japan from April 30 to May 1, 1999, Australia proposed a totally new research approach that could include an EFP. This would have set aside an additional increase of TAC that each Party might use for scientific purposes. The additional increase of TAC proposed by Australia was 1,200 mt, which would include allocation to a tagging survey to be conducted by Australia. This increase fell significantly short of the levels considered necessary by Japan for a meaningful EFP to be completed during the period of three years. Also, the proposal involved several fundamental issues such as the establishment of a technical review panel and the requirement of levy of A$6/Kg of the quota for research, which required careful discussion. But there was insufficient time to negotiate all the details, and Japan urged Australia to focus on practical discussions to finalize the 1999 EFP. At an earlier stage, proposing an alternative EFP might have appeared cooperative, but to the contrary, by proposing a totally new approach and a significantly lower amount of catch, it contributed effectively to preventing an agreed EFP.

During the resumed Fifth Annual Meeting of the Commission from May 9-13, 1999, the Parties spent most of the time in discussion of the 1999 EFP. Australia proposed a 1,400 mt increase above the TAC for the EFP (including allocation to a tagging survey). However, the Parties could not reach consensus on the 1999 EFP.

A further final but unsuccessful effort by a high-level Japanese delegation sent to Australia and New Zealand took place at the end of May 1999. At the time, Australia increased its proposal for an additional increase above the TAC to 1,500 mt. In this connection, New Zealand produced a "Summary of Key Issues relating to an Experimental Fishing Programme, 28 May 1999," which demonstrated with striking cogency the limitation of the dispute to matters related to the implementation of the CCSBT:

> This paper outlines New Zealand's view of the progress that has been made as a result of the extensive discussions between the parties since the Article 16 dispute negotiations in December 1998 that established the EFP working group process. It also summarises those areas where New Zealand has compromised on the negotiating position we took to these discussions, and the areas where further work is needed in order to embark on an EFP based on a consensus decision of the parties.

> 1. Areas of Agreement

>> i) The parties have agreed that the EFP should be a three year programme with the objective of generating information that will provide a basis for the Commission to make management decisions at the conclusion of the programme.

>> ii) The parties have agreed on some principles for the development and implementation of decision rules based on the draft developed by the Chair and external scientists involved in the EFP working group process.

iii) The principle of using independent scientists to assist in resolving assessment questions and to develop comprehensive decision rules has been settled, but further work is necessary to define a process and terms of reference.

iv) The programme will include both catch rate and tagging elements, with the tagging initially undertaken on a feasibility basis.

2. Areas where New Zealand has compromised

i) New Zealand has compromised from our position that it was critical that comprehensive decision rules be in place prior to implementation of an EFP. We regarded this as very important to ensure that an EFP is implemented in a manner consistent with the agreed design and that the risk to the stock could be mitigated if the EFP failed to meet its objectives.

ii) We have conceded that agreed analysis methods can be developed concurrently with the implementation of a three year programme. This remains a critical issue in order to ensure that the EFP results can be used to improve management decisions.

iii) We have sought to negotiate improvements to Japan's proposed design for the EFP component of a programme rather than develop a design collaboratively that would maximise reduction in uncertainty and minimise removals from the stock.

3. Key issues to resolve

Despite New Zealand's best attempts through the four meetings of the EFP working group process since December, and the discussion held during CCSBT5(2), differences remained in a number of key areas following the adjournment of CCSBT5(2). These include:

i) An acceptable annual catch level for the EFP needs to be resolved, along with mechanisms to constrain the catch to the agreed amount.

ii) The parties need to determine a mechanism to allocate the catch and agree on the manner in which that will influence future allocation decisions.

iii) Improvements to the deployment of vessels fishing during 1999 are necessary to address problems evident in data from Japan's 1998 unilateral EFP.

iv) The areas and times to be surveyed over the three years of the programme need to be agreed in principle.

v) Japan has agreed to feasibility level tagging on their EFP vessels, but the parties have still to determine how to resource and undertake tagging from pole vessels in the Australian zone.

vi) Arrangements for the provision of
monitoring information need to be
concluded.

vii) A process to develop agreed analysis
methods is necessary to ensure EFP results
can be used to improve management
decisions.

viii) The sharing of data between the parties
needs to be resolved to allow for reasonable
access to data that would allow for
independent analysis.

ix) The parties need to decide on the related
issue of the TAC that will apply over the
course of the EFP.

It may be noted that this document did not identify a single key
issue requiring resolution in which it would be necessary or
possible to have recourse to UNCLOS.

On June 1, 1999, Japan commenced its three-year EFP. It
informed Australia on the same day, stating that Japan had made
extraordinary efforts to reach an agreement in the negotiations and
that it had accepted as much as possible requests from ANZ,
including a tagging survey. On June 4, 1999, Japan conveyed the
same information to New Zealand, stating that it had made its best
efforts to accommodate the position of New Zealand "on such
issues as improvements of the deployment of vessels and observer
coverage, tagging survey and a part of random sampling survey."
Japan also stated that it was "ready to adjust its EFP when a
consensus is reached among the parties." To this end, it urged the
continuation of the dialogue between the Parties.

On June 23, 1999, Japan proposed mediation under CCSBT to
Australia and by an identical note on June 24, 1999, made the

same proposal to New Zealand. In these notes, Japan proposed that the Indian Ocean Tuna Commission (IOTC), the UN Food and Agriculture Organization, the European Union and the United States could appropriately serve as mediators. Japan had, in fact, already raised the matter with each of them and had secured their general agreement to play a role as a mediator. By identical notes dated June 30, 1999, Australia and New Zealand replied that such mediation could only take place if Japan were to agree to cease its unilateral EFP by July 5 and if the mediation were to be completed by August 31, 1999. A Japanese offer in July to arbitrate in accordance with CCSBT encountered a similar response.

Notes

[1] The most concise source for the factual statements in the text is Annexes 1-4 of the Response of the Government of Japan to Request for Provisional Measures & Counter-Request For Provisional Measures (Japan's Response). They are: 1) "Southern Bluefin Tuna: Panel Statement on Experimental Fishing Program," by J. J. Maguire, Patrick Sullivan, Robert Mohn, and Syoiti Tanaka (August 4, 1999); 2) Statement of Douglas S. Butterworth, Ph.D (August 5, 1999); 3) Declaration of Dr. Sachiko Tsuji (August 5, 1999); and 4) Declaration of Masayuki Komatsu. These quote from and rely upon many documents relating to the Parties' previous efforts at cooperation respecting Southern Bluefin Tuna. Many of those documents appear in other Annexes to Japan's Response.

[2] In M. H. Nordquist and J. N. Moore, eds., *Current Fisheries Issues and the Food and Agriculture Organization of the United Nations* (hereinafter *Current Fisheries Issues*) (Netherlands: Kluwer Law International, 2000), Serge M. Garcia comments on page 523 in "The Precautionary Approach to Fisheries, Progress Review and Main Issues: 1995-2000," paper presented on March 16-17, 2000, at the conference co-hosted by the Center for Oceans Law and Policy, University of Virginia School of Law, and FAO, and presented to various fisheries organizations in draft at the ICES/NAFO/ICCAT/FAO CWP Working Group on precautionary approach terminology, Copenhagen, Denmark, February 14-16, 2000: "[I]t is well known that decimating juveniles before they could grow and reproduce is biological nonsense, jeopardizing stock growth and reproduction, and reducing resilience."

[3] The quote is from the Report of the Second Special Meeting of the Commission for the Conservation of the Southern Bluefin Tuna, April 29–May 3, 1996, Annex 20 to Japan's Response to the requests for provisional measures.

[4] The record does not indicate whether or when the papers filed on July 15 were distributed to the judges.

[5] Among other things, Japan argued that the dispute resolution provisions of the Tuna Treaty "excluded any further procedure," such as UNCLOS arbitration, so that the UNCLOS dispute resolution procedures are inapplicable, as expressly provided in UNCLOS, article 281, paragraph 1.

[6] Japan submitted a compilation of treaties to the arbitrators that included sixty-six such treaties, and extensive diplomatic correspondence about the negotiation of the Tuna Treaty, not all of which was available to ITLOS.

[7] There is, of course, no inconsistency between a finding that the very low threshold of *prima facie* jurisdiction in a provisional measures proceeding is satisfied and a subsequent decision that jurisdiction is lacking. The point in the text is, however, that given the broad range of disputes that may come before the

Tribunal, some stated reasons for its finding of *prima facie* jurisdiction would have been desirable.

[8] Australia's July 15 Request was four pages long. Its July 30 Request was nine pages long.

[9] At Japan's request, the response time was extended on August 4 to Monday August 9. Japan submitted documents in both English and French; parties are encouraged to submit documents to the Tribunal in both. See Gudmundur Eiriksson, "The Working Methods of the International Tribunal for the Law of the Sea," in M. H. Nordquist and J. N. Moore, eds., *Oceans Policy, New Institutions, Challenges and Opportunities* (Netherlands: Kluwer Law International, 1999), 123.

[10] At the close of the oral hearing on August 20, the President announced that the Tribunal had tentatively scheduled a decision on August 27. By adhering to its tentative decision date, the Tribunal allowed itself only a week following the rebuttal presentations.

[11] Annex 1 to Japan's Response.

[12] August 18, morning transcript, 28.

[13] Judge Laing's separate opinion notes at paragraph 18 that the Order includes the "concept of payback for catch taken over quota in 1999," without, however, dealing with the fact that there was no quota established for 1999 under the Tuna Convention or explaining how a quota had been established under UNCLOS. Judge Wolfrum subsequently did elaborate on jurisdictional and urgency issues, but without discussing Pay Back or other aspects of Japan's defense. "The Role of the International Tribunal for the Law of the Sea," *Current Fisheries Issues, supra* note 2, 369-385.

[14] The issue arises generally under UNCLOS, article 290, section 1, ("appropriate under the circumstances to preserve the respective rights of the parties or to prevent serious harm to the marine environment") and more specifically, pending the constitution of an arbitral tribunal, under section 5 ("the urgency of the situation so requires").

[15] Japan's Response, 16-19; August 19, morning transcript, 24.

[16] August 18, morning transcript, 28.

[17] August 18, afternoon transcript, 24, 27.

[18] This was addressed in Separate Opinions but not in a dispositive manner.

[19] One difference was that ANZ had requested an outright prohibition of the EFP, apparently on the basis that they had a right to prevent Japan from acting without their approval. The Tribunal allowed the EFP to continue provided it reduced Japan's commercial catch.

[20] This issue was discussed in the Separate Opinion of Judge *ad hoc* Shearer.

[21] "Matters for further elaboration by the Parties—Answers submitted by Australia and New Zealand" (20 August 1999), Answer to Question 2.

[22] S. M. Garcia, *supra* note 2, 479-481.

[23] *Id.*, 507.

---

[24] *Id.*, 508.

[25] *Id.*, 487, 509-510, 541, Figure 2. Garcia also calls (page 510) for a threshold reference point within the buffer zone, to warn that the catch is approaching a designated limit such as MSY and some corrective action is advisable.

[26] *Id.*, 508.

[27] Judge Laing's separate opinion states that UNCLOS adopts a precautionary approach and that the Order does so also.

[28] The Precautionary Principle has been the subject of much recent consideration within the European Union. On December 14, 2000, the European Parliament broadly endorsed ideas from the European Commission on how to apply the Precautionary Principle in product safety, environmental, and public health policies. The Commission would invoke the Principle when there "are reasonable grounds for concern of the possible occurrence of effects which are potentially dangerous" and "incompatible with the level of protection chosen." BNA Product Safety Reporter (January 1, 2001), 16 (emphasis added). Some chosen level of protection is necessary, and cannot be derived from the Principle itself; the same is true for biological reference points.

[29] See, for example, Lon Fuller, "Adjudication and the Rule of Law," Proceedings of the American Society of International Law, April 28-30 (published by the Society, 1960), 3. ("[A]djudication is a process of decision badly suited to the solution of polycentric problems.")

[30] Order, para. 71.

[31] August 18, morning transcript, 29 ("historically low levels"). Paragraph 11 of Australia's Request for Provisional Measures also refers to "historically low levels."

[32] See Annex 4 to Australia's Request for Provisional Measures, "A Scientific Overview of the Status of the Southern Bluefin Tuna Stock" by T. Polacheck and A. Preece, at Annex One thereto, quoting "historically low levels" from the Scientific Committee Reports of 1990, 1991, and 1998.

[33] Paragraph 79, however, recognized that there was no agreement among the Parties whether the stock had improved.

[34] Jean-Jacques Maguire, "Southern Bluefin Tuna Dispute," in *Current Fisheries Issues, supra* note 2, 218. ("If the stock has already started to recover, then it might be possible to increase the TAC with associated increased benefits for society at large.")

[35] After observing that the Tribunal applied a precautionary approach, Maguire, *supra* note 34, 216-217, states: "The fishing industry may see in the Tribunal's decision the materialization of their worst fears with the implementation of the precautionary approach: if precaution is applied at every stage [*e.g.*, scientific and management] of the process, the overall system will become unduly precautionary, and it will soon become impossible to do any fishing."

[36] See, for example, T. C. Hartley, *The Foundations of European Community Law*, 4th ed. (Oxford University Press, 1998), 56 ("The advocate general's opinion is usually much easier to read than the [European] Court's judgment. The latter, being the work of a committee, is often lacking in logical rigor; its terse and formal style is unattractive, at least to those brought up in the common law tradition—while the need to achieve consensus may produce obscurities and inconsistencies."); C. Baudenbacher, "Between Homogeneity and Independence: The Legal Position of the EFTA Court in the European Economic Area," 3 *Colum. J. Eur. L.* 169 (1997): 210-211. ("As is known, the European Court of Justice cultivates a peculiar judicial style. . . . Even more important than these rather more formal reservations is the criticism that has been primarily (but not exclusively) voiced by German authors, to the effect that the rulings given by the ECJ often lack sufficient reasons.")

[37] Hartley, *supra* note 36, 75. ("The second expedient . . . instead of putting something in to please both groups, the Court deletes anything which might displease either. The result is that no reasons of substance are given at all.")

[38] As Professor Fuller observed in his paper on the rule of law, *supra* note 29, 2, the fundamental characteristic of adjudication is "the institutionally protected opportunity [for a litigant] to present proofs and arguments for a decision in his favor."

[39] *Ibid.*

[40] "In its second prompt-release case, the Tribunal once again demonstrated its capacity for swift action. In these cases, the Tribunal is, quite rightly, functioning primarily as an efficient and effective adjudicator of petitions to be set free in the most literal sense, and properly continues to resist the invitation to give primacy to formulating finely framed dictum explicated *in extenso*." Bernard H. Oxman & Vincent P. Bantz, "The 'Camouco,'" 94 *AJIL* 713 (2000): 719; ITLOS Press Release of 17 July 2000, "OFFICIAL OPENING OF THE HEADQUARTERS BUILDING OF THE TRIBUNAL, United Nations SECRETARY-GENERAL praises Tribunal as 'MODERN COURT THAT CAN RESPOND QUICKLY'" ("Mr. Annan . . . was 'delighted to note that in its first four years the Tribunal has already built a reputation among international lawyers as a modern court that can respond quickly.'").

[41] August 18, morning transcript, 38; afternoon transcript, 9. In a bold and apparently effective move to avoid the implications of Professor Beddington's testimony, Counsel for ANZ accepted that his recommendation was to "reduce the TAC " but said, "we did not put him forward in support of an argument for that proposition." *Id.*, 11. The Separate Opinion of Judge *ad hoc* Shearer argued forcefully that the Tribunal could not order a reduction of the catch. The Separate Opinion of Judges Wolfrum, Caminos, Rangel, Yankov, Anderson, and Eiriksson suggests they may have been willing to order a reduction in the catch, but they were well short of a majority.

[42] As one of the Tuna Commission's invited external experts has observed, "The
southern bluefin tuna situation is quite clear: either existing management
measures have been sufficient and stock recovery has begun, or they have not.
Given that the data are not sufficient to convincingly answer this question, there
is urgent need for collecting additional information, in order to resolve this
issue. Otherwise, the consequences could be catastrophic." Maguire, *supra* note
34, 218.

[43] The source of the statements in the Appendix is paragraphs 17-19, 29-35, 37-
59, 62-63, 78-84, 86, 90, and 93 of Japan's Memorial on Jurisdiction that was
submitted in 2000 to the arbitral tribunal. The Memorial and other arbitration
papers are available at: <www.worldbank.org/icsid>.

PANEL IV

Roundtable on Issues of Interest for International Tribunals

MAIN FEATURES OF COURTS AND TRIBUNALS DEALING WITH LAW OF THE SEA CASES

*Budislav Vukas**

The purpose of this brief paper is to point out some of the main characteristics and problems arising out of the use of compulsory procedures entailing binding decisions in the settlement of disputes system established under the Law of the Sea Convention.

The system is based on four different fora for the peaceful settlement of disputes listed in article 287: two types of arbitral tribunals, the International Court of Justice, and the International Tribunal for the Law of the Sea. The principle that every dispute concerning the interpretation or application of the Convention can eventually be submitted at the request of any party to the dispute to a compulsory procedure entailing binding decisions has often been pointed out as one of the main contributions of the Third United Nations Conference to the development of the law of the sea.[1] In the Convention, this principle has been implemented by many specific rules. It has, however, also been considerably restricted in its application.

The first characteristic of the system is the right of States Parties to the Convention to choose one or more of the courts and tribunals listed in article 287. To date, twenty-four States have made a declaration concerning their choice. Fifteen States have indicated the Tribunal as the only, their preferred, or one of the preferred means for the settlement of disputes. An equal number of States have expressed such preference for the ICJ. Two States have expressly rejected the ICJ as a means for the resolution of disputes under the Convention.[2]

The small number of States having made a declaration expressing their choice renders even more important the rule according to which a State Party to the Convention, which is a party to a dispute not covered by a declaration in force, shall be

---

* Judge, International Tribunal for the Law of the Sea.

M.H. Nordquist and J.N. Moore (eds.),
Current Marine Environmental Issues and the International Tribunal for the Law of the Sea, 217–222.

deemed to have accepted arbitration.[3] In addition to this rule, there is the provision that arbitration shall be applied to disputes where the parties have not accepted the same procedure.[4] The importance of this provision does not depend upon the number of declarations but rather on the variety of means chosen. Thus, in a dispute involving two States that have opted for permanent courts—one for the ICJ and the other for ITLOS—the regulations concerning arbitration in accordance with Annex VII will apply! This solution does not seem very logical.

Be that as it may, we must recall that under article 282 of the Convention, any disputes settlement mechanism that is binding on the disputing parties is favored over the courts and tribunals listed in article 287. According to article 282, if the States Parties to the Convention that are parties to a dispute concerning the interpretation or application of the Convention have agreed that such dispute shall, at the request of any party to the dispute, be submitted to a procedure that entails a binding decision, that procedure shall apply in lieu of the procedures provided in article 287. It is interesting to note that Judge Treves includes in those procedures, agreed outside the Convention's system, even the ICJ itself, in case all parties to a dispute have accepted the Court's compulsory jurisdiction under article 36, paragraph 2, of the Court's Statute.[5] Although the conclusion seems plausible, it should be stressed that article 282 would seem to give priority to procedures that fall outside of Part XV of the Convention, while in respect of the disputes concerning the interpretation or application of the Law of the Sea Convention, the ICJ is one of the procedures on which the system of article 287 is based.

If the variety of the fora for the settlement of disputes offered to States should have the effect of increasing the number of cases brought before the courts and tribunals, the restrictions of their jurisdiction *ratione materiae* have the opposite effect. The Convention contains a poorly drafted article on limitations on applicability of compulsory procedures entailing binding decisions[6] and an impressive list of optional exceptions to applicability of such procedures.[7] Fortunately, only twelve States have to date made declarations concerning non-acceptance of the procedures entailing binding decisions with respect to one or more of the categories of disputes listed in article 298.[8]

It is also interesting to note that eight States have made reservations excluding various disputes concerning law of the sea issues from their acceptance of the jurisdiction of the International Court of Justice further to article 36, paragraph 2, of its Statute.[9]

Notwithstanding the general equality of the courts and tribunals listed in article 287, the differences of their jurisdiction *ratione personae* and *ratione materiae* inevitably affect their present and future activities. A great advantage of the ICJ and arbitration outside the Convention's framework is the fact that their jurisdiction is not limited to the law of the sea. Therefore, for example, they can deal with a dispute concerning land and maritime delimitation, while under article 287, jurisdiction could only be established in respect of maritime delimitation. The arbitral tribunals established in accordance with Annex VIII would have the most limited jurisdiction of all the means set out in article 287.

On the other hand, only the ITLOS Seabed Disputes Chamber has jurisdiction in respect of disputes and requests for advisory opinions concerning activities in the Area.[10] As those activities at present are almost nonexistent, this jurisdiction is not likely to generate cases or requests for advisory opinions in the near future.

However, the provisions on the jurisdiction of the Seabed Disputes Chamber disclose more clearly than any other part of the Convention the broad jurisdiction of ITLOS *ratione personae*. The Chamber is open to States Parties, the International Seabed Authority, its Enterprise, state enterprises, and natural or juridical persons.[11] Furthermore, the Tribunal itself has to be open to all those entitled to become parties to the Convention: States, self-governing associated States, non-fully independent territories, and international organizations.[12]

In addition to the exclusive jurisdiction of ITLOS in respect of the activities in the Area, the Tribunal has some priority in respect of two specific issues: the prompt release of vessels and crews, and the prescription of provisional measures.[13] This priority established under the provisions of the Convention has resulted in several cases dealt with by the Tribunal in the first four years of its work.[14]

Finally, an important advantage of the ICJ in comparison with all other courts and tribunals should be mentioned. Article 94, paragraph 2, of the United Nations Charter reads:

> If any party to a case fails to perform the obligations incumbent upon it under a judgment rendered by the Court, the other party may have recourse to the Security Council, which may, if it deems necessary, make recommendations or decide upon measures to be taken to give effect to the judgment.

States Parties to the Law of the Sea Convention should find a solution that would contribute to the enforcement of the judgments rendered by the tribunals established under the Convention. A solution permitting a party to address the Meeting of States Parties and/or the General Assembly of the United Nations, if the other party fails to perform the obligations incumbent upon it under a judgment rendered by ITLOS or an arbitral tribunal should be found.

A conclusion at the end of these brief remarks would be out of place. Let me only add a final note.

The development of the law of the sea in the last thirty-five years is but another proof of the chaotic development of international law and international institutions. The revision of this part of international law was commenced because of the impression created by the developed countries that the exploitation of mineral resources of the ocean floor was imminent. Due to this conviction, half of the text of the Law of the Sea Convention deals with this presently nonexisting activity.

The adoption of the disputes settlement system was also partly due to the perceived necessity of resolving disputes concerning the exploration and exploitation of the Area. The structure and the system of dispute settlement under the Convention as well as the attribution of competences to the ICJ and the tribunals were also tailored to the new vision of what was viewed as the "most important" activities at sea.

The reality of today is quite different from what was expected in the euphoria of the 1960s and 1970s. The courts and tribunals, not only those mentioned in article 287, are left with the traditional disputes concerning law of the sea and maritime issues. Nevertheless, there will be more and more problems and disputes concerning the conservation and exploitation of the living resources of the sea and the protection of the environment. Yet, it seems to me that the existing dispute settlement system is able to cope with all the developments in the foreseeable future.

Notes

[1] See article 286 of the Convention in: *The Law of the Sea, Official Text of the United Nations Convention on the Law of the Sea with Annexes and Index* (New York: United Nations, 1983).

[2] *Oceans and Law of the Sea*, Division for Ocean Affairs and the Law of the Sea, Settlement of Disputes Mechanism, <http://www:un.org/Depts/los/los_sdm1.htm>.

[3] Article 287, para. 3.

[4] Article 287, para. 5.

[5] T. Treves, "Conflicts between the International Tribunal for the Law of the Sea and the International Court of Justice," 31 *New York University Journal of International Law and Politics* (1999): 812.

[6] Article 297.

[7] Article 298.

[8] Declarations made upon ratification of, accession to, or succession with respect to the Convention: < http://www.un.org/Depts/los/los_decl.htm>.

[9] Declarations recognizing as compulsory the jurisdiction of the International Court of Justice: <http://www.icj-cij.org/icjww/ibasicdocuments/ibasictext/ibasicdeclarations.htm>.

[10] See articles 187 and 191.

[11] See article 187.

[12] See article 305.

[13] See articles 292 and 290.

[14] *M/V Saiga* (Prompt Release) (1997); *M/V Saiga* (Provisional Measures) (1998); *Southern Bluefin Tuna* Cases (1999); *Camouco* (2000); and *Monte Confurco* (2000).

CURRENT FISHERIES DISPUTES AND THE INTERNATIONAL TRIBUNAL FOR THE LAW OF THE SEA

*Alexander Yankov**

INTRODUCTION

The international maritime disputes have acquired a prominent part in international adjudication in the course of the last three decades. This trend has been evidenced by the noticeable increase of maritime cases in relation to the aggregate number of other cases before international judicial institutions.

A differentiated comparison between the two categories of disputes would reveal the evolving progression of maritime cases.

Thus, the Permanent Court of International Justice in its judicial activities of eighteen years, between 1922 and 1940, has handled thirty-six cases of a contentious nature and twenty-eight requests for advisory opinions. Out of the sixty-four cases, only five, or less than eight percent, pertained to law of the sea matters.

During the first two decades (1947-1967), the International Court of Justice (ICJ) had before it, out of fifty-nine cases, only three law of the sea cases, or about five percent, of the total number of cases. But in the next two decades (1968-1988), a dramatic change took place. Disputes relating to delimitation of marine boundaries, coastal State jurisdiction on its continental shelf, establishment of special fisheries zones or exclusive economic zones, to mention only the main contentious issues, made almost half of the cases before the ICJ. At present, the situation is not the same. But there still have been a number of pending cases of a law of the sea nature on the current list of cases of the ICJ. In addition, the last Report of the Secretary-General of the United Nations on ocean affairs and the law of the sea pointed out that there are about 150 national claims on maritime matters

---

* Judge, International Tribunal for the Law of the Sea.

M.H. Nordquist and J.N. Moore (eds.),
Current Marine Environmental Issues and the International Tribunal for the Law of the Sea, 223–238.
© 2001 *Kluwer Law International. Printed in the Netherlands.*

and a significant number of potential international disputes on marine boundary delimitation.

In general, fisheries disputes have been among the topical law of the sea matters before international judicial institutions. There has been a certain tendency of shifting from matters of jurisdiction over special fisheries zones or sovereign rights of fisheries in the exclusive economic zones towards disputes concerning compliance with and enforcement of fisheries rules and regulations in conservation and management.

Taking into account these new developments, it is helpful to briefly examine the practice of the International Tribunal for the Law of the Sea (ITLOS) relating directly or indirectly to fisheries. It is also helpful, in this connection, to consider some recent legislative, administrative, and technical measures for establishing an international regime of responsible fisheries. This topical issue in current and, most probably, future fishing activities, has been a response to the increasing concern about the over-exploitation and depletion of important fish stocks constituting serious damage to the ecosystems in marine areas under national jurisdiction and in the high seas.

PROBLEMS OF CONSERVATION AND MANAGEMENT OF MARINE LIVING RESOURCES IN THE RECENT PRACTICE OF ITLOS

The examination of the main characteristics of the current fisheries disputes in the judicial practice of ITLOS, though limited in their quantity and scope, is quite symptomatic for the emerging new approach to the treatment of fisheries claims. The fisheries disputes before the ICJ, from 1949 up to 1974, were centered mainly on claims regarding the exploitation of fisheries resources and establishing special fisheries zones.[1] However, in recent time an evolving trend has been observed, attributing greater significance to conservation and management of living resources, including compliance and enforcement measures against illegal, unreported, and unregulated fishing activities. This new approach is in line with the policy of responsible fisheries.

All cases dealt with by ITLOS so far, with the exception of the Southern Bluefin Tuna cases of 1999,[2] were related to prompt release of fishing vessels and their crews under article 292 of UNCLOS. In these cases, issues relating to fisheries were raised in passing, particularly in respect to allegations concerning violation of rules and regulations, as legal grounds for the detention of foreign fishing vessels.

The proceedings of the Southern Bluefin Tuna cases were instituted by New Zealand and Australia against Japan with a Request for prescription of provisional measures under article 290, paragraph 5, of UNCLOS.[3] Paragraph 1 of this article stipulates that:

> . . . the court or the tribunal may prescribe any provisional measures which it considers appropriate under the circumstances to preserve the respective rights of the parties to the dispute or to prevent serious harm to the marine environment, pending the final decision.

This provision is very indicative for the specific legal features of the jurisdiction of the court or tribunal to prescribe provisional measures within the framework of incidental proceedings. First of all, it defines the authority of the respective judicial institution to prescribe the provisional measures that *"it considers appropriate under the circumstances"* (emphasis supplied) of the case. Secondly, the competent judicial institutions are competent to consider any matters of substance directly related to the prescription of provisional measures, which have preventive function.

The scope of the competence of the court or tribunal, though concentrated on the prescription of prompt provisional measures, is wide-open. It implies examination and assessment of relevant facts, evaluation of the possible consequences of the conduct of the parties, the protection of their interests pending the final decision of the case, prevention of serious harm to the marine environment, and other related issues concerning the merits of the case.

An essential objective of the provisional measures in fisheries disputes, is the conservation and management of the contested living resources as an important part of the incidental proceedings. In this connection the court or tribunal, in the exercise of its jurisdiction, may also proceed to the interpretation or application of UNCLOS and other relevant international legal instruments.

Thus, the judicial functions of the court or tribunal may go beyond the scope of some other kinds of incidental proceedings, such as preliminary objections or prompt release of vessels and crews. The prescription of prompt provisional measures, therefore, is a particular kind of incidental proceeding that is confined not only to procedural matters but also have certain bearing on the merits of the case.

Of course, the procedural requirements of incidental proceedings for prescription of provisional measures under article 290 of UNCLOS and articles 89 to 95 of the Rules, take up a significant part of the Tribunal's Order. Special attention is attributed to questions of jurisdiction of UNCLOS, admissibility of the applications, the authority of UNCLOS under article 290, paragraph 5, to satisfy itself that *prima facie* the arbitral tribunal, which is to be constituted, would have jurisdiction, the urgency of the case, and time-limits prescribed by the relevant procedural rules.

For the purposes of the present study, the emphasis is placed on the specific character of the incidental proceedings for prescription of provisional measures in the Southern Bluefin Tuna cases, which encompass procedural and related substantive matters. These peculiar features of the provisional measures are reflected in the Statements of Claim by New Zealand and Australia, and Statement in Response by Japan, in the written proceedings, as well as their final submissions at the oral proceedings.[4] However, for the jurisprudence of ITLOS, in its first case on fisheries, though confined to provisional measures, it might be appropriate to examine some issues on the merits referred to in the dispositive of the Order.

When prescribing provisional measures, the topical issues having a bearing on matters of substance, which ITLOS has pointed out, have been concentrated on the problem of conservation and management or optimum utilization of Southern Bluefin Tuna (SBT) stock. The main reason for this approach was the concern about the harmful effect on these highly migratory species as a result of over-exploitation. The scientific evidence provided by the parties in the written and oral proceedings, including the testimony and cross-examination of the experts, proved the state of deterioration of the marine ecosystem in the disputed area. Consequently, the Tribunal stated in paragraph 71 of the Order that:

> . . . there is no disagreement between the parties that the stock of southern bluefin tuna is severely depleted and is at its historically lowest levels and that this is a cause for serious biological concern.

This assertion was further substantiated by the Joint Declaration of several Judges, emphasizing that:

> Cooperation among the members of the Commission for the Conservation of Southern Bluefin Tuna, at both the scientific and governmental levels, has not been effective in recent years; and during this same period catches by non-members of the Commission and new entrants to the fishery have risen significantly.
> In the circumstances, a reduction in the catches of all those concerned in the fishery in the immediate short term would assist the stock to recover over the medium to long term.[5]

The reference to conservation and management is expressed in several aspects in the Order. First of all, it is identified as a general duty of the coastal State and other States, under article 64, paragraph 1, of UNCLOS, to "cooperate directly or through appropriate international organizations with a view to ensuring conservation and promoting the objective of optimum utilization" of highly migratory species both within and beyond the exclusive economic zone. The Tribunal further specifies in paragraph 48 of the Order, exercising its authority of interpretation of UNCLOS, that:

> . . . under article 64, read together with articles 116 to 119, of the Convention, States Parties to the Convention have the duty to cooperate directly or through appropriate international organizations with a view to ensuring conservation and promoting the objective of optimum utilization of highly migratory species.

This interpretation reiterates the application of the general rule of article 64 beyond the exclusive economic zones in the high seas. Article 118, on the cooperation of States, employs the expression "conservation and management of living resources in the areas of the high seas," instead of the term "optimum utilization." It is a more comprehensive and adequate statement for present fishing activities in the high seas. It covers all living resources in the high seas and, by the term "management," corresponds better to the scope of modern fisheries. The term "management," or "sustainable utilisation," of marine living resources seems preferable since it carries with it the meaning of integration between exploitation and protection and preservation of marine living resources.

Furthermore, by the *dictum* expressed in paragraph 70 of the Order that "the conservation of the living resources of the seas is an element in the protection and preservation of the marine environment," the Tribunal has made a contribution to the jurisprudence in the law of the sea, in general, and the international environmental law, in particular. This authoritative statement of ITLOS has brought the concept of conservation and management in conformity with the modern integrated approach of sustainable utilization of the marine living resources and the protection and preservation of the marine environment. The living resources are considered an essential organic component of the marine environment. This concept is in line with the modern notion of marine environment, comprising also the marine living resources and providing the grounds for a comprehensive and updated interpretation of article 1, paragraph 1(4), of UNCLOS.

The Southern Bluefin Tuna cases have offered ITLOS an opportunity to tackle some aspects of the relatively novel concept of precautionary principle or precautionary approach.[6] The precautionary principle is intrinsically connected with the obligations of conservation and sustainable management.[7] This principle so far has been applied in the field of environmental law and policy, primarily in fisheries.[8] It has been subject to a significant number of studies and state practice, including a relatively limited jurisprudence.[9]

The reference to the substance of the precautionary principle was among the key issues of the Southern Bluefin Tuna cases within the proceedings of provisional measures. The Tribunal had to consider the implications of this principle, since the Applicants had referred to it in their Statements of Claim and final submissions. They substantiated their request for provisional measures, among other reasons, also on the grounds that the Respondent had breached its obligations under articles 64 and 116 to 119 of UNCLOS by "otherwise failing in its obligations under UNCLOS in respect of the conservation and management of SBT, having regard to the requirements of *the precautionary principle*" (emphasis supplied).[10] In their joint final submissions, New Zealand and Australia requested "that the parties act consistently with *the precautionary principle* in fishing for SBT pending a final settlement of the dispute" (emphasis supplied).[11]

On the other hand, Japan contended that there was "no urgency for the prescription of provisional measures in the circumstances of this case" and that the scientific evidence available showed that the implementation of its experimental fishing program would cause no further threat to the SBT stock.[12]

The Tribunal took note of the statements and submissions of the parties on the applicability of the precautionary principle or some of its relevant constitutive elements. In this connection, the views of the Tribunal on the urgency of the provisional measures, potential risk for serious harm to or deterioration of the marine environment, and assessment of the scientific evidence for further deleterious effect on the SBT stock, have a bearing on the content and scope of the precautionary principle.[13] None of these statements, however, refer explicitly to that principle. Nevertheless, there are some statements of the Tribunal in the Order that appear to reveal its stand in favor of essential elements of the precautionary approach.

In this connection, paragraph 80 of the Order deserves special attention as a kind of a synthesis of precautionary measures or precautionary approach. After an examination and assessment of the views of the parties in respect to the urgency of the measures to be prescribed, the scientific uncertainty of their possible effect and the conduct of the parties, the Tribunal states that:

> . . . although the Tribunal cannot conclusively assess the scientific evidence presented by the parties, it finds that the measures should be taken as a matter of urgency to preserve the rights of the parties and to avert further deterioration of the southern bluefin tuna stock.[14]

This assertion about the urgency of the appropriate conservatory measures to prevent the risk of further deterioration of the SBT stock, on the one hand, and the differing views of the parties and lack of conclusive scientific evidence, on the other hand, led the Tribunal to adopt a "flexible" precautionary approach. This is evident by the use of the "soft" term "should," instead of "shall," concerning the provisional measures to be taken, as pointed out in paragraph 80.

The overall assessment of the provisional measures prescribed by the Tribunal need to be considered in conjunction with some other parts of the Order and relevant provisions of UNCLOS, applicable in this case. It is appropriate to refer to paragraph 77, which states that:

> . . . in the view of the Tribunal, the parties should in the circumstances act with prudence and caution to ensure that effective conservation measures are taken to prevent serious harm to the stock of southern bluefin tuna.

The notion of "serious harm," or "irreparable damage," have acquired recognition in treaty law, other international instruments, national legislation, and jurisprudence, as an important element and threshold in conservation measures, based on the precautionary approach. The establishment precisely of this threshold, on the basis of reliable data and expertise, makes the identification and application of the precautionary principle very difficult.

The case under consideration is within the incidental proceedings for provisional measures "to preserve the respective rights of the parties to the dispute or to prevent serious harm to the marine environment, *pending the final* decision" (emphasis supplied), as stipulated by article 290, paragraph 1, of UNCLOS. There is no legal obstacle for ITLOS to take a decision on matters relating to the application of the precautionary principle. However, it should be pointed out that normally such a decision would require more time for thorough examination of the merits of the case, including appropriate scientific and technical expertise. The application of the precautionary principle is dependent upon lengthy and comprehensive environmental impact assessment. But the core of the proceedings still remains the urgency and need of prompt provisional measures.

The proceedings under article 290, paragraph 5, contemplate that the arbitral tribunal to be constituted, is competent to modify, revoke, or affirm the provisional measures, and may handle the case, including the implementation of the precautionary principle, when necessary. Therefore, the recourse to the precautionary principle in some circumstances might be more apt to be handled in proceedings on the merits of the case. The prescription of provisional measures must always keep its priority over all other proceedings in accordance with article 90, paragraph 1, of the Rules of ITLOS. Perhaps in the future, with accumulation of state practice and jurisprudence, at the national and international level, ITLOS and the parties to a dispute will be in a better position to respond to the challenges of the complex legal issues, like the relatively novel precautionary principle.

The problem of the precautionary approach was considered during the deliberations of the Tribunal. Some of the judges who constituted the majority expressed their particular views in separate opinions or in the Joint Declaration.[15] Despite critical observations about the reluctance of the Tribunal to take firmer position and prescribe legally binding provisional measures invoking the precautionary principle, in general, the handling of the case was considered to be reasonable, taking into account the incidental character of the proceedings, the perplexity of the subject matter, and insufficient jurisprudence. The attempt of ITLOS to consider some topical aspects of the precautionary principle has been acknowledged, in some reviews, as a step in the development of its jurisprudence in new areas of international environmental law relating to marine affairs.[16]

Another subject of legal interest with jurisprudential significance has been the consideration by ITLOS of the relationship between the 1993 Convention for the Conservation of Southern Bluefin Tuna (the 1993 Convention) and UNCLOS. The Tribunal expressed its views on this issue in several paragraphs of the Order.[17] It pointed out that the conduct of the parties to the 1993 Convention in their relations with non-parties to that Convention "is relevant to an evaluation of the extent to which the parties are in compliance with their obligations under the Convention on the Law of the Sea."[18] This statement is in conformity with article 311, paragraphs 2 and 3, of UNCLOS. The Tribunal expressed its positive opinion concerning the right of the parties to the 1993 Convention to invoke the provisions of UNCLOS in respect to conservation and management of SBT stock. In addition, it was stated " . . . that the fact that the Convention of 1993 applies between the parties does not preclude recourse to procedures in Part XV, section 2, of the Convention on the Law of the Sea."[19] This assertion of the Tribunal declined the claim of the Respondent that the only available means for the settlement of a dispute between the parties to the 1993 Convention are the procedures contemplated by that Convention.

In connection with the problem of determining the *prima facie* jurisdiction of the arbitral tribunal to be established under article 290, paragraph 5, of UNCLOS, ITLOS specified that the provisions of UNCLOS "appear to afford a basis on which the jurisdiction of the arbitral tribunal might be founded."[20]

All these statements of ITLOS concerning the relation between UNCLOS and other international agreements, including procedural matters, are based on the interpretation of articles 286, 287, 290, paragraph 5, and the relevant provisions of article 311, of UNCLOS.

ENHANCING THE LEGAL STATUS OF FISHING VESSELS AND THE REGIME OF RESPONSIBLE FISHING ON THE HIGH SEAS

The problems of the legitimate status of fishing vessels, their genuine link with the flag state and compliance with and enforcement of the rules and regulations for responsible fishing activities, count among the current fisheries disputes. Out of eight cases on the list of cases of ITLOS, seven are on prompt release of vessels and their crews. The prevailing number of contentious cases on prompt release, under article 292 of UNCLOS, has been centered on the status of the vessel. In most instances the dispute between the parties has been on irregularities of the registration of the vessel or its nationality, lack of sufficient evidence of the genuine link with the flag State, and allegations of non-compliance with international rules and regulations in fisheries, on the high seas or within the exclusive economic zone of the coastal State concerned.

International rules and regulations and national legislation in respect to registration and granting nationality to fishing vessels, have to be complied with by the state and the master of the ship flying its flag. The requirements set out in article 91 of UNCLOS, on the registration and nationality of the ship, and article 92, on its status, must be applied strictly. It is the primary duty of the Tribunal to proceed with utmost care to the examination of the regularity of the certificate and other documents referred to in article 91, paragraph 2, of UNCLOS. The Tribunal should take the opportunity, at the earliest possible stage of the proceedings, to clear up any *prima facie* doubts on the registration and nationality of the vessel, and should require supplementary information by the applicant, in accordance with the relevant provisions of the Rules and the Guidelines concerning the Preparation and Presentation of Cases before the Tribunal.[21] These requirements will provide reliable documentary evidence on the nationality and status of the vessel and, thus, prevent documentary uncertainties during the proceedings.

The outcome of the proceedings and the Order of the *Grand Prince* case, should serve as a good lesson in this respect. Precautionary measures of this kind are indispensable in view of the increasing use of fishing vessels flying "flags of convenience" or reflagging on the high seas, which has become a widespread phenomenon in the illegal, unregulated, and unreported fishing activities on the high seas and some parts of the exclusive economic zones of foreign coastal States. It is, therefore, a duty within the authority of the Tribunal to perform its mission of judicial custodian of the implementation of UNCLOS and other international agreements in the field of the law of the sea, including rules and regulations on responsible fisheries.

ITLOS is also called, through its judicial activities and within its competence, to promote the compliance of flag states with international law concerning their duties, deriving from international treaties.

A significant number of international instruments have been adopted, which entail specific obligations and responsibilities of flag states. They have the duty to exercise effective control over fishing vessels flying their flags. Though some of the international agreements have not been ratified, their provisions have been widely recognized in practice. Article III.1(a) of the FAO Compliance Agreement stipulates that appropriate measures shall be taken in order to ensure that fishing vessels entitled to fly the flag of a flag State Party " . . . do not engage in any activity that undermines the effectiveness of international conservation and management measures."

Under articles 18.1 and 19.1 of the Straddling Fish Stocks Agreement and Highly Migratory Fish Stocks of 1995, it is the duty and responsibility of the flag state to take appropriate measures necessary to ensure that vessels flying its flag comply with conservation and management rules and regulations. The same articles authorize the coastal State and the flag state and, in some circumstances, the port state, to undertake enforcement measures, including investigation, physical inspection, institution of proceedings in case of alleged violation of conservation, and management. It is obvious that this problem area may be subject to disputes before international arbitration and adjudication.

Notes

[1] Between 1949 and 1974, there were several fisheries cases handled by ICJ. The first one was between the United Kingdom and Norway (see I. C. J. Reports 1949, Pleadings, and I. C. J. Reports, Judgment). All the other fisheries cases, mainly on jurisdiction, were between the United Kingdom and Iceland, and the Federal Republic of Germany and Iceland (see I. C. J. Reports 1972, *Fisheries Jurisdiction (United Kingdom v. Iceland)*, Judgment; I. C. J. Reports 1973; and I. C. J. Reports 1974, *Merits, Judgement*; and I. C. J. Reports 1974, Fisheries Jurisdiction, *Merits, Judgement (Federal Republic of Germany v. Iceland)*.

[2] See ITLOS 1999, *Southern Bluefin Tuna Cases*, nos. 3 and 4 (New Zealand v. Japan; Australia v. Japan) (August 27, 1999), "Request for Provisional Measures," Order.

[3] *Supra* note 2, paras. 2 and 5.

[4] *Supra* note 2, Statements of Claims and Submissions by New Zealand and Australia, paras. 28-32, and Statement of Response and Submissions by Japan, para. 33.

[5] *Supra* note 2, Joint Declaration of Vice-President Wolfrum and Judges Caminos, Marotta Rangel, Yankov, Anderson and Eiriksson.

[6] There have been many denominations of the precautionary principle since it had emerged first in doctrinal studies followed by state practice during the last two or three decades. Depending upon the context within which the reference is made, there have been various terms employed, such "as precautionary concept," "precautionary approach and principle," "precautionary duty," "precautionary action," "precautionary measures," "precautionary management," etc. This great variety of labels was symptomatic of the conceptual novelty, lack of reliable experience, and unusual legal implications of this new phenomenon in environmental policy and law. For more details, see the publications listed in notes 7 and 9.

[7] See "The Challenge of Implementation," in *The Precautionary Principle and International Law*, David Freestone and Ellen Hey, eds., (The Hague: Kluwer Law International, 1996), 261 (" . . . a precautionary interpretation derived from the primary obligation of conservation . . .").

[8] *Ibid.*, 249.

[9] *Supra* note 7, as well as some other publications on the subject, such as: Dr. jur. H. Hohmann, *Precautionary Legal Duties and Principles of Modern International Environmental Law* (Graham & Trotman, Martinus Nijhoff); L. Gündling, "The Status of International Law of the Principle of Precautionary Act," 5 *International Journal of Estuarine and Coastal Law*, nos. 1, 2, and 3, Spec. Issue, David Freestone and Ton Ijlstra, eds. (February 3, 1990); FAO, *Precautionary Approach to Capture Fisheries and Species Introduction* (Rome, 1996); Marc Iynedjian, "Le principe de précaution en droit international public," 78 *Revue de Droit International* 3 (Geneva, Septembre-décembre 2000): 247; John M. MacDonald, "Appreciating the Precautionary Principle as an Ethical

Evolution in Ocean Management," 25 *Ocean Development and International Law* 1 (January-March 1994); Pascale Martin-Bidou, "Le principe de précaution en droit international de l'environment," *RGDIP*, Tome 103/1999/3. As to State practice, the precautionary principle has been embodied in the Convention on the Drift Net Fishing on the High Seas, of 1991, and the Agreement for the Implementation of the United Nations Convention on the Law of the Sea of December 10, 1982, Relating to the Conservation and Management of Straddling Fish Stocks and Highly Migratory Fish Stocks of 1995 (articles 5 and 6, and Annex II, Guidelines for the Application of Precautionary Reference Points in Conservation and Management of Straddling Fish Stocks and Highly Migratory Fish Stocks). The recent practice of the European Union, and the Conferences on the Protection of the Environment, since 1983, and, in particular, the recognition of the legal effects of the precautionary principle. To these international treaty instruments should be added Agenda 21 of UNCED, where reference has been made to the precautionary and anticipatory approach, particularly in chapter 17 on the protection, rational use, and development of the marine living resources (Part 17, para. 17.21). By way of illustration could be listed some cases before the ICJ, though the judicial practice is still limited. Nevertheless, there are some cases in which reference has been made, directly or indirectly, to precautionary principle or precautionary approach, such as "Legality of the Threat or Use of Nuclear Weapons" (I. C. J. Reports 1995, and I. C. J. Reports 1996; *Nuclear Tests* [New Zealand v. France] I. C. J. Reports 1995); and "Case Concerning the Gabčikovo-Nagymaros Project" (Hungary/Slovakia) I. C. J. Reports 1997.

[10] Para. 28 (1)(e).

[11] Para. 34 (3).

[12] Paras. 66 and 73.

[13] Paras. 77, 78, 79, and 80.

[14] Para. 80.

[15] See the Separate Opinion of Judge Laing and the Separate Opinion of Judge Treves. Judge Laing considers that the thrust of the notion of "environmental precaution" is to "provide guidance to administrative and other decision-makers." He further points out that "serious harm to the marine environment" "is a crucial, perhaps the crucial criterion or condition to provisional measures." He maintains that "the Tribunal has adopted the concept of precautionary approach, rather than a principle." Judge Treves placed the emphasis on the requirement of urgency as a "part of the very nature of provisional measures." In his view for the prescription of provisional measures in the present case "it is not necessary to hold the view that this approach is dictated by a rule of international law." In this connection, Judge Treves takes a stand, which is opposite to those who consider that customary law is the legal source of the

precautionary principle. The existence of a number of international treaty instruments in which this principle is incorporated are not in support of the exclusive significance of customary rules as the only legal foundation of the precautionary principle. Ad Hoc Judge Shearer in his Separate Opinion also deals with the precautionary principle. His Conclusion notes that though the Tribunal "has not found it necessary to enter into the discussion of the precautionary principle/approach . . . the measures ordered by the Tribunal are rightly based upon considerations deriving from a precautionary approach." The Joint Declaration expressed its support for the views of the Tribunal, to the effect that "there is no disagreement between the parties that the stock of SBF is severely depleted and is at its historically [*sic*] levels and that this is a cause for serious biological concern." It is indicated that the signatories of the Joint Declaration share the statement of the Tribunal that the parties "should act with prudence and caution to ensure that effective conservation measures are taken to prevent serious harm to the stock of southern bluefin tuna." They also agree fully with paragraph 80 of the Order prescribing the provisional measures that the parties should take. The most important provision of the Joint Declaration, from the point of view of the meaning of the precautionary principle, is the conclusion that "a reduction in the catches of all those concerned in the fishery in the immediate short term would assist the stock to recover over the medium to long term."

[16] See Barbara Kwiatkowska, "The Southern Bluefin Tuna (New Zealand v. Japan; Australia v. Japan) Cases," 15 *The International Journal of Marine and Coastal Law* 1 (March 2000); Kwiatkowska, "Southern Bluefin Tuna (New Zealand v. Japan; Australia v. Japan), Order on Provisional Measures (ITLOS Cases Nos. 3 and 4)" 94 *AJIL* 1 (January 2000): 150; Kristina Leggel, "The Southern Bluefin Tuna Cases; ITLOS Order on Provisional Measures," 9 *RECIEL* 1 (2000): 75; and Simon Marr, "The Southern Bluefin Tuna Cases; The Precautionary Approach and Conservation and Management of Fish Resources," 11 *European Journal of International Law* 4 (December 2000): 815.

[17] Paras. 45, 46, 50, 51, 54, 55, 57, and 76.

[18] International Tribunal for the Law of the Sea, *Reports of Judgments, Advisory Opinions and Orders* (1997), para. 43.

[19] Para. 55.

[20] Para. 52.

[21] See *International Tribunal for the Law of the Sea. Basic Texts. Textes de Base 1998* (The Hague: Kluwer Law International, 1999).

NATIONAL LEGISLATION IN THE LIGHT OF UNCLOS AND THE PRACTICE OF THE INTERNATIONAL TRIBUNAL FOR THE LAW OF THE SEA

Anatoly L. Kolodkin*

Thank you, Mr. Chairman, first of all for allowing me to express high appreciation to the Center for Oceans Law and Policy, to Professor John Norton Moore, and to Myron Nordquist for the invitation to come here. I would also like to express many thanks to the President, Vice President, and Registrar of the Tribunal for the organization of this Conference with the Center for Oceans Law and Policy.

UNCLOS is called the Constitution of the Seas and Oceans. In my mind, UNCLOS has priority in respect to national legislation, a national approach to ocean policy. Unfortunately, the cases coming to ITLOS show that UNCLOS is not observed everywhere. Many states aim to transfer certain elements of the regime of the territorial sea to the EEZ. A large portion of the sea still does not recognize certain provisions of the Convention. I will talk more about this later.

Several speakers have referred to the Saiga case. I was astonished that Guinea and representatives of the state referred to custom jurisdiction in the EEZ as a normal situation. To my way of thinking, the Convention in article 56, and in other articles, does not mention custom jurisdiction. I fully agreed with Judge Anderson who, in his presentation in Brussels, said that the implementation of legislation concerning custom jurisdiction in the EEZ is unlawful. Unfortunately, in my country two of our main laws make reference to the state customs committee, and there are other laws concerning the customs. These laws mention the activity of the state customs committee in the EEZ. I participated in elaborating these laws in our parliament. The voice of a lawyer

---

* Judge, International Tribunal for the Law of the Sea.

M.H. Nordquist and J.N. Moore (eds.),
Current Marine Environmental Issues and the International Tribunal for the Law of the Sea, 239–241.
© 2001 *Kluwer Law International. Printed in the Netherlands.*

will not be heard, however, and this provision has been included in our law concerning the exclusive economic zone.

The other point concerning the Saiga case is bunkering. In this case, bunkering was not connected with fisheries. It was connected only with the navigation of free Italian fishing vessels that went to the capital of Guinea. It was not unlawful fishing nor was it in violation of article 56 of the Convention. Rather, as I understood during the hearing, Guinea referred instead to the violation of its economic rights.

I would also like to refer to other points concerning the prior notification and punishment in French legislation of 1966, which was amended in 1997. In spite of the fact that France ratified the Convention, its legislation retains the provision concerning the punishment for the failure of prior notification. I fully agree with Professor Oxman who, in the *American Journal of International Law* (4) of last year, pointed out that it was even more surprising that the application conceded that imposing a fine for failure to advise of entry into an EEZ was normal and may form part of the means a coastal State has to control access to its EEZ. The captains in two cases, Camouco and Confurco, both indicated that they had no intention to fish in the EEZ, but only to pass through these areas. That is where it seems to me that France was in violation of article 58 of the Convention concerning the freedom of navigation in the waters of an exclusive economic zone.

My last point concerns the new approach of states with regard to the Draft Convention on Protection of Underwater Cultural Heritage. As you know, we now have several drafts. One is the main draft being prepared by UNESCO in conjunction with the United Nations Department of Ocean Affairs and Law of the Sea and the International Maritime Organization. The International Law Association is preparing the second draft. A compromise has not yet been reached. In spite of article 303 of the Convention, one part of the community comprised of developing countries such as Latin American countries insisted on jurisdiction and control in the EEZ and continental shelf concerning these activities with regard to underwater cultural heritage. Other countries, including the United States, Great Britain, Russia, France, Germany, the

Netherlands, Norway, and others, strongly opposed this approach. In accordance with the Convention, in particular article 303, the coastal States could have jurisdiction and control with regard to this activity only within the twenty-four mile contiguous zone. No more.

I was surprised two days ago when during a meeting of ITLOS, the Siracusa Declaration on the Submarine Cultural Heritage of the Mediterranean Sea was distributed. There was absolutely nothing about UNCLOS. UNCLOS simply doesn't exist. Only the ICOMOS charter (ICOMOS is the International Council on Monuments and Sites) is mentioned. There is nothing else. No references are made to the articles of the United Nations Convention on the Law of the Sea. This approach, of course, is not acceptable.

In conclusion, I would like to stress that during and after the Third United Nations Conference on the Law of the Sea, the Soviet Union and other countries criticized developing countries that violate the Convention with the excuse that they did not understand the main provisions of international law of the sea. During our session so far with the Tribunal and in the process of considering some cases with regard to this Draft, I see that developed countries have changed slightly in their approach. With regard to the Draft Convention on cultural heritage, some developed countries of Europe, for example Denmark, Greece, Ireland, and Portugal, joined with the developing countries. And this approach, as I said before and I would like to emphasize again, is not acceptable. Thank you.

INTERIM MEASURES OF PROTECTION BEFORE THE INTERNATIONAL TRIBUNAL FOR THE LAW OF THE SEA

Philippe Gautier[*]

INTRODUCTION

As a preliminary remark to the present topic concerning interim measures of protection, it may be interesting to note that, of the seven cases that have so far been submitted to the Tribunal, three proceedings[1] have been instituted by a request for the prescription of provisional measures under article 290 of the United Nations Convention on the Law of the Sea (hereinafter the Convention). In fact, two of these cases were joined,[2] but if we take into account the number of judicial decisions (six) rendered by the Tribunal, two of them, two orders, have been made to prescribe provisional measures. This shows that this subject is of interest not only from the point of view of the legal doctrine but also for practitioners.

The purpose of this paper is not to give a comprehensive and systematic overview of provisional measures proceedings before the International Tribunal for the Law of the Sea, but rather to make some comments on selected issues that may be of interest to international tribunals, the subject matter of this panel. To that end, I intend to focus on the differences existing between the procedures for provisional measures before the Tribunal and the corresponding procedures before the International Court of Justice.[3] It may be added that this task is greatly facilitated by the fact that several articles on the legal doctrine have already underlined the main differences between the two courts with regard to questions of procedure.[4]

---

[*] Deputy Registrar, International Tribunal for the Law of the Sea; Visiting Professor, Catholic University of Louvain (Louvain-la-Neuve).

M.H. Nordquist and J.N. Moore (eds.),
Current Marine Environmental Issues and the International Tribunal for the Law of the Sea, 243–253.

PRESCRIPTION OF PROVISIONAL MEASURES

The first difference between the two courts may be encapsulated in three words: *indicate or prescribe*. Indeed, contrary to the International Court of Justice, which indicates provisional measures, the Tribunal prescribes them. The latter term expresses without any doubt the binding character of such measures, while the binding value of the measures indicated by the Court is a matter for discussion.[5] Incidentally, we may note that this ambiguity is to some extent reflected in a difference between the French and English versions of article 41 of the Statute of the Court. While the English version states: "indicate . . . any provisional measures . . . which ought to be taken," the French says "indiquer . . . quelles mesures conservatoires . . . doivent être prises à titre provisoire" [indicate any provisional measures . . . which must/shall be taken]. The difference is also reflected in the French and English versions of certain Orders of the Court.[6] This is perhaps an example of what is usually described as constructive ambiguity. From the point of view of the registry, it demonstrates the difficulty of dealing with different official languages and the importance to be attached to questions of drafting and translation in the official languages of the Tribunal.

While the binding character of the provisional measures prescribed by the Tribunal is undisputed, it should be noted that the Tribunal has decided in some cases not to use this power but to recommend certain measures. This approach was taken in the Orders adopted by the Tribunal in the *M/V "SAIGA" (No. 2)* case and the *Southern Bluefin Tuna* cases. In the *M/V "SAIGA" (No. 2)* case, the Tribunal "recommended" that the parties ensure that no action be taken that could aggravate the dispute, and this recommendation was not part of the provisional measure prescribed under paragraph 1 of the operative part of the Order. In the declaration appended to this Order, Judge Vukas took the view that the Tribunal should have prescribed the measure, given the importance to be attached to the obligation of parties to refrain from actions that might aggravate or extend the dispute. He was also of the opinion that under the Convention, the Tribunal was only competent to "prescribe provisional measures" and not to recommend them. In the *Southern Bluefin Tuna* cases, another technique was used. Of the six measures introduced by the expression "prescribes," two were drafted in a non-mandatory form by using the word "should" instead of "shall." These two measures concerned the duty to resume negotiations between the parties and efforts to be made to reach agreement between the parties and other States and entities engaged in fishery activities.

The fact that the measures are binding also explains why article 95 of the Rules of the Tribunal imposes on each party the obligation to report on steps taken in order to comply with the measures prescribed. In this respect, article 78 of the Rules of Court is less mandatory. It provides that the Court "may request information from the parties" in the matter of implementation of provisional measures.

Thus the power conferred on the Tribunal to order binding provisional measures is an important prerogative given to an international court. That is why this power is limited. Unlike the Court, the Tribunal cannot act *proprio motu* and will only prescribe provisional measures at the request of a party. But, according to article 89, paragraph 5, of the Rules, once a request has been made, the Tribunal may prescribe measures different in whole or in part from those requested. That is what it did in the *Southern Bluefin Tuna* cases by inserting measures concerning the duty of parties not to aggravate the dispute and directing them to seek agreement with other States engaged in fishing activities. In his separate opinion appended to this Order, Judge *ad hoc* Shearer expressed the view that article 89, paragraph 5, of the Rules should be applied in a cautious manner. According to him, if this rule

> purports to give a power to the Tribunal to act beyond the bounds of what has been requested (*ultra petita*), then . . . that rule is not authorized by the Convention. . . . If, on the other hand, it is properly to be interpreted as meaning only that the Tribunal may, in addition to the alternatives of

acceding completely to, or rejecting completely, the requested measures, prescribe measures that represent a partial grant or a modified version of the requested measures, the rule would be within power.

However, he considered that the Tribunal had not exceeded its powers in prescribing the two additional measures that had not been formally requested by the parties. As regards the non-aggravation clause, he considered that this measure was part of provisional measures that may be prescribed "by tradition"[7] and that the other measure, directing the parties to seek agreement with other States and entities engaged in fishing activities, was "closely related to other measures sought by the parties" and, therefore, its validity was not questioned.

PROVISIONAL MEASURES AND JURISDICTION OF THE TRIBUNAL

It is important to mention that the competence of the Tribunal to prescribe provisional measures may be activated in two different ways. The first relates to the ordinary meaning of provisional measures and is contemplated under article 290, paragraph 1, of the Convention. It arises when provisional measures are requested by a party as proceedings incidental to the main proceedings dealing with a dispute submitted to the Tribunal. The other procedure represents an innovation introduced by the Convention under article 290, paragraph 5. It confers on the Tribunal compulsory jurisdiction in the following circumstances: pending the constitution of an arbitral tribunal to which a dispute is submitted, a request for the prescription of provisional measures may be unilaterally brought before the Tribunal if the parties do not agree on another court or tribunal within a period of two weeks following the request for provisional measures. As regards this time-limit of two weeks, the question could arise concerning to which authority this initial request needs to be addressed. This question has been answered by article 89, paragraph 2, of the Rules of the Tribunal, which identifies the other party as the addressee of the request. In other words, the time-limit of two weeks is calculated from the date of the notification to the other party of a request for provisional measures. Under article 290, paragraph 5, the Tribunal has a residuary but compulsory jurisdiction and, in these circumstances, is likely to become the regular forum used by parties in such a case. It is, therefore, not fortuitous that the two requests for provisional measures that have so far been submitted to the Tribunal were both, at least initially,[8] based on this provision.

As is the case for other disputes brought before the Tribunal, provisional measures proceedings may be dealt with by a chamber of the Tribunal if so agreed by the parties. In addition to this option offered to parties, the Statute of the Tribunal gives a particular role to the Chamber of Summary Procedure, formed annually and composed of five judges. Article 25 of the Statute provides for the prescription of provisional measures by this Chamber "[i]f the Tribunal is not in session or a sufficient number of members is not available to constitute a quorum." It may also be added that the Seabed Disputes Chamber of the Tribunal is competent to prescribe provisional measures in matters falling within its jurisdiction under the Convention.

The Tribunal will prescribe provisional measures only if it considers that "*prima facie* it has jurisdiction" or, in the case of article 290, paragraph 5, that the arbitral tribunal to be constituted would have jurisdiction. A *prima facie* approach corresponds to the test applied by the Court in provisional measures proceedings. However, it does not prevent the respondent from questioning the jurisdiction of the Tribunal. We may observe that in the cases brought before the Tribunal, objections to jurisdiction have, in fact, been raised. In the *M/V "SAIGA" (No. 2)* case, the respondent invoked article 297, paragraph 3 (a), of the Convention (relating to disputes concerning sovereign rights of the coastal State with respect to the living resources in the exclusive economic zone) and argued that the dispute did not fall within the jurisdiction of the Tribunal, while the applicant based the jurisdiction of the Tribunal on article 297, paragraph 1, of the Convention (concerning an alleged breach of freedom of navigation by the coastal State). The Tribunal simply concluded that article 297, paragraph 1, offered *prima facie* a basis for its jurisdiction. In the *Southern Bluefin Tuna* cases, the respondent disputed the jurisdiction of the arbitral tribunal on several grounds: the dispute was scientific rather than legal; it concerned an agreement on southern bluefin tuna concluded in 1993 and not the Convention and, therefore, should have been submitted to the dispute settlement mechanism provided by that agreement; and, lastly, the parties had not exhausted diplomatic procedures. The Tribunal considered that "the requirements for invoking the procedures under Part XV, section 2, of the Convention have been fulfilled."[9] In particular, it took the view that the existence of another treaty on the same matter did not exclude the right to invoke this provision of the Convention and that its jurisdiction was unaffected by the dispute settlement procedure provided by the agreement of 1993, since that procedure did not entail a binding decision, as required by article 292 of the Convention. The answers provided by the Tribunal on these points are well known and do not need to be commented upon here. I will only add, as a footnote, that while the test of jurisdiction is a *prima facie* one, the Tribunal had to devote a substantial part of its reasoning to the question of jurisdiction. If we disregard the formal part of the judgments ("les qualités"), about half of the legal reasoning of the Tribunal was devoted to this issue in the *Southern Bluefin Tuna* cases and one-fifth in the *M/V "SAIGA" (No. 2)* case. There is probably no reason to be surprised at the importance assumed by objections to jurisdiction in provisional measures proceedings. It must be borne in mind that the cases were submitted by virtue of article 290, paragraph 5, of the Convention, independently of any expression of consent other than the ratification of, or accession to, the Convention. This means that the submission of the dispute was not based on a special agreement or a notification submitted by virtue of declarations made under article 287 of the Convention, but was based directly on the compulsory jurisdiction conferred on the Tribunal by the Convention.

Another comparison between the Court and the Tribunal may be made as regards the rights or legal interests the provisional measures are intended to protect. Both the Tribunal and the Court may adopt provisional measures to preserve the respective rights of the parties, pending a final decision. In addition to this classical function of interim measures of protection, article 290 of the Convention provides that provisional measures may also be prescribed "to prevent serious harm to the marine environment." This illustrates the importance given to the environment in the Convention. That being said, we may ask, however, whether the prevention of serious harm to the environment is to be considered as completely separate from the protection of the rights of a party to the dispute. Indeed, the fact that a case has been submitted to the Tribunal normally implies that a party to the dispute is alleging that its rights have been violated by an unlawful action of the other party. In this context, when a party requests the prescription of provisional measures to prevent serious harm to the environment, this request is likely to be based on a vested right, or rather a duty, to protect the environment or to ensure the conservation of the living resources of the sea. If this alleged right or duty is, in fact, the subject of the dispute, a provisional measure prescribed to prevent serious harm to the environment will probably not be very different from a provisional measure prescribed to preserve the respective rights of the parties.[10] However, the recognition of protection of the environment in article 290 of the Convention as a separate and independent ground for prescribing provisional measures presents clear advantages in a situation where the rights in dispute do not directly include a duty to protect the environment or where the right to request provisional measures is challenged on the basis that the party concerned would not have *locus standi* because it would not be "injured" by harm caused to the environment, for example, in areas beyond maritime zones under national jurisdiction.

According to the practice of the International Court of Justice, provisional measures are adopted when the right to be protected is likely to suffer irreparable damage. It presupposes that in the absence of provisional measures, the prejudice caused to the rights of the party concerned would affect the possibility of their full restoration in the event of a judgment in its favor. It means that full restoration of the rights would be affected. It does not mean that any damage that might occur could not be compensated for or subject to reparation.[11] In the *Southern Bluefin Tuna* cases, a threat to a fish stock was at stake. Both parties agreed that the stock was severely depleted. While Japan maintained that its experimental fishing program would cause no further threat to the stock, Australia and New Zealand contended that this fishing program "could endanger the existence of the stock." In its Order, the Tribunal did not itself pronounce on the question of irreparability. Paragraph 80 of the Order refers to the need to take provisional measures "to preserve the rights of the parties and to avert further deterioration of the southern bluefin tuna stock." This reference to the protection of the environment should be noted. Indeed, when provisional measures are prescribed to protect the environment, the Convention provides expressly for a specific standard, that is, "serious harm," which is different from the concept of irreparable damage.[12]

PROVISIONAL MEASURES AND THE TIME FACTOR

Like article 41 of the Statute of the Court, article 290, paragraph 1, of the Convention does not expressly refer to the criterion of urgency. However, time undoubtedly plays an important role in provisional measures proceedings. These proceedings are intended to lead to a "provisional" decision, "pending the final decision" in the case. This is why the International Court of Justice considers that provisional measures "are only justified if there is urgency."[13] This "procedural urgency" is undisputed, even if views may differ on the extent to which "substantive urgency" is a separate factor to be taken into account in assessing whether provisional measures are appropriate in the circumstances of a case.[14] Urgency is, nevertheless, mentioned expressly in article 290, paragraph 5, of the

Convention. This insistence on the urgency may be explained by the fact that the measures are prescribed pending the constitution of an arbitral tribunal that may subsequently modify, revoke, or affirm the measures taken. In other words, once a request for provisional measures is submitted under article 290, paragraph 5, the Tribunal will not only consider whether the right to be protected is likely to suffer irreparable damage pending a final decision but will also consider whether "the measures requested could, without prejudice to the rights to be protected, be granted by the arbitral tribunal once constituted."[15]

The urgent character of provisional measures proceedings is reflected in the Rules and practice of the Tribunal. According to article 90 of the Rules, a request for the prescription of provisional measures "has priority over all other proceedings," with the exception of prompt release cases. In the two cases submitted to the Tribunal, the whole procedure took less than two months (fifty-seven days) in the *M/V "SAIGA" (No. 2)* case and less than one month (twenty-eight days) in the *Southern Bluefin Tuna* cases. The short duration of these proceedings has consequences, not only for the judges and members of the Registry, who have to work under time constraints, but also for the parties, which need to provide the Tribunal with pleadings and relevant documentation within the time frame available. In these circumstances, compliance with the Rules does not preclude the possibility of adopting a flexible approach, in order, for example, to enable the parties to submit additional documents.[16] This may certainly help the parties to present their arguments in full and contribute, in the interest of international justice, towards alleviating certain difficulties caused by reduced time-limits.

Notes

[1] The *M/V "SAIGA" (No. 2)* case *(Saint Vincent and the Grenadines* v. *Guinea), Provisional Measures; Southern Bluefin Tuna* cases *(New Zealand* v. *Japan), Provisional Measures;* and *Southern Bluefin Tuna* cases *(Australia* v. *Japan), Provisional Measures.*

[2] Cases nos. 3 and 4 *(Southern Bluefin Tuna* cases *[New Zealand* v. *Japan], Provisional Measures;* and *Southern Bluefin Tuna* cases *[Australia* v. *Japan], Provisional Measures)* were joined by the Order of the Tribunal of 16 August 1999.

[3] As regards provisional measures before the ICJ, see, for example, S. Rosenne, *The Law and Practice of the International Court of Justice 1920-1996,* vol. III, 1419-1462; J. Sztucki, *Interim Measures in the Hague Court—An Attempt at a Scrutiny;* S. Oda, "Provisional Measures, the Practice of the International Court of Justice," in V. Lowe and M. Fitzmaurice, eds., *Fifty Years of the International Court of Justice—Essays in Honour of Sir Robert Jennings,* 541-556; B. Oxman, "Jurisdiction and the Power to Indicate Provisional Measures," in L. F. Damrosch, ed., *The International Court of Justice at a Crossroads,* 323-354.

[4] See, for example, T. Treves, "The Procedure Before the International Tribunal for the Law of the Sea: The Rules of the Tribunal and Related Documents," in 11 *Leiden Journal of International Law* 565-594 (1998): 582-586; S. Rosenne, "The International Tribunal for the Law of the Sea and the International Court of Justice: Some points of difference," in R. Platzöder and P. Verlaan, eds., *New Developments in National Policies and International Cooperation,* 200-215.

[5] See, for example, B. Oxman, *op.cit,* 331-333; S. Oda, *op.cit.,* 554-556.

[6] See, for example, the following Orders where, in the operative parts, the English texts refer to the expression "should" while the French texts use the verb "devoir" in the present tense [shall/must]: *Application of the Convention on the Prevention and Punishment of the Crime of Genocide, Provisional Measures, Order of 8 April 1993, I.C.J. Reports 1993; Vienna Convention on Consular Relations (Paraguay* v. *United States of America), Provisional Measures, Order of 9 April 1998; Vienna Convention on Consular Relations (Germany* v. *United States of America), Provisional Measures, Order of 3 March 1999.* The practice of the Court seems to vary concerning the French texts of the orders; see, for instances, the following Orders, where the French texts use the present tense ("Les deux Parties veillent . . ." [both Parties ensure . . ."]), while the English texts use the conditional ("Both Parties should ensure"): *Military and Paramilitary Activities in and against Nicaragua (Nicaragua* v. *United States of America), Provisional Measures, Order of 10 May 1984, I.C.J. Reports 1984; Land and Maritime Boundary between Cameroon and Nigeria, Provisional Measures, Order of 15 March 1996, I.C.J. Reports 1996.*

[7] It may be noted that in his dissenting opinion, Judge Eiriksson expressed his disagreement with the prescription of such a general measure. In his view, the

measure was "of so general a nature that a party cannot be entirely clear when contemplating any given action whether or not it falls within its scope."

[8] In the *M/V "SAIGA" (No. 2)* case, the request for the prescription of provisional measures of 13 January 1998 was based on article 290, paragraph 5, of the Convention. Subsequently, following the conclusion of a special agreement to submit the main dispute to the Tribunal, the Tribunal adopted its Order of 20 February 1998, by which it decided that the request should be "considered as having been duly submitted to the Tribunal under article 290, paragraph 1, of the Convention. . . ."

[9] See para. 61 of the Order.

[10] We may refer, for example, to paragraph 80 of the Order of the Tribunal in the *Southern Bluefin Tuna* cases, where the Tribunal found that provisional measures should be taken "to preserve the rights of the parties and to avert further deterioration of the southern bluefin tuna stock."

[11] In this regard, it may be observed that in the jurisprudence of the Court, provisional measures were requested to prevent prejudice to rights of a financial nature, which are more easily compensated. In *Interhandel, Interim Protection, Order of 24 October 1957, I.C.J. Reports 1957*, 111-112, the Court considered the request to the Government of the United States not to sell the shares of a company claimed by the Swiss Government as the property of its nationals.

[12] On this question, see the separate opinion of Judge Treves concerning the Order of the Tribunal of 27 August 1999 (*Southern Bluefin Tuna* cases).

[13] *Land and Maritime Boundary between Cameroon and Nigeria, Provisional Measures, Order of 15 March 1996, I.C.J. Reports 1996*, 22. See also *Military and Paramilitary Activities in and against Nicaragua (Nicaragua v. United States of America), Provisional Measures, Order of 10 May 1984, I.C.J. Reports 1984*, 179.

[14] On this question, see separate opinions of Judge Laing concerning the Order of 11 March 1998 (*M/V "SAIGA" [No. 2]* case) and the Order of 27 August 1999 (*Southern Bluefin Tuna* cases).

[15] Separate opinion of Judge Treves concerning the Order of the Tribunal of 27 August 1999 (*Southern Bluefin Tuna* cases), para. 4.

[16] In the *M/V "SAIGA" (No. 2)* case, in addition to the request and a statement in response submitted by the parties, each party was able to submit an additional written pleading. In the *Southern Bluefin Tuna* cases, when additional documents were submitted by one party in the course of oral proceedings, the other party requested also to be authorized to file new documents. This request was granted by the Tribunal.

THE ROLE OF THE COMMISSION ON THE LIMITS OF THE CONTINENTAL SHELF IN THE INTERPRETATION AND APPLICATION OF THE CONVENTION

*L. D. M. Nelson**

The prime function of the Commission, as set out in the Convention, is to consider "the data and other material" submitted by coastal States concerning the outer limits of the continental shelf where those limits extend beyond 200 miles and to make recommendations on their establishment. "The limits of the shelf established by a coastal State on the basis of these recommendations shall be final and binding."[1] What if the coastal State disagrees with the recommendations of the Commission? The Convention specifically provides that in such a situation the coastal State shall, within a *reasonable* time, make a revised or new submission to the Commission (Annex II, article 8). The next step is not specified in the Convention and, consequently, is uncertain. Presumably this process can and perhaps should be continued until some accommodation is reached. It is certain however, that the Commission has not been granted the power to submit any dispute concerning the outer limit of a coastal State's continental shelf to any court or tribunal. Questions regarding a possible appeals procedure and the relationship between the Commission with "the proposed dispute settlement procedures under the new Convention" were raised in the Evensen Group, but the matter never seems to have gone further.[2]

It may be useful here to recall that during the course of the prolonged and difficult negotiations on article 76, the expression "taking into account these recommendations" was replaced by the words "on the basis of these recommendations" (article 76, para. 8). Several wide-margined coastal States were unhappy with this

---

* Judge and Vice-President of the International Tribunal for the Law of the Sea. This paper is partly based on an article entitled "The Continental Shelf: Interplay between Law and Science," which is to be published in the forthcoming Festschrift for Judge Oda.

M.H. Nordquist and J.N. Moore (eds.),
Current Marine Environmental Issues and the International Tribunal for the Law of the Sea, 255–261.
© 2001 *Kluwer Law International. Printed in the Netherlands.*

amendment.[3] It was viewed as an attempt to erode the sovereign rights of coastal States. Indeed, the United Kingdom had proposed a formal amendment seeking to reverse the change.[4] That amendment was later withdrawn. The Commission has not been given the power to impose its recommendations on the coastal State, thus determining the outer limit of the continental shelves of coastal States.[5] That is why it seems important that both the Commission and the coastal State concerned should strive to the maximum extent possible to reach some accommodation.

Besides making recommendations to coastal States on the establishment of their continental shelves, the Commission has other functions that are of no less importance. It is also the business of the Commission to provide scientific and technical advice, if requested by the coastal State concerned during the preparation of the relevant data (Annex II, article 3, para. 1[b]).[6] It will also in the nature of things provide useful guidance on the interpretation and application of the technical requirements to be found in article 76 that would surely influence the practice of both parties and non-parties.

An important function of the Commission that is not expressly referred to in the Convention has to do with the interpretation or application of the Convention. Recent developments in the Commission have thrown this role into high relief. It can be argued that the Scientific and Technical Guidelines of the Commission on the Limits of the Continental Shelf adopted on 13 May 1999 (CLCS/11) represent in essence an interpretation of the Convention—in particular of article 76.

The Commission is aware of its role in the interpretation and application of the relevant provisions of the Convention. It has made the following observations with respect to the Guidelines, and I quote them *in extenso*:

> . . . the Commission aims also to clarify its interpretation of scientific, technical and legal terms contained in the Convention. Clarification is required in particular because the Convention makes use of scientific terms in a legal context which at times departs significantly from accepted

scientific definitions and terminology. In other cases, clarification is required because various terms in the Convention might be left open to several possible and equally acceptable interpretations. It is also possible that it may not have been felt necessary at the time of the Third United Nations Conference on the Law of the Sea to determine the precise definition of various scientific and technical terms. In still other cases, the need for clarification arises as a result of the complexity of several provisions and the potential scientific and technical difficulties which might be encountered by States in making a single and unequivocal interpretation of each of them.[7]

This may be termed a comprehensive exposition of what the Commission, in a sense, is all about.

The Commission is engaged in clarifying the ambiguities in article 76 and giving a precise definition of the meaning and scope of that complex provision. The well-known definition of interpretation given by the Permanent Court of Justice will be recalled: ". . . the Court is of the opinion that the expression 'to construe' (<interprétation> in French) must be understood as meaning to give a precise definition of the meaning and scope" of a legal instrument.[8] The process involves interplay between law and science. It is all the more surprising that legal expertise was deliberately not included in the membership of the Commission.[9]

It must be stated that these Guidelines are not legally binding, but they come close to being an authoritative interpretation of the technical provisions to be found in article 76 relating to such issues as: i) the location of the foot of the slope; ii) the sediment thickness test; iii) the selection of the 2,500 meter isobath; and iv) ridges.

The Convention states that the actions of the Commission shall not prejudice matters relating to the delimitation of boundaries between the States with opposite or adjacent coasts. The

Commission must, therefore, avoid dealing with submissions that may prejudice matters relating to the delimitation of boundaries between States.

The Committee has drafted rules to deal with this problem.[10] First, the Commission expressly recognizes that the competence with respect to matters regarding disputes that may arise in connection with the establishment of the outer limits of the continental shelf rests with States. Second, where there is a dispute on the delimitation of the continental shelf between States with opposite or adjacent coastlines or in other cases of unresolved land or maritime disputes, the coastal State making a submission must inform the Commission of the dispute and must ensure to the extent possible that the submission will not prejudice matters relating to the delimitation of boundaries between States. Third, two or more States are entitled to make joint or separate submission by agreement. Fourth, and perhaps most importantly:

> [i]n cases where a land or maritime dispute exists, the Commission shall not examine and qualify a submission made by any of the States concerned in the dispute. However, the Commission may examine one or more submissions in the areas under dispute with prior consent given by all States that are parties to such a dispute.[11]

There remains, of course, the basic duty of the Commission itself that its own actions do not prejudice matters relating to the delimitation of boundaries between States.

The work of the Commission, however, will have effects, albeit indirect, on the delimitation of the outer continental shelves between States with opposite or adjacent coasts. International tribunals dealing with such maritime boundary disputes will surely be guided by the Scientific and Technical Guidelines of the Commission with respect to the interpretation and application of the relevant provisions of the Convention. In this regard, the actual practice of the Commission in dealing with submissions will also be a source of guidance for international tribunals. It is reasonable to expect that States—parties and non-parties to the Convention—

will rely on the work of the Commission not only in establishing the limits of their outer continental shelves, but also in negotiating the maritime boundaries of the outer continental shelf between States with opposite or adjacent coastlines.

The Commission, in preparing the Scientific and Technical Guidelines, has had to operate in the interface between law and science. It was faced with a legal provision (article 76) utilizing a host of scientific and technical terms. The task of the Guidelines was to interpret and apply these scientific terms within the context of the law. In that sense, the Commission has been engaged in interpreting and applying a key provision of the Convention on the Law of the Sea—a provision that has as its object the establishment of the common boundary between areas falling under national jurisdiction and the international seabed area. The Commission is now ready to receive submissions from coastal States and to provide scientific and technical advice that States preparing submissions may require. The Commission, in applying its Guidelines, should take very much into account the need for "negotiating differences" that may arise between itself and the coastal State concerned, so as to avoid disputes for which there is as yet no clear forum for their resolution.

Notes

---

[1] Article 76, para. 8, and Annex II, article 3, para.1(a).

[2] Fourth Revision of the Evensen Text on the Continental Shelf dated 6 May 1975, on which see *The United Nations Convention on the Law of the Sea 1982: A Commentary*, vol. II (1993), 850. It may be remembered that the 1970 Draft United Nations Convention on the International Seabed Area had indeed given the International Seabed Boundary Review Commission the power to make such a submission. Article 45 read in part as follows:

> The International Seabed Boundary Review Commission shall: a) Review the delineation of boundaries submitted by Contracting Parties in accordance with Articles 1 and 26 to see that they conform to the provisions of this convention, negotiate any differences with Contracting Parties, and if these differences are not resolved initiate proceedings before the Tribunal. . . .

S. Oda, *The International Law of the Ocean Development: Basic documents*, (1972), 83.

[3] Canada, for instance, declared that:

> . . . The commission is primarily an instrument which will provide the international community with reassurances that coastal States will establish their continental shelf limits in strict accordance with the provisions of article 76. It has never been intended, nor should it be intended, as a means to impose on coastal States limits that differ from those already recognized in article 76. Thus to suggest that the coastal States limits shall be established "on the basis" of the commission's recommendations rather than on the basis of article 76, could be interpreted as giving the commission the function and power to determine the outer limits of the continental shelf of a coastal State.

Off. Rec. Third UN Conference on the Law of the Sea, XIII, 102, para. 15. To the same effect, see also Australia, *ibid.*, 33, para. 13; Pakistan, *ibid.*, 21, para. 140; The United Kingdom, *ibid.*, 25, para. 15; Venezuela, *ibid.*, 20, para. 136; and Uruguay, *ibid.*, 35-36, para. 50. The Canadian statement seems, to this writer, to disregard a significant function (though unexpressed) of the Commission—that is, to interpret and apply the provisions of article 76.

[4] For amendment, see A/CONF.62/L.126 of 13 April 1982, *Off. Rec. Third UN Conference on the Law of the Sea*, XVI, 233.

[5] *The Law of the Sea, Definition of the Continental Shelf*, 29, para. 86.

[6] A trust fund has been established to help developing countries in the preparation of relevant data and information for submission to the Commission

on the Limits of the Continental Shelf. See Annex II to GA Resolution A/55/10 of 20 October 2000.

[7] Scientific and Technical Guidelines of the Commission on the Limits of the Continental Shelf, CLCS/11 of 13 May 1999, 7. The U.S. Government had recommended that this provision should be deleted, remarking that "[i]t is much too broadly stated" (CLCS/CRP.15 of 18 April 1999, 3). On the other hand, it may be argued that this is the type of function that the Commission must carry out.

[8] Interpretation of Judgments Nos. 7 and 8 (The Chorzów Factory), Series A, Judgment No. 11, 10.

[9] Annex II, article 2, para. 1, reads as follows:

> The Commission shall consist of 21 members who shall be experts in the field of geology, geophysics or hydrography, elected by States Parties to this Convention from among their nationals, having due regard to the need to ensure equitable geographical representation, who shall serve in their personal capacities.

[10] Rule 44 and Annex I of the Rules of Procedure of the Commission that were adopted on 4 September 1998 (CLCS/3/Rev.2).

[11] Annex I, para. 5(a), of the Rules of Procedure of the Commission.

PANEL V

Accidents, Insurance and Classification

THE *ERIKA* ACCIDENT AND ITS EFFECTS ON EU MARITIME REGULATION

Henrik Ringbom [*]

INTRODUCTION

Maritime accidents that are ill-fated enough to provoke profound changes to the regulatory regime for shipping as a whole appear to occur with a certain regularity. For some reason, there has been a sequence of eleven years between the most high-profile marine pollution accidents. The first modern oil tanker incident to shake up the international maritime legal regime was the grounding of the *Torrey Canyon* off Land's End, UK, in 1967, which led to the development of several new international conventions. The stranding of the *Amoco Cadiz* in Brittany, France, in 1978, provoked the inclusion of some important new provisions into the United Nations Convention on the Law of the Sea, while, again eleven years later, the *Exxon Valdez* ran aground in Prince William Sound, Alaska, in 1989, giving rise to the U.S. Oil Pollution Act, OPA 90. In line with this rate of recurrence, the next accident of this type should have happened in the year 2000. Yet, the *Erika* sank a couple of weeks before the entry into that year, on December 12, 1999.

As opposed to previous disastrous oil spills in European waters, the sinking of the *Erika* occurred at a time when the European Union (EU) had already established a comprehensive maritime safety policy of its own. Therefore, once the scale of the accident became clear, it was natural that the EU took up the issue of tanker regulation, and in particular it was understandable that

---

[*] Administrator, Maritime Safety Unit, Directorate General for Energy and Transport, European Commission. The views expressed in this article are solely those of the author and do not necessarily correspond to those of the European Commission.

M.H. Nordquist and J.N. Moore (eds.),
Current Marine Environmental Issues and the International Tribunal for the Law of the Sea, 265–290.
© 2001 *Kluwer Law International. Printed in the Netherlands.*

the European Commission, being the institution responsible for proposing EU regulation, decided to take an especially active role in the follow-up to this accident.[1]

WHY THE *ERIKA*?

Why, then, did this particular accident spark off such an intense response? Of the many different underlying reasons, some seem particularly relevant. First of all, the *Erika* incident was particularly damaging in terms of the pollution it caused. Although the amount of oil spilled (some 20,000 tons) was not exceptionally great, heavy fuel oil is, by its nature, a very persistent, slowly dissipating oil that is difficult to clean. The *Erika* furthermore sank relatively far—some thirty miles—off the nearest coast, whereby the area affected by the pollution was very vast. On top of that, extreme winter storms hit the region in the immediate aftermath of the accident, seriously hampering any efforts to mitigate the damage at sea. In the end, more than 400 kilometers of the French Atlantic coastline was polluted by *Erika*'s cargo. The final costs of the accident are still to be assessed, but the *Erika* is beyond doubt going to be the most expensive oil spill in the history of the International Oil Pollution Compensation (IOPC) Funds.

Such a massive pollution of a sensitive coastline naturally created a tremendous public reaction. While this was expected, the actual intensity of this public reaction probably came as a surprise to many. The European Commission alone received thousands of postcards and letters in which citizens expressed their concerns about the existing safety situation in shipping and repeatedly urged for drastic improvements to the regulatory regime. It was made very clear by the people living in the most exposed parts of the European coast that citizens' tolerance towards oil spills or other environmental disasters caused by ships was by now more or less nonexistent.

The animosity of those affected by the pollution was further magnified by the way in which the accident was handled by those most directly involved. In the immediate aftermath of the accident, all parties known to have been implicated in the ship and its cargo, such as the classification society, charterer, cargo owner, insurers, and flag State (all of which incidentally happened to be European, making it largely an EU—or enlarged EU—"internal affair"), only came forward to declare the absence of any responsibility on their part. The actual owner and manager of the ship were not identified at all, until several weeks after the oil had landed on the beaches of Brittany. Such a display of a lack of accountability of those involved caused severe damage to the public image of the shipping industry as a whole. Consequently, pressure was strong for restoring confidence in it. This pressure was particularly felt within the industry itself and among regulators and other public authorities.[2]

Apart from the problems referred to above, there was another aspect to the *Erika* accident that was of particular concern to the public authorities, such as the European Commission. This particular case demonstrated the shortcomings of the existing network in place for preventing incidents of this kind with an awkward bluntness. While certain weaknesses, particularly as regards the implementation of applicable rules, were known to most, the *Erika* represented to many the "ultimate confirmation," as it were, of the inherent failings of the existing regulatory system. The *Erika* was inspected, and approved, by nearly all kinds of controls, ranging from flag State and class controls, including various safety management audits, to port State control inspections of various profundity and private industry vetting mechanisms established to ensure the suitability of the ships for the trade.[3] Despite this, the ship simply broke in two when the weather got rough. Hence there were fair grounds to question the quality of controls that are undertaken by various bodies.

THE COMMISSION'S RESPONSE: ERIKA 1

Given the international character of maritime transport, not all types of regulation are appropriate at a regional level. Various considerations, following both from the international law of the sea and from the practicalities of the shipping world, impose certain limitations as to what can effectively be achieved through regional rule-making in maritime safety. Generally speaking, the EU measures on maritime safety have tended to focus on conditions applying to all ships, whatever their flag, entering EU ports, while the flag State perspective has been limited to setting standards for EU maritime administrations and regulating their relationship with the classification societies. The first set of proposals following the sinking of the *Erika*, which was adopted only three months after the accident, followed this pattern. The three proposals, the so-called "Erika 1 package," cover the following elements:[4]

- Amendments to the existing Directive on classification societies;
- Amendments to the existing Directive on port State control; and
- A new proposal aiming at the phasing-out of single hull tankers from EU waters

Classification Societies

Classification societies are specialized private organizations responsible for inspecting and monitoring ships' structures. The societies assess the condition of a ship against their own technical standards and issue a "class certificate" for the ship upon request of the shipowner. In addition, classification societies are often authorized to act on behalf of flag States to verify the ship's compliance with safety and environmental requirements laid down in the international conventions and to issue the relevant statutory certificates. This dual role of the classification societies and the tension between their commercial interests on the one hand and public control functions on the other hand can cause problems of consistency for the societies, which, in particular, may affect their diligence in the latter role.

Since 1994, there has been a European system in place for accepting classification societies through an EU-wide recognition of certain societies.[5] EU Member States, in their capacity as flag States, can only rely on those recognized societies when authorizing classification societies to do statutory tasks on their behalf. For the moment, twelve classification societies are recognized, including all ten members of the International Association of Classification Societies. Through this recognition, and through the periodic monitoring it involves, a certain degree of control over the major classification societies is achieved. While only twelve out of fifty or so classification societies worldwide are EU-recognized, this is not overly restricted, as most ships (some ninety percent in terms of tonnage and some fifty percent in number) are classed with the ten largest classification societies.

The experience of the regime in place has indicated certain shortcomings, both regarding the way in which classification societies are recognized and regarding the way the performance of the recognized societies is followed up. The procedure for recognizing classification societies, for example, is left to individual Member States without *ex ante* harmonized control of the society as to the fulfilment of the common criteria. The same lack of a common approach applies to the periodic controls of the recognized organizations. Furthermore, the overall safety and pollution prevention performance record of the classification societies—measured in respect of all their classed ships, irrespective of the flag they fly—is not regarded as a *conditio sine qua non* for obtaining and maintaining EU recognition.

Through the post-*Erika* amendments, the criteria and control of this recognition are considerably strengthened as well as the remedies to take action when classification societies fail to meet the necessary criteria. In addition, a procedural streamlining is undertaken by further strengthening the role of the Commission, at the expense of individual Member States, in the assessment and evaluation process.

The proposed establishment of clear performance criteria seeks to lay considerably more emphasis on the overall safety performance record of classification societies worldwide. In addition, certain new requirements on the procedures to be applied when ships transfer from one society to another and on increased exchange of information between classification societies and port State control are introduced. The most controversial issue of the new proposal has proven to be the specific requirements on the sharing of the financial liability between the flag State and the classification society in cases where the flag State is held liable but the cause is linked to the operation of the classification society performing duties on its behalf.[6]

As regards the remedies against badly performing classification societies, the Commission's role in the withdrawal of recognition is also significantly strengthened through procedural changes. Furthermore, the "all-or-nothing" regime is somewhat moderated by the introduction of a new remedy for non-performing societies: a one-year suspension of the recognition, which is followed by withdrawal in case the shortcomings giving rise to the suspension are not rectified during that period.

Port State Control

The *Erika* accident also prompted proposals for a considerable strengthening of the European port State control regime. Since the early 1980s, port State control has been the second line of defense against flag States who fail to ensure that their ships meet the required international standards. It has proven to be a useful and rather effective tool in ensuring a certain level of standards of the ships entering ports in a given region. Since 1995, an EU-wide law on the subject and the process of fine-tuning the regime and targeting the ships to be inspected has been continuous involving regular amendments of the Directive.[7]

With the amendments of March 2000, some additional, rather remarkable changes are being proposed. Notably, the concept of *mandatory* inspections of certain categories of ships is introduced. So far, the method has been to target certain ships by giving them points based on various characteristics, but there has not been a clear-cut obligation for port State control authority to inspect a certain ship. This is now proposed to change and, in particular, so-called environmental high-risk ships, such as oil and chemical tankers as well as ships for which the "target factor" exceeds a certain limit, would be the focus of this mandatory inspection regime, which represents a detailed form of inspection.[8]

The other major novelty is the increased facility of *banning* certain ships with an exceptionally bad performance record from all EU ports. The possibility for EU States to ban individual ships from all EU ports existed before, in exceptional circumstances. The criteria for resorting to this remedy are now being considerably widened. The new criteria are linked primarily to the detention records of the individual ship and, significantly, to the performance in general of the flag State concerned.[9]

Other changes to the existing port State control regime include increased cooperation between port State control authorities and classification societies and extending the range of information to be published on detained ships, to include new items such as the identity of the ship's charterer and data on the latest class survey and port State control inspections.

Phasing-out of Single-hulled Oil Tankers

The third proposal, on the phasing-out of single-hulled oil tankers, was by far the most controversial one in the first Erika package. The background for this proposal is that the international community had already, through amendments to the Marpol 73/78 Convention in 1992, agreed that single-hulled oil tankers should be phased out. According to these rules, all tankers built after 1996 need to have a double-hull or an equivalent structure. The phasing-out scheme of the remaining older ships (built before 1996) was based on the age and type of the ship. This had the effect that all tankers above certain size limits would be required to be double-hulled by 2026 at the latest.

The United States, however, did not adhere to this set of rules and chose to continue with the regime of OPA 90, which establishes certain end-dates, the year 2010, or for certain ships 2015, by which all tankers in U.S. waters shall be double-hulled. The United States also introduced its own technical requirements as to what is regarded as a double-hulled ship, which differ from those of the Marpol criteria.

This state of affairs was rather problematic for the EU, as it meant that within a few years' time, a number of relatively old tankers posing an increased pollution risk that had been banned from U.S. waters would be free to continue trading for many years in the EU. After the *Erika*, a twenty-four year old tanker soon to be taken out of service, this was increasingly difficult to justify.

The idea of the Commission's proposal was very simple: to stick with the construction requirements of the Marpol regime, but to bring forward the phasing-out dates in order to bring them more in line with those of the U.S. regime. The proposal did not establish new criteria or standards for oil tankers' technical construction.

Mostly because of the economic implications of this proposal, it created substantial unrest within the international maritime community. The debate that followed was primarily based on economic and political considerations, but some arguments of a legal nature were also raised in this context, relating to the possibility of port States, according to the law of the sea, to deviate from internationally agreed standards regarding the construction and design of ships.[10]

By now, however, much of the steam has gone out of this debate, the reason being the transfer of the discussions to a global level. The International Maritime Organization (IMO) rapidly included this item on its agenda, and there are now far-reaching plans to introduce a phasing-out scheme at the international level, which contains many of the elements proposed by the European Commission. The end-dates are likely to be much the same, but the IMO scheme introduces a certain flexibility in the requirements in order to avoid peak years, where a large number of tankers would need to be taken out of service at the same time.[11] The final details of this proposed amendment to Marpol 73/78 are still to be discussed. Only after that the EU bodies will decide on how to proceed with the original proposal.[12]

Perhaps surprisingly, the international maritime community, with some exceptions, seems to be largely content with the measures now being proposed by the IMO, despite their evident similarities with the controversial Commission proposal. To some extent, this reaction certainly follows from a general change of attitude towards older oil tankers in the market and within the industry as a whole. However, in light of the initial indignation expressed at the Commission's proposal, the generally positive reception of the global phasing-out rules by the international maritime community is nevertheless interesting. It may be seen as another illustration of the firmness within the maritime world that what really matters is that the rules, whatever they may be, shall apply for everybody and shall thus be adopted at a global level.

ERIKA 2

On December 6, 2000, the Commission, as already announced in its first Communication, presented three new proposals, the so-called "Erika 2 package."[13] The proposed measures contained herein are the following: 1) the creation of a European Maritime Safety Agency; 2) improvements to the international system for liability and compensation of oil pollution damage; and 3) a new regime for the surveillance and control of navigation in EU coastal waters.

A European Maritime Safety Agency

The main purpose of the proposed European Maritime Safety Agency is to provide the Commission and the EU Member States with the technical support necessary for ensuring the uniform application of the growing bulk of EU maritime safety regulations, and to help monitor compliance with EU law in this area. The background for this measure lies in the incontestable reality that also within the EU there are sometimes shortcomings and discrepancies in the way the rules are applied. A larger Union involving a number of new important maritime States will further accentuate the need for a proper implementation of EU rules.

More specifically, the proposed agency will perform a particularly important role in monitoring the functioning of the EU port State control regime and the EU-recognized classification societies. Other tasks include the collection of ship safety related information, the operation of databases, the coordination of EU marine accident investigation procedures, and the organization of training activities for Member State officials.

This measure is essentially of an administrative character. Through its organization, which is modeled on other comparable European agencies, it is designed to serve the interests of both the EU as a whole and the individual Member States. Given its tasks and mandate, it is obvious that the proposed Agency's relationship to Member States' maritime administrations would be of a complementary, rather than of an alternative character. Accordingly, the Agency is not intended to interfere in the decision-making procedures, whether nationally, regionally, or globally.

Liability and Compensation

It was relatively clear from the outset that the *Erika* accident was going to be a very expensive one in terms of the pollution damage it caused. Fears for the insufficiency of the international compensation system in place were, therefore, raised early on, which prompted the Commission to analyze the adequacy of the existing international system for liability and compensation of oil pollution damage in some detail.

The international system for liability and compensation of oil pollution damage caused by tankers consists of a two-tier system based on two international conventions.[14] The first tier, the CLC Convention, provides for strict liability and compulsory insurance for the registered shipowner but, on the other hand, provides a right for the owner, in most cases, to limit this liability to a sum that is related to the size of the ship. If this limited liability is insufficient to cover the costs of the damage caused by an incident, the second tier, the IOPC Fund, which is financed by oil receivers in States Parties, will step in to provide the remaining compensation. The maximum limit of the shipowner's liability is around $80 million for the largest ships while the IOPC Fund's compensation is capped at around $180 million.[15]

The Commission established three criteria against which the adequacy of a liability and compensation system needs to be assessed.

(1) It should provide prompt compensation to victims without having to rely on extensive and lengthy judicial procedures.

(2) The maximum compensation limit should be set at a sufficiently high level to cover claims from any foreseeable disaster occurring as a result of an oil tanker accident.

(3) The regime should contribute to discouraging tanker operators and cargo interests from transporting oil in anything other than tankers of an impeccable quality.

The Commission's assessment, which is described in the "explanatory memorandum" of the proposal, is that the international liability and compensation regime largely satisfies the first assessment criterion but entails important shortcomings as to the two others.

The most important and urgent shortcoming was considered to be that related to the second criterion, that is, the insufficiency of the existing maximum compensation limits. There is thus a real risk of incomplete compensation, even if the validity of the claims has been confirmed. In certain cases, such as the *Erika*, too low limits also produce the effect that the level of compensation of victims is dependent on voluntary undertakings by the government and the oil company concerned. In the view of the Commission, such effects were "unacceptable."

Another consequence of low compensation limits that was underlined by the Commission is the so-called "pro-rating" problem, which may lead to considerable delays in the compensation of victims of accidents that exceed or threaten to exceed the limit. Following from Article 5.4 of the IOPC Fund,[16] only a certain percentage of the eligible compensation can be paid until the final costs of the accident are known, in order for the IOPC Fund to avoid overpayment or unequal treatment of claimants. Given that this prorating procedure has been resorted to relatively frequently and the fact that it may often take several years to establish the final costs of an accident, its detrimental implications for pollution victims are important. The Commission considered that this problem is primarily caused by low overall compensation limits rather than failings in the compensation procedures as such.

As regards the third criterion, the Commission noted that some features of the international regime in place did not represent an appropriate balance between the responsibilities of various players involved in the shipment of oil and their exposure to liability. In particular, shipowners' almost unbreakable right to limit the liability in accordance with Article V.2 of the CLC[17] and the protection of a number of key players from any liability at all[18] were considered to be counterproductive in not providing sufficient incentives for the parties involved to take the necessary precautions to avoid accidents. In addition, the Commission considered that compensation of environmental damage should be scrutinized with a view to widening the available compensation for damage to the environment *per se.*

The international regime prohibits any additional compensation claims to be made outside the convention regime. Accordingly, it is very difficult for individual States or the EU to introduce rules imposing individual liabilities on shipowners or any of the protected parties that go beyond those established in the conventions without being in conflict with international law. In effect, therefore, the Commission's choice was between proposing to build upon the existing regime, despite its perceived shortcomings, or to propose a completely separate liability and compensation system for the EU, involving the denunciation by all Member States of the two international conventions. Because of the various advantages offered by an international system, the Commission opted for the first option. This, however, was subject to some important qualifications. The proposed line of action constitutes a three-step approach for developing the applicable liability and compensation regime.

First, in order to address what was considered to be the most urgent concern, the Commission proposed a five-fold increase of the maximum compensation limits (up to €1 billion, corresponding to some $900 million). The additional funding is raised through the creation of a fund for the compensation of oil pollution damage in European waters, the COPE Fund, which will be financed by oil companies receiving oil in Europe. It is, in many respects, very similar to the existing IOPC Fund, but it will be placed "on top" of that one, as a "third tier," in order to provide compensation to victims in case the international fund's money is not sufficient. The COPE Fund will be based on the same criteria and similar procedures as the existing system, and will base its compensation on the IOPC Fund's claims assessment in order to avoid a duplication of tasks and confusion for victims.

In addition, the proposal also includes the introduction of a financial penalty to be imposed on any party, whether shipowner, charterer, classification society, or anybody else, who has contributed to the oil pollution by his grossly negligent conduct or omissions. This sanction is of a penal nature, hence not related to the compensation of damage, and would cover all oil spill incidents, not only those originating in oil tankers. The underlying idea is to achieve the individual disincentive for various industry players, which is lacking in the COPE fund approach.

Finally, the proposal also lays down the Commission's views as to how the international system should be amended and improved to achieve a better balance between the responsibilities involved in the transport of oil by sea and the exposure to liability. Three concrete amendments to the CLC Convention were proposed:

(1) The liability of the shipowner shall be unlimited if it is proven that the pollution damage resulted from gross negligence on his part;

(2) The prohibition of compensation claims for pollution damage against the charterer, manager and operator of the ship shall be removed from Article III.4(c) of the Liability Convention;

(3) Compensation of damage caused to the environment should be reviewed and widened in light of comparable compensation regimes established under Community law.

Finally, it is stated in the proposal that depending on how the process of amending the international conventions in this sense will succeed, the Commission may return to these issues, perhaps through a proposal for a completely EU-based liability and compensation regime.

Traffic Monitoring, Control, and Information System

The proposed Directive on traffic monitoring introduces a number of measures enabling European coastal States to strengthen the monitoring of ships outside their coasts and their cargoes and reinforces the possibilities and obligations of EU Member States to take action before, during, and after a maritime emergency situation. The measures proposed in the Directive are rather diverse in nature but may be divided into the following three main categories:

1) Simplification of the existing regime for the notification of dangerous goods on board ships bound for EU ports.

2) Establishment of common rules on ship reporting and traffic monitoring in EU waters.

3) Additional measures in respect of environmentally "high risk" ships.

The first category follows from the need to update the so-called "Hazmat" Directive of 1993[19] in light of the experience gained over the years and in light of recent legal and technological developments. The main measures proposed relate to the increased use of electronic data transmission and a greater flexibility for ship operators and shore-based stations as to the format of transmissions. One underlying idea is that once the necessary information on the dangerous goods has been received, it should be shared by all Member States along the ship's route rather than requiring repeated submissions by the ship operator.

The second category deals with the improvement of the monitoring of traffic along the EU coasts. The first type of measures included here builds upon traffic reporting, routing, and VTS systems approved by the IMO. The link to IMO-approved systems is laid down in the provisions of the Directive, and obligations on third States' vessels is made conditional on such international approval, unless the system is within the limits of the territorial sea of the coastal State. The added value of bringing such systems under the auspices of EU law is primarily that a certain standardization of the EU systems can be achieved in this way. Other implications are that the obligations following from such traffic monitoring systems, notably those of Member States having established the systems, will be enforceable under EU law.

Another type of measures under the monitoring heading relates to certain equipment requirements for ships calling at EU ports. More precisely, the proposed Directive provides for automatic identification systems, or "transponders," to be carried on board all vessels bound for EU-ports, according to a certain timetable that corresponds to what has been established internationally.[20] It also provides for the mandatory carriage of voyage data recorders, or "black boxes." Here the Commission's proposal is broader than the international rules, as it extends the obligation to existing cargo ships, on which the IMO's Maritime Safety Committee failed to reach an agreement when adopting the new Regulation 20 of SOLAS Chapter V in December 2000.

The third category of measures consists of various provisions aimed at increasing the monitoring and intervention powers regarding what are considered to be "high-risk" ships. They include obligations on ships' masters to notify incidents and accidents at sea to the authorities of the coastal State, obligations on Member States to take "appropriate measures" in the event of such incidents and accidents, and the remedy to refuse ships carrying dangerous goods to leave the port in very severe weather conditions in case there is a "serious threat of pollution." In addition, the proposed Directive requires Member States to ensure the availability of so-called "ports of refuge" or shelter-areas for ships in distress. Finally, there is an article on the implementation of the Directive, which provides for financial penalties on shipowners, operators, masters, and others who fail to comply with the obligations imposed by the Directive or, in some cases, the withdrawal of the ship's ISM certification.

CONCLUDING REMARKS

It is evident that the European Union's activities in the field of maritime safety have increased substantially during the past decade. As a consequence, the EU institutions, particularly the European Commission, have become increasingly involved in matters relating to the safety at sea and ship-source pollution. This trend has been continuous ever since the formulation of an EU-wide policy in this field through the adoption and approval of "A Common Policy on Safe Seas" in 1993.

The *Erika* accident signified a considerable leap forward in this continuous process, by more or less directly giving rise to six new legislative proposals, most of which relate to key issues in maritime regulation. To some extent, the two "Erika packages," as proposed by the Commission, may be seen as representing a shift in focus of the EU maritime policy. While the proposed measures still build on the four "pillars" outlined in 1993, some of the proposals signify a more independent approach in relation to the international regulatory regime. Apart from seeking to ensure the adequate *implementation* of the international rules, which still underlies the gist of the proposed measures, some of the proposals actually seek to *improve* the international rules where the prevailing regime is considered to provide insufficient protection. This is particularly evident in the proposal for the accelerated phasing-out of single-hulled oil tankers and the proposal to establish the COPE Fund. Many aspects of the Erika proposals moreover address issues that have so far remained outside the scope of EU-regulation, thereby widening the range of measures considered to be of a "Community-interest." This expansion is particularly notable in the area of civil liability and compensation of damage.[21]

Strictly speaking, however, any appraisal of the Erika proposals needs to be cautious, given that the proposals reflect the aims and ambitions of the European Commission, rather than those of the European Union as such. It should be borne in mind that at the time of writing (March 2001), none of the proposed measures have been formally adopted, though several look set to be adopted within the near future. Whether the same significance of the *Erika* accident will pertain for the policy of the EU as a whole remains to be seen and will depend on if and when the proposed measures are finally adopted.

It may still be too early to predict the details of how the six Erika proposals will finally be reflected in terms of changes to EU law. Generally, however, Commission proposals in the area of maritime safety have tended to be adopted, albeit in a more or less modified form.[22] Based on the discussions within the EU so far, this seems to be the case for most of the Erika proposals as well. On the amendments to the classification society and port State control Directives, there is already a substantial agreement on the key points between the EU co-legislators, the European Parliament, and the Council of Ministers. As to the accelerated phasing-out of single-hulled oil tankers, the EU governments decided to bring the issue forward within the international framework before continuing the discussions within the EU. Even in this area, however, results may be expected shortly, as the IMO looks set to adopt the proposed measures. If it fails to do so, the Council has committed itself to proceed with the adoption of a European measure, the essence of which is already agreed.[23]

The discussions on the second set of measures are less advanced. However, at a political level there seems to be considerable understanding within the EU institutions for the need to improve the vessel traffic monitoring and control regime in EU waters and for the usefulness of establishing a maritime safety agency. While a number of amendments to the Commission's proposals may be expected, there seems to be no immediate reason to doubt the eventual adoption of these two measures. The necessity of significant improvements to the compensation regime is equally recognized, notably as regards raising the maximum level of cover, but whether the required action should be taken at EU-level or internationally within the framework of the existing

IMO/IOPC Fund regime is still subject to debate. In this respect, the IOPC Fund has recently established a working group to consider revisions to the existing liability and compensation system. The creation of an optional supplementary third tier fund, which in essence would be an international version of the proposed COPE Fund, has emerged as one of the key items for discussion.[24]

It thus seems that the EU is prepared to go ahead in one form or another with all six of the Erika proposals. In light of the implications of the measures at issue, that in itself may be considered to be noteworthy. It is probably fair to say that the *Erika* accident and the problems it has highlighted have served to underline the benefits of a common EU-based approach to maritime safety as opposed to national solutions. Perhaps the most significant indication of such a common approach is the endorsement, in principle, of the setting up of a new institution, an agency, for ensuring the uniform implementation of international and European maritime safety rules in all fifteen Member States.

It appears, however, that the readiness of the EU legislators, in particular of the Council, to go ahead with EU proposals depends to a large extent on the relationship of the measure to the international regulatory regime. Adopting measures that concern the implementation of applicable international or EU commitments is significantly less problematic than finding an agreement on measures that depart from the general regulatory regime, or seek to "improve" the international rules at the EU level.[25] There is still considerable hesitation among the EU governments to take "unilateral" EU-wide action by adopting rules that differ from those applicable worldwide. This applies for subject matters where there are easily understood advantages with global rules, such as requirements on ships' design and construction, as well as for matters where such benefits are less self-evident, such as in the field of compensation of pollution damage.

On the other hand, in the deliberations of the Erika proposals, the EU institutions have on several occasions signaled their independence vis-à-vis the international regulatory bodies by showing preparedness to take the necessary action at EU-level, should the international regime fail to produce satisfactory results. Significantly, the Council has been prepared to resort to this line of action even in matters that relate to substantial aspects of the construction and equipment of ships and, thus, are of major relevance for the regulatory regime of maritime transport as a whole.[26] Such a preparedness is noteworthy, as agreeing on elements of a "fall-back position" in the form of EU legislation in advance of the relevant international negotiations indicates an altered, more autonomous approach of the EU Member States in relation to the international community. Inevitably such an approach also increases the pressure for the international community to reach an agreement that principally corresponds to the EU policy in order to avoid a fragmentation of maritime regulation.

One of the dilemmas facing the EU Member States in maritime regulation is the need to strike a balance between the often unquestionable benefits of coordinated and common EU approaches in this field and the ensuing restraints on the national freedom of choice that common EU-policies inevitably entail. So far, the outcome of such strains has been a continuous expansion of the scope of EU legislation. Since the inception of the EU maritime policy, all such changes have unfailingly been "coastal" rather than "maritime" in nature, in that they have been aimed at increasing the protection of people and coastlines rather than at safeguarding navigational freedoms.

The *Erika* accident and its follow-up measures have certainly strengthened these tendencies. It is evident that the process of gradually creating a comprehensive EU maritime safety policy has been considerably accelerated over the past year. At the moment there are few indications of a reversal of that trend. Rather, to the contrary, it would seem that an ever-broader range of issues considered to be of "Community interest," increased influence and legislative powers of the European Parliament and the (potential) establishment of a European Maritime Safety Agency, are important indications of a continued expanding role of the EU in the development and enforcement of rules on maritime safety and environmental protection.

Notes

[1] The European Commission is a key institution within the EU, being at the same time the only body with a full and unconditional right of legal initiative and the "guardian of the Treaty," responsible for monitoring the proper implementation of EU law in the fifteen Member States. In the field of transport safety, as in most other areas of the EU's activities, the regulatory process starts with a proposal from the Commission. This proposal, normally for a Regulation or a Directive, will be discussed by the European Parliament and the Council of Ministers, the latter representing the governments of all fifteen Member States. The act is not adopted until the Parliament and Council find an agreement on the text.

Despite some earlier efforts by the Commission to propose Community-wide measures in the area of maritime safety in the late 1970s, it was not until 1993 that the EU established a comprehensive maritime safety policy. The Commission's Communication "A Common Policy for Safe Seas" (COM[93]66 Final, 24 February 1993) marked the point of departure for this policy by outlining the four cornerstones, or "pillars," of the EU maritime safety policy, largely based on the need for convergent implementation of the international rules, and by presenting an ambitious action plan for the ten years to follow. The principles of this policy were endorsed by the Council in Council Resolution of 8 June 1993 on a Common Policy for Safe Seas (Official Journal of the European Communities [OJ] 1993, C 271).

The action plan of 1993 has now been largely implemented. The EU measures in force already encompass some twenty legal instruments covering matters such as classification societies, port State control, passenger and fishing vessel safety, the so-called "human element," obligations to use and provide waste reception facilities in ports, and a number of other issues. For more details, see J. de Dieu, "EU Policies Concerning Ship Safety and Pollution Prevention Versus International Rule-Making," in H. Ringbom, ed., *Competing Norms in the Law of Marine Environmental Protection—Focus on Ship Safety and Pollution Prevention* (Kluwer Law International, 1997).

[2] Following the *Erika* accident and, in particular, during the French Presidency of the European Union in the latter half of the year 2000, maritime safety issues were frequently discussed at an exceptionally high political level. This was the case at the meetings of EU Heads of States in Biarritz in October and in Nice in December (see, for example, paragraphs 41-43 of the Presidency's conclusions of the Nice Summit at <http://ue.eu.int/en/Info/eurocouncil/index.htm>) and during the G8 Summit in Okinawa in July 2000 (see, for example, paragraphs 69 and 70 of the G8 Communiqué of 23 July 2000, available at, for example, <http://www.g7.utoronto.ca/g7/summit/2000okinawa/finalcom.htm>).

[3] For more detailed information on the *Erika* accident, see, for example, the French and Maltese accident investigation reports at <http://www.mareenoire.com/erika/ rapport_detail.asp> and <http://www.keskom.co.uk/Erika.pdf >.

[4] COM (2000)142 final, 21.3.2000.

[5] Council Directive 94/57/EC of 22 November 1994 on common rules and standards for ship inspection and survey organizations and for the relevant activities of maritime administrations. OJ 1994, L 319. The minimum criteria to be met by recognized societies, listed in the Annex of the Directive, include both quantitative and qualitative requirements.

[6] The proposed revision of article 6 of the Directive provides for unlimited liability for the classification societies where the loss or damage is caused by willful acts or omissions or gross negligence of the classification society, and a financially limited liability for negligence or recklessness. While the European Parliament has endorsed this approach, the Council has considered that the liability of the societies should be potentially unlimited even in the latter case. See the First Reading Report of the European Parliament PE R5-0534/2000 of 30 November 2000 and the Council's Common Position No. 14/2001 of 26 February 2001, OJ 2001, C 101, 1.

[7] Council Directive 95/21/EC of June 1995, concerning the enforcement, in respect of shipping using Community ports and sailing in the waters under the jurisdiction of the Member States, of international standards for ship safety, pollution prevention, and shipboard living conditions (port State control) (OJ 1995, L 157, 1), as amended by Council Directive 98/25/EC (OJ 1998, L 133, 19), Commission Directive 98/42/EC (OJ 1998, L 184, 40), Commission Directive 1999/97/EC (OJ 1999, L 331, 67).

[8] See, in particular, article 7 of the proposal. However, the article has been subject to some considerable amendments, in particular during the Council discussions. See Common Position No. 15/2001 of 26 February 2001, OJ 2001, C 101, 15. For the European Parliament's first reading report, see Doc. PE R5-0343/2000 of 30 November 2000.

[9] The proposed article 7a includes criteria, such as the age of the ship, its detention record in the EU over the preceding twenty-four months, and the average detention rate of the flag State. The Commission will publish a list of such banned ships every six month. A procedure is laid down in article 11.6 by which the "ban" of a ship may be lifted, following a thorough inspection of the ship at the request of the shipowner.

[10] Despite its importance for the whole nature of the regulatory regime of shipping, the question of jurisdictional rights of port States to legislate for matters that are already subject to international regulation has received relatively little attention in the legal literature. For a recent and comprehensive

analysis, see E. J. Molenaar: *Coastal State Jurisdiction over Vessel-Source Pollution* (Kluwer Law International, 1998), 110-117.

[11] See IMO Document MEPC/45/WP.5 and the article by Mr. J. Angelo in this volume, pp. 309-317.

[12] See note 23 below.

[13] COM (2000) 802 Final, 6 December 2000.

[14] The 1969 International Convention on Civil Liability for Oil Pollution (CLC) and the 1971 International Convention setting up the Oil Pollution Compensation Fund (Fund Convention), as amended by the 1992 Protocols to them.

[15] For more details, see, for example, the Annual Report of the International Oil Pollution Compensation Fund, available at <http://www.iopcfund.org/ eng2000ar.pdf >.

[16] Article 4.5 of the Fund Convention reads:

> Where the amount of established claims against the Fund exceeds the aggregate amount of compensation payable . . . , the amount available shall be distributed in such a manner that the proportion between any established claim and the amount of compensation actually recovered by the claimant under this Convention shall be the same for all claimants.

[17] Article V.2 of the CLC provides that:

> The owner shall not be entitled to limit his liability under this Convention if it is proved that the pollution damage resulted from his personal act or omission, committed with the intent to cause such damage, or recklessly and with knowledge that such damage would probably result.

[18] Article III.4 of the CLC reads:

> No claim for compensation for pollution damage may be made against the owner otherwise than in accordance with this Convention. Subject to paragraph 5 of this Article, no claim for compensation for pollution damage under this Convention or otherwise may be made against:
>
> (a) the servants or agents of the owner or the members of the crew;
> (b) the pilot or any other person who, without being a member of the crew, performs services for the ship;

(c) any charterer (howsoever described, including a bareboat charterer), manager or operator of the ship;

(d) any person performing salvage operations with the consent of the owner or on the instructions of a competent public authority;

(e) any person taking preventive measures; and

(f) all servants or agents of persons mentioned in subparagraphs (c), (d) and (e); unless the damage resulted from their personal act or omission, committed with the intent to cause such damage, or recklessly and with knowledge that such damage would probably result.

[19] Council Directive 93/75/EEC of 13 September 1993 concerning minimum requirements for vessels bound for or leaving Community ports and carrying dangerous or polluting goods (OJ 1993, L 247, 19). This Directive requires all ships bound for Community ports to make advance notification of dangerous goods on board the ship, a principal aim being that authorities have such information readily available in the case of accidents.

[20] The EU timetable is laid down in Annex II-I of the Directive, while the most recent internationally agreed rules, the Regulations of SOLAS chapter V, are to be found in IMO Doc. MSC 73/21/Add.2.

[21] There are signs that this subject will continue to remain of interest to the Commission. With regard to other forms of liability than oil pollution, the Commission has pointed at the "highly unsatisfactory" situation as regards the absence of any regime in force for liability and compensation for hazardous and noxious substances other than oil (COM[2000]802 Final, 62), while a new proposal for a Directive on shipowners' liability vis-à-vis passengers is included in the Commission's work program for the year 2001 (COM[2001]28 Final, Annex 1, item 2001/190).

[22] Of the twenty or so proposals made by the Commission up to 1999, only one has failed to be adopted. See J. de Dieu, *supra* note 1, 160. Generally speaking, the Council has tended to somewhat "reduce" the level of ambition of the Commission's proposals. In this respect, it is worth noting that following the entry into force of the Amsterdam Treaty (revising the Treaty establishing European Community) in 1999, maritime safety rules are adopted by the so-called co-decision procedures, giving equal powers to the Council and the European Parliament (see article 251 of the Treaty, OJ 1997, C 340). This may have significant effects, as the European Parliament normally tends to be prepared to go further than the Commission proposals. See also the Cadwallader Annual Memorial Lecture of 2000 by Mrs. Georgette Lalis, the European

Commission's Director for Maritime Transport, published in the *Lloyd's List Newspaper* (18 September 2000): 8.

[23] At the Transport Council meeting on October 2, 2000, the EU ministers agreed on a "common approach" to the accelerated introduction of double-hulled tankers, to be defended in the IMO discussions the same month. (See Press Release No. 11711/00 [Presse 347] of 2 October 2000.) At the following meeting on December 20, the Council undertook to adopt by June 2001 a common position incorporating that approach, should the IMO during its April meeting fail to reach agreement including the "essential points" of the common approach (Press Release 14004/00 [Presse 470] 20 December 2000).

[24] See in particular IOPC Doc. 92FUND/WG.3/6.

[25] It should be noted, however, that there are some EU measures that involve some reinforcements of the international rules in the form of additional regulatory requirements for ships bound for EU ports. See, in particular, Council Regulation 3051/95/EC (introducing an earlier date for the implementation of the International Safety Management Code in the EU than what was required internationally, OJ 1995, L 320, 14) and Council Directive 94/58/EC (imposing some additional operational requirements on crews on board oil tankers, OJ 1994, L 319, 24). See also H. Ringbom: "Preventing Pollution from Ships—Reflections on the 'Adequacy' of Existing Rules," in *Review of European Community and International Environmental Law*, no. 1 (Blackwell Publishers Ltd., 1999), 21-28.

[26] See *supra* note 23. Apart from the phasing-out of single-hulled tankers, the Council, at its meeting on December 20, 2000, also agreed on a similar approach for the retrofitting of voyage data recorders (VDRs or maritime "black boxes") for cargo ships, on which the IMO had failed to reach agreement some months earlier. The Council agreed that VDRs:

> should be made mandatory within five years for cargo ships built before 1 July 2002 calling at Community ports. [The Council] encourages Member States to continue their effort in the IMO framework to achieve this end and agrees, if this is not possible, to legislate at Community level (Press Release 14004/00 [Presse 470] 20 December 2000).

The issue of mandatory introduction of VDRs has been of particular importance to the European Parliament. See Doc. PE R5-0343/2000 of 30 November 2000.

INSURER AND CLASS AND MARINE ACCIDENTS

Hans G. Payer*

> The fundamental problem with class societies and with P&I clubs is that the good owners, who are invited on to the committees of such organisations in a gesture towards an attempt to oversee and regulate them, are genuinely ignorant of what the bad owners are capable of.

This was stated by Andrew Craig-Bennett in *Lloyd's List* a few years ago. Although I do not agree with some of the other statements he has published about class, what he says here is correct.

Shipping is an industry where public and political interest and accountability have sharply increased in recent years, despite the continuous progress made by the partners involved with ship safety. The world fleet continues to grow and is getting more complex. Accidents have, however, as short-term statistics show, decreased. Nevertheless, this is not a call for complacency. Each accident, every life lost at sea, every case of pollution of the environment is one too many. This was dramatically demonstrated with the ERIKA accident, the 30,000 dwt tanker that broke in two and sank off the Atlantic coast of France on December 12, 1999. We have to continue to find ways to further reduce risks and improve quality and safety in shipping.

In some ways, insurers and class are sitting in the same boat. I also assume that we both are trying to do everything within our possibilities to improve ship safety and reduce the risks involved with shipping. Or are we?

Sometimes we from class have the impression that we do not get sufficient support from the insurers. It would seem so logical, that the two of us work closely together: Class looks after the ships and the risks involved, and the insurer gives benefits to those owners

---

* Executive Board, Germanischer Lloyd, and Past-Chairman of the International Association of Classification Societies.

M.H. Nordquist and J.N. Moore (eds.),
Current Marine Environmental Issues and the International Tribunal for the Law of the Sea, 291–299.
© 2001 *Kluwer Law International. Printed in the Netherlands.*

who do more than the minimum and severely punish those few black sheep who try to cut corners, evade requirements, and, therefore, pose a highly elevated risk. But reality is quite different.

Let us look at the situation a bit closer. After addressing the situation of the Classification Societies, we will discuss the relation between class and insurer and see whether we can find ways for improvement in our cooperation.

SHIP CLASSIFICATION AND SOLAS

Since the start of IACS—The International Association of Ship Classification Societies—thirty-three years ago, the maritime industry spent much effort battling excessive competition in the world shipping market resulting from continuous over-capacity. At the same time, there was a general shift from traditional company fleets managed with pride in the quality of their fleet and its operation to a more fragmented state, with far less personal ties of owners or operators to their ships. This was the arena where substandard ships could develop and, in fact, operate at a commercial advantage by cutting corners regarding maintenance, evading regulations, and avoiding new investments.

This situation placed increasing demand on the technical skills, knowledge, and experience available in the class societies. The unique level of know-how in IACS and its member class societies, and the resulting contributions it could make to the industry regarding safety and rules was recognized by IMO—the International Maritime Organization—which gave IACS consultative status within the first year of its existence in 1969. Even today, IACS remains the only non-governmental organization with this status that is able to develop and apply structural rules. IACS is also cooperating closely with IMO regarding MARPOL, the International Convention for the Prevention of Pollution from Ships, through MEPC, IMO's Marine Environmental Protection Committee. Many of the specialists from IACS working groups are also participating in the work-teams of the relevant IMO Committees.

The key influencers for safer shipping—shipowners and their associations, the IMO, flag states, and port states as well as the insurer—each respect class rules for structural design and essential engineering systems as the technical foundation for a safer world fleet. Recognizing this central role of class, the July 1, 1998, revision to SOLAS 74 on "Recognised Organisations" requires that:

> ships be designed, constructed and maintained in compliance
> with the structural, mechanical and electrical requirements of
> a classification society, recognised by the Administration, or
> with applicable national standards of the Administration
> which provide an equivalent level of safety.

This is a precondition for meeting other SOLAS safety standards for new ships. In turn, compliance with IMO Conventions is the basis of the ISM Code—the yardstick of international shipping safety for both Flag State and Port State Control regimes.

CLASS AND THE MARINE INDUSTRY

Today's marine industry, its technology, and its challenges are dramatically different from 1968, when IACS was formally created. Since then class, too, has changed. There was a time of crisis in the late eighties and early nineties, where suspicion came up that due to excessive competition between class societies, the quality standards for ship new-buildings as well as ships in operation did deteriorate to some degree.

With the introduction of new and much more detailed analysis methods in the seventies, such as the finite element method, the evaluation of ships, new and in service, has been moved from the largely empirical to a more rational approach. This has made classification societies bolder, with structural optimization of new-buildings—leading to minimum scantlings—but also regarding the judgment on older ships. Whoever was more advanced with these new methods bragged about it. Competition developed on minimum scantlings and requirements: "Come to us and your ship will be

293

lighter." This has undoubtedly resulted in a certain mistrust towards class, also from the side of the insurers, as well as between safety partners in shipping generally. It was suspected that there was a conflict of interest with class developing the very rules they then apply within a competitive environment.

Our rules cover all aspects of the ship hardware, structures and strength, machinery, electrical equipment, safety equipment and devices, automation, etc. Class is the best and only institution to develop and upkeep these rules. Class has the specialists, and class gathers the most extensive experience from surveys of their fleet of ships of all type throughout their life span. Today there is increased exchange of this experience within IACS and rules are becoming more harmonized. Therefore, it is not possible for one society to try to attract business by making softer (money-saving) rules.

A ship tends to require more maintenance and repairs as it gets older. If the necessary maintenance is not performed or neglected, the ship becomes substandard and this can happen very quickly. Although significant progress has been made in improving safety and quality standards at sea, there are still too many substandard ships operating even today. A ship is substandard when it does not meet the minimum prescribed and commonly accepted standards and requirements from IMO, IACS, and others. Here class plays an important role. It is, however, a fact that a ship that passed the last annual class survey on the assumption of normal maintenance, can deteriorate dramatically if maintenance is neglected. Additionally, owners have in the past, when they did not like the requirements and recommendations for their ship expressed by the surveyor of their class, changed to a different class.

The IACS Transfer of Class Agreement (TOCA) stopped this practice of what is called class-hopping. Today, a new class can not accept a ship before all the requirements from the previous class have been met and surveyed. Older ships can be accepted by an IACS class only after this society has assured itself of the condition of the vessel by a special survey.

SUBSTANDARD SHIPS AND THE ROLE OF CLASS

For a conference on Quality Shipping in Singapore in the spring of 2000, Michael Grey stated in *Lloyd's List*:

> Substandard shipping, like the common cold, is a universal complaint, and may be encountered in any maritime region. It is difficult to eradicate, with its symptoms found in a minority of ships, seafarers and operators. If there is greater stress on quality shipping then half the battle to eliminate substandard elements of shipping is won.

Classification Societies have come under considerable pressure with each spectacular accident in recent years. This has two aspects. One aspect is that IACS and the member class societies have not yet been successful in getting rid completely of high risk substandard ships. The other aspect is that tolerance for accidents by the public has generally sharply decreased. Everyone—including politicians—is looking at class to handle the situation. This falls together with a basic change of classification societies from a more bureaucratic/administrative role to a service-oriented, business partner role.

Are most substandard ships attended by non-IACS class societies? I would guess that non-IACS societies probably have a higher percentage of substandard ships in their class than IACS member societies. With the increasing pressure on such ships within IACS, this percentage may further increase. But we have to remind ourselves that, altogether, only about five to eight percent of the world's tonnage is outside IACS. So it makes a lot of difference if IACS is successful with their fight against substandard ships or not. During the past three or four years, IACS has closely looked at how to handle the evasive owner and how to reduce risks particularly with older ships. And IACS has made decisions that will be felt.

The enhanced surveys for older ships, the strengthening of the special surveys by prescribing at least two class surveyors in order to see more, but mainly to be able to better resist pressure from the owner's superintendent, together with the tightened Transfer of Class Agreement within IACS, will make a lot of difference in this respect.

Who is mainly to blame for substandard shipping—the class or the substandard owner, the substandard charterers, or the insurer? Class has limited possibilities for policing. Class can refuse to issue or can withdraw a certificate. But class attends the ships only on a set schedule, with class renewal after five years and only limited inspections at the annual surveys. This schedule is based on the assumption of normal maintenance and conscientious repair. The typical substandard owner will, however, save on maintenance and repair. The ship can deteriorate very quickly, within a period of months, and the risk of something serious going wrong rises sharply.

Class has very limited possibilities to give economic incentives to encourage quality shipping. This is where we need the cooperation with our other partners, particularly the insurers.

HOW CAN INSURER AND CLASS COOPERATE IN THE FIGHT AGAINST SUBSTANDARD SHIPS?

Behind every substandard ship, it is likely that there is not only a substandard owner, substandard operator, and substandard charterer, but also an insurer who may not be too fussy about what he has insured. There may be bankers involved who may not have taken the trouble to examine what they are financing, and there may be others who willingly or unwillingly support a low-grade, high risk operation of a vessel.

Looking at the total cost of marine incidents, however, the insurers must be interested in reducing the risks in shipping: At a Mare Forum Conference 99 in Amsterdam, research results from the marine insurance sector were quoted, putting the annual worldwide cost of vessel incidents between U.S. \$3.6 and \$6 billion. Many, if not most, of these accidents and incidents are avoidable.

The insurer often says that he fully relies on class. But does he care about which society the ship is classed with? Does he make a difference between a ship classed by an IACS class or not? Does he look at the performance of the different classification societies? Does he ask the class for a differentiation on the risk involved with a particular ship? Is there enough technical expertise in the insurance industry? How will the insurance companies ever respond to quality shipping companies? Perhaps the quality owner has tried in some cases and has not received a helpful answer.

Class and the insurers have to talk with each other more openly and constructively. What can class offer the insurer? I would like to mention a few aspects for better cooperation in the future.

Risk assessment. Class has the technical know-how and the necessary information to make a risk assessment of a vessel. This may appear strange, as we usually issue class certificates like 100A5, meaning full (100%) fulfilment of the class requirements for a class period of five years. But there are differences. One ship may just barely fulfil these requirements and another one, the quality ship from a quality owner, may be way beyond these minimum requirements. The insurer should know this and give credit to the owner. The class can assist him in this.

Regulatory evasion, where the evader is able to avoid regulatory scrutiny, saves increasing amounts of money that the quality operator is forced to spend in order to remain fully compliant. This has to be changed, and we all can help to do this.

I believe that class and insurer together can make a lot of difference regarding quality in shipping. Together we need to set up incentives. In this we can follow a stick and carrot philosophy. This would offer a number of attractions to the good owner and operator. The majority of good practitioners are forced to bear much of the regulatory burden that is imposed because of the minority of poor performers. As incentive: the high quality owners and operators should be trusted to undertake parts of their own supervisions, inspections, and surveys, leaving the regulators to concentrate on eliminating the substandard and policing those that need policing.

This could be one of the carrots: More self-regulation for the good owner leading to less frequent inspections. This could mean savings in time and cost for the quality ship.

Today we are at a time of transition from the prescriptive rules and regulations common in the past to a more self-regulatory and self-responsible attitude and culture being developed and implemented by those seriously interested in quality shipping for the future. Class today sees itself at the heart of modern industry self-regulation, and IACS is a driving force behind this move. We have experience, and we can make progress with the assistance of our partners, particularly the insurer.

What could be a stick? Apart from the evaluation of a ship by the class, a rating system could be introduced. This could, for instance, be based on port state control statistics and other factors. Lower ratings would call for higher fees for class services, or for their insurance. With this (additional) possibility—if we from class may suggest—the insurer could set insurance premiums with differentiation according to a bonus and malus system.

And finally, what can the insurer offer to class? Insurance companies can assist us in our fight against substandard ships. You can assist us by supporting class with some policing power. Refuse insurance to the evasive, non-cooperative owner. I believe there are many ways where insurer and class together could make a lot of progress.

CONCLUSION

There is no viable alternative to IACS and the class system. It has become somewhat fashionable to kick IACS and class. The industry, including insurers and the press, could, however, contribute to improvements in ship safety by declining to blame and tarnish classification societies and IACS, and instead by supporting them. IACS is moving in the right direction, so "never kick a willing horse!"

Class is only one link in the maritime safety chain. We can work constructively together. This applies particularly to the relation between class and the insurer. Originally class was created to provide a technical basis for insuring a ship. Basically this is so even today, although our world has become much more complex. This complexity has led to a lack of communication. We no longer simply meet at the Lloyd's Cafe in London's City. Therefore, our activities, the activities of the insurers and the class, run parallel, sometimes even in opposing directions. We can assist each other in our goals. We can do more together. Let's do it.

PANEL VI

Maritime Transport

INTRODUCTION TO MARITIME TRANSPORT

Barbara S. Moore[*]

Good morning and welcome to the panel on marine transportation. It is my pleasure to be here today and to be chairing this session. I always enjoy participating in discussions on ocean law, though I tend to view the discussions from a perspective different from many of the participants. I have had the honor of being invited to many of the Center's conferences for two reasons—one, as the wife of the Director of the organization that sponsors the meetings, I come as part of a packaged deal with my husband; and second, with my background in science rather than law, I tend to view ocean issues through a different set of lenses and am frequently asked to add these views.

I think you will agree that we have an interesting set of presentations on this panel, covering a variety of issues in marine transportation. As we start, I would like to offer a few comments.

When I think of marine transportation, one of the first things I think about is the transport of oil, which leads me to thinking about oil spills. A number of years ago, I worked in the areas of oil spills and pollution to the marine environment. Since I have not been active in this field for some time, I thought it might be interesting to go back and look at the data to see what has happened in the years since I lost touch.

Being someone who understands information better in the form of pictures, I couldn't resist preparing a few slides to present this data in graphical form. Fortunately, the Canadian government, through Environment Canada, maintains an excellent database on oil spills from vessels. Using their information for the past twenty-three years from the Worldwide Tanker Spill Database, the following charts have been developed.

---

[*] Director, National Undersea Research Program, National Oceanic and Atmospheric Administration (NOAA).

M.H. Nordquist and J.N. Moore (eds.),
Current Marine Environmental Issues and the International Tribunal for the Law of the Sea, 303–307.
© 2001 *Kluwer Law International. Printed in the Netherlands.*

Figure 1[1] shows the number of accidental tanker oil spills per year (greater than one thousand barrels) from 1974 to 1997. The figures show a dramatic decrease from an average of about fifty-five per year in 1974 to twelve to fourteen per year in 1997.

Figure 2[2] shows the volume of these spills, which has also shown a general decrease except for a few unusual years.

1978 shows a spike because of the spill from the famous Amoco Cadiz off the Brittany coast of France. This was one of the largest tanker spills in history.

Figure 3[3] lists the largest oil spills in history from a different database (International Oil Spill Statistics, 1997). It includes spills that occurred on land as well as spills that were not accidental (acts of terrorism). The largest spill in history resulted from the intentional destruction of oil wells by Iraqi forces at the end of the Persian Gulf War. Second and third largest were accidental oil well blowouts in the Gulf of Mexico and in Uzbekistan. The largest oil spill from a tanker, the Amoco Cadiz ranks as sixth largest spill, and the much-publicized Exxon Valdez spill in 1989 ranks as thirty-eighth.

Figure 4[4] shows a graphical comparison of the spills resulting from acts of terrorism in Kuwait as compared with the largest tanker spill in history and the total combined volume of spills from all tankers.

Notes

1

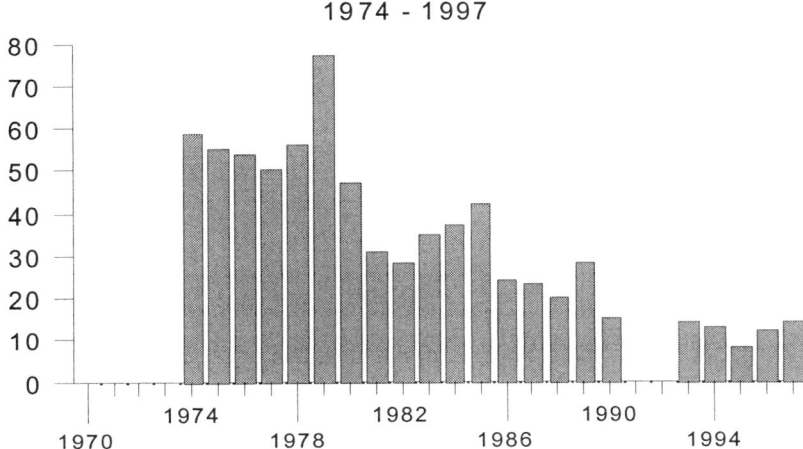

Number of Oil Spills from Vessels
1974 - 1997

2

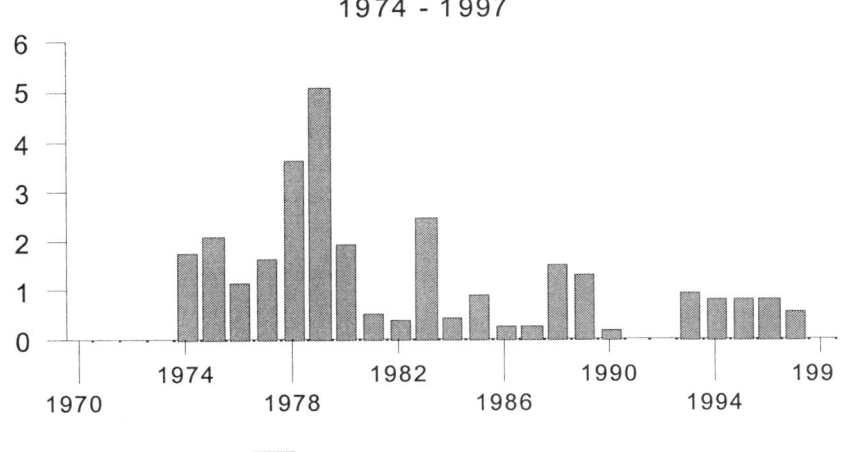

Volume of Oil Spilled by Vessels
1974 - 1997

Million Barrels Oil

3

Oil Spilled
Comparison by Source 1974 - 1997

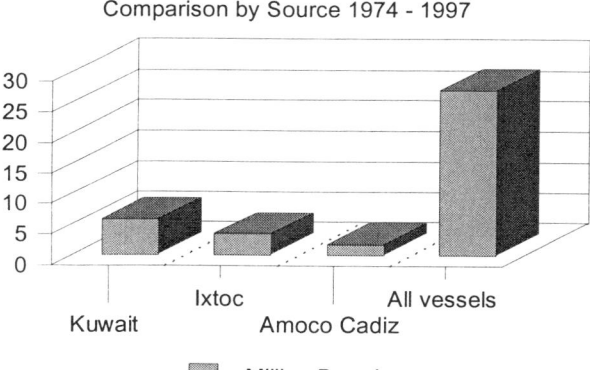

Million Barrels

4

Largest Oil Spills Worldwide

(Excerpted from International Oil Spill Statistics, 1997)

Rank	Incident	Millions of Gallons	Millions of Barrels
1	26 January 1991; terminals, tankers; 8 sources total *Sea Island installations; Kuwait;* off coast in Persian Gulf and in Saudi Arabia	240.0	5.71
2	03 June 1979; exploratory well *Ixtoc I well; Mexico*; Gulf of Mexico, Bahia Del Campeche, 80 km NW of Ciudad del Carmen, Campeche	140.0	3.33
3	02 March 1992; oil well; Uzbekistan; Fergana Valley	88.0	2.1
4	04 February 1983; platform No. 3 well (Nowruz); Iran; Persian Gulf, Nowruz Field	80.0	1.9
5	06 August 1983; tanker Castillo de Bellver; South Africa; Atlantic Ocean, 64 km off Table Bay	78.5	1.87
6	16 March 1978; tanker *Amoco Cadiz; France*; Atlantic Ocean, off Portsall, Brittany	68.7	1.62
7	10 November 1988; tanker Odyssey; Canada; North Atlantic Ocean, 1,175 km NE of Saint John's, Newfoundland	43.1	1.02
8	19 July 1979; tanker *Atlantic Empress; Trinidad and Tobago*; Caribbean Sea, 32 km northeast of Trinidad-Tobago	42.7[1]	1.02

9	01 August 1980; production well D-103 concession well; 800 km southeast of Tripoli, Libya	42.0	1.0
10	11 April 1991; tanker Haven; Italy; Mediterranean Sea, port of Genoa	42.0	1.0
11	02 August 1979; tanker *Atlantic Empress; 450 km east of Barbados*	41.5[1]	.99
12	18 March 1967; tanker *Torrey Canyon; United Kingdom*; Lands End	38.2	.91

307

ERIKA AFTERMATH: DEVELOPMENTS AT IMO ON DOUBLE HULLS (A U.S. PERSPECTIVE)

*Joseph Angelo**

On behalf of the U.S. Coast Guard, I would like to thank the Center for Oceans Law and Policy for inviting us to participate in this conference. I called up Myron and asked him what he wanted me to speak on. He said it was up to my discretion, so I thought I'd talk about the Erika aftermath, not realizing that it would fit in so nicely with the information Mr. Ringbom has just provided for us.

My presentation focuses on what Mr. Ringbom has identified as, and I think we all agree, the most controversial aspect of what has come out of the Erika, and that is the phasing out of single hull tankers with the requirement for double hull tankers. This is significant because it directly impacts the world's oil supplies. It could impact each of us here, depending on what happens.

This presentation gives you two perspectives. The first perspective addresses what is happening at the International Maritime Organization (IMO) in the development of negotiating new requirements for phasing out the single hull tankers. The second perspective addresses what is happening relative to what the U.S. interests are in these issues. As Mr. Ringbom has pointed out, we have the Oil Pollution Act of 1990 that has different implementation dates for double hulls, and the United States is the only country in the world that is not party to the double hull standards agreed upon internationally.

As we know, the Erika is a relatively small tanker that was built in 1975. It broke in two off the coast of Brittany back in December of 1999. More than 10,000 tons of oil spilled into the water off the coast of Brittany. This was a minor spill, relatively speaking, when compared to all of the other spills that have

---

* Director of Standards, U.S. Coast Guard; and Head, U.S. Delegation to the Marine Environmental Protection Committee of the International Maritime Organization.

M.H. Nordquist and J.N. Moore (eds.),
Current Marine Environmental Issues and the International Tribunal for the Law of the Sea, 309–317.
© 2001 *Kluwer Law International. Printed in the Netherlands.*

occurred around the world. However, because of the political concern over this, it potentially has the biggest impact the world could face relative to oil supplies.

The European Union (EU) did, in fact, have their Erika 1 and Erika 2 initiatives to prevent future occurrences. As we have heard, Erika 1 focused on phasing out single hull tankers. But rather than go unilateral within the EU, the decision was made to bring the proposal to IMO first. So the French, cosponsored with Germany and Belgium, submitted a proposal for accelerating the phase out of single hull tankers.

As soon as that was put on the table, a number of alternative proposals were also put forward by several countries and international organizations, each feeling that theirs was a better solution to address this issue. Also of significance was that the Secretary General of IMO, Mr. Bill O'Neil, feeling very strongly that he wanted IMO to take action as opposed to the EU taking unilateral action, initiated a study to be conducted by the industry under his leadership to provide technical data relative to the impacts of what was included in the French proposal.

What is so significant is that when the French put their proposal on the table at IMO, they basically brought into play two major issues. The first is the effectiveness of IMO. If the IMO could not or cannot reach a solution on this issue, then, of course, the EU will go ahead and do its own thing unilaterally. If they do, that will significantly weaken IMO in establishing international standards. In the future, other countries that have major incidents will say, "Look, the French attempted to reach a solution at IMO. They were not able to. Why should we?" And it could bring about unilateral action around the world. This is something that we would not like to see. I know that I would, speaking somewhat tongue in cheek, because of OPA90. But it's still true that we would prefer not to see unilateral action in regulating international shipping.

The second issue, which is perhaps the most significant, is the impact the accelerated phase out of single hull tankers will have on the delivery of the world's oil supplies. This is very significant, as you'll see when we get to the various proposals.

At its meeting last year, the IMO had a number of different proposals to deal with in trying to reach a solution in a one-week time period. What ended up happening was that the Denmark-United Kingdom-Netherlands proposal was considered to be the most feasible and was used as a basis to work from.

As I have mentioned, the Secretary General conducted a study in cooperation with industry organizations to address a number of issues: the volume of oil, number of tankers available, the world's shipbuilding capacity, world ship recycling capacity, and initial assessment of costs to tanker industry. What was most significant from this study and had the most impact on the IMO was, in fact, the world's shipbuilding capacity. If there was going to be a phasing out of single hull tankers and an increase in the need for building of new double hull tankers, there had to be enough shipbuilding capacity to deal with this issue.

The most significant impact of the Secretary General's study is that it became very clear to the delegates at the IMO that the proposal by France was not going to be acceptable. The French proposals were too rigorous, too onerous, and if they were accepted, they would have devastating effects on the world's shipbuilding capacity, which would have a significant impact on the world's oil supplies and economies. This is what resulted in compromise at IMO in trying to reach a solution in order to move forward.

There are three tanker categories in the compromise solutions agreed to at IMO. Category 1 includes tankers above 20,000 dwt that are not in compliance with certain international requirements. Category 2 includes tankers above 20,000 dwt that are in compliance with certain requirements. These are mostly the newer tankers that were built after 1982. Category 3 includes all the small tankers of 5,000 dwt or more, but less than that specified in Categories 1 and 2.

The compromise achieved at IMO was tentative because all that happened at the meeting was an agreement to circulate this proposal for final adoption at our upcoming session in April 2001, which is next month. The proposal attempted to pick when the ship was built and, based on when the ship was built, it then said when it had to be phased out.

They did attempt to use some of the key dates that were there in OPA90, in particular 2010 and 2015, but by no means were the French proposals or what was agreed to in the compromise the same as what is in OPA90. There is a very simple reason for that. OPA90 was established eleven years ago and allowed for a more gradual phase-in. If those dates were to be used now, it would be much too onerous on the industry.

In Category 2, there was some disagreement on whether the end date should be 2015 or 2017. Certain segments of the industry felt that for the newer Category 2 tankers, the final compliance date should be stretched out to 2017. This was, perhaps, one of the more controversial issues that we dealt with at IMO.

For the Category 2 alternatives, there was one group that supported alternative A and wanted to have a phase out by 2015. This would be consistent worldwide with OPA90 and addressed, of course, the political concerns the French administration had to face, as well as the concerns of the EU. The counter argument for alternative B, which was to go two more years to 2017, was that 2015 would penalize the tanker owner who built the tanker in 1996 in full compliance with all the standards. He would have a tanker that would be allowed to operate for just over eighteen years, which is not very much time.

There is also some indication in the Secretary General's study that perhaps there would not be sufficient shipbuilding capacity if the 2015 date was picked. Since that has occurred, I think European Parliament met in December last year and indicated that as far as the European Union is concerned, they want 2015. This will likely dictate their negotiating position when they come to the MEPC next month. That is what happened at MEPC 45. Now these outstanding issues remain for MEPC 46 when it meets next month.

The first outstanding issue as I mentioned is alternative A or alternative B, 2015 or 2017. I frankly don't see that as being very controversial now.

The second one is what is called the Conditional Assessment Scheme (CAS). What is being discussed here is whether a tanker should be allowed to extend its life without having a more rigorous inspection. The Conditional Assessment Scheme is basically a verification check to allow prolongation of the tanker's life. For Category 1 tankers, it would allow the extension to 2007. For Category 2 tankers, it would allow the extension beyond 2010. So when we talk about 2015 or 2017, you can only get there under the current regime if you have a Conditional Assessment Scheme.

There was a meeting at IMO back in January about this. It was somewhat controversial. The major issue centered on verification. Who should be doing this verification? The European countries are looking for a second opinion; that is, once the verification is done, they want a second opinion to be brought in to check that initial verification. Others are saying that under their sovereign rights, once they make a decision, it should be sufficient. So this is going to be one of the more controversial issues that we will be discussing at the meeting in April.

But third, and what I believe may be the most significant, is the concern by developing countries over the possible disruption to their oil supplies. To emphasize this, Brazil has submitted a paper to this upcoming meeting very emphatically stating that they do not believe IMO should take any action at this meeting in April. They believe that the issues that are being raised by France and others are not being specifically addressed as a result of the Erika accident. They are saying that a double hull would not have solved the problem. And they are concerned about their oil supplies. They raised this at the previous session and, in fact, a number of developing countries supported them.

From my perspective as head of the U.S. delegation, I believe the Brazilian paper is going to be the most controversial, to see how the developing countries and the open registries react to this. Are they more concerned about IMO taking action to show that IMO can respond so that there's not any unilateral action, or are they more concerned about these issues that they're raising? This is what remains to be seen.

With that, I want to quickly mention some future events. I mentioned that the meeting in January (January 31-February 2) to talk about a Conditional Assessment Scheme was somewhat controversial, but we were able to move forward there. Coming at the end of April will be the actual forty-sixth session of the Marine Environmental Protection Committee to consider the formal adoption of these amendments. I have given you the background of what will be considered there.

If the amendments are adopted, when would these amendments enter into force? Well, naturally, if we are going to go forward with this at IMO, we would be looking for the earliest possible dates. The earliest date under the current IMO structure would be January 1, 2003. We will see if that occurs.

I would like to turn now to the U.S. perspective, because we have OPA90 and are not party to 13G. First, what did we do at that MEPC 45 meeting? To the surprise of many people, we spoke in support of the French proposals in principle. Not in detail, but in principle. And the reason we spoke in support of the French proposals in principle was two-fold. First, the phase out dates were more consistent with what was in OPA90. They were not identical, but they were more consistent. Secondly, and I believe more importantly, although somewhat hypocritically, is that we would prefer to see IMO take action rather than to see the EU take unilateral action. Our concern is that unilateral action in this area would significantly weaken IMO.

The second thing we did at MEPC 45 was to propose the OPA90 dates. Since dates were being proposed, we had an obligation to put OPA90 dates on the table. We were politely thanked, but the OPA90 dates were rejected. Because of that and because we're not party to 13G, we had to reserve opposition on the amendments that were approved and that have been circulated for adoption.

Let me talk a little bit about OPA90 and how this fits in, because we're watching what happens at IMO very closely in the United States. What happens at IMO could, in fact, have a big impact in the United States. Under OPA90, the phase out dates are based on the vessel's age, size, and design. And by design I mean whether it's single hull, double hull, or whether it has a double bottom or double sides. There are exceptions, though. If the vessel is less than 5,000 gross tons (GRT), it has until 2015. If it is unloading at a deepwater port or if it is offloading in a designated lightering zone, it has until 2015. None of the other dates come into play.

These last two have become the most significant, because as you'll see, the biggest differences between OPA90 and what currently exists in 13G as amended, which we'll be considering next month, is, in fact, less than 5,000 GRT. This is of no consequence to the United States, because less than 5,000 GRT is basically only impacting U.S. tankers. There are but a very few foreign tankers coming to the U.S. of that size, so it has no impact. But those that lighter in designated lightering zones or those that call at loop have a big impact on oil coming into the United States.

In the Gulf of Mexico, there are designated lightering zone areas. Tankers must be in these particular areas to lighter their cargo. By lighter, I mean a larger ship comes in, they unload their cargo to a smaller tanker, and then the smaller tanker brings the oil into the United States to one of these ports or the vessel calls at loop to Louisiana Offshore Oil Production Platform, which is just south of Louisiana.

Now, why do I point this out so much? We took a look at the statistics, and it turns out that approximately twenty-five percent of U.S. oil imports comes from loop or designated lightering zones. That is quite a significant amount of oil. And if you recall, I pointed out that the tankers that come to these areas don't have to have a double hull until the year 2015 under our law. Oil imports from loop have increased thirty percent over the past year and those ships that are calling at designated lightering zones doubled last year. Why? As the phase out date for the single hull tanker is reached and that vessel cannot come into the United States, it then knows it can go to the lightering zone and continue its life in calling at the United States under OPA90. So we expect to see an increase in oil imports coming from loop and from the designated lightering zones.

In comparing OPA90 to the 13G proposed phase out, the OPA90 dates are earlier than everything being proposed under the proposed 13G, whether it be alternative A, alternative B, Category 1, or Category 2. So from the standpoint of a tanker calling at the United States, we're not concerned. But from the standpoint of a tanker calling at loop or a designated lightering zone, we are concerned because, very simply put, the modified 13G is going to require certain tankers to come out of service four to five years sooner than they currently would right now. This could have a big impact on oil coming to the United States. So this is why the United States is watching this very closely and is concerned about it.

Now in closing, I would simply say there are some unknowns. We don't know what is going to happen. I can give you my personal perspectives, though. The first is: Will IMO take appropriate action or will the EU go its own way? From what I have seen, I think everybody that has participated in the discussions at IMO would prefer IMO to take action. They would prefer not to see the EU take regional action. Of course, the wild card is Brazil, and what support that may garner, we are not sure of at this point. But I think that in the long run, IMO will prevail and there will be an agreement. In prevailing, will it result in an accelerated phase out of single hull tankers that impacts the world's oil supplies? Again, if we go with the dates that have been agreed to at MEPC 45, I don't think there will be a problem worldwide. There may be some consequences on a very small individual basis for some countries, but that will be almost impossible to predict.

Will the United States become a party to the amended 13G? We're currently not a party to the existing 13G. Will what comes out of IMO in April be something that we could live with and be linked to? In other words, will OPA90 be amended to reflect the amended 13G? On this issue I have spoken to U.S. ship operators, U.S. shipbuilding interests, environmentalists, and certain members of Congress, and they agree that OPA 90 has served the United States well and they see no need to amend it. Therefore, I do not think OPA90 is going to be amended, and if OPA90 is not amended, then it's very unlikely that the United States would become a party to the amended 13G.

With that, I conclude my presentation. Thank you very much for this opportunity. I hope this has been helpful.

THE PANAMA CANAL: *AN OVERVIEW*, ONE YEAR AFTER THE REVERSION FROM THE UNITED STATES TO THE SOVEREIGN REPUBLIC OF PANAMA

C. Thomas Burke*

Panama is the southernmost country in Central America with a population of nearly three million people. Around sixty percent are Mestizos (mixed AmerIndian and Spanish descent), about twenty percent are of African heritage, whites account for ten percent, and full-blooded AmerIndians comprise eight percent. The country is bound by the Caribbean Sea to the north, the Pacific Ocean to the south, Costa Rica to the west, and Colombia to the east. There are over 500 rivers. Average rainfall varies from 70 inches to 100 inches depending on the region. The climate is tropical with little seasonal variation and humidity around eighty percent year round. The main exports are bananas, coffee, petroleum products, shrimps, and sugar.

A contemporary look at the country of Panama is necessary in order to understand the internal issues and dilemmas challenging the government of President Moscoso and dramatically impacting the Panamanian people. President Moscoso was elected in May 1999 and took office in September as the final steps in the reversion of property from the U.S. to Panama were being completed. This overview examines the national context within which the historic and controversial 1977 Carter-Torrijos treaty has been implemented. Panama faces a period of transition. There is potential for transformation that could dramatically alter its economic, political, and social identity.

On August 15, 1999, the Panama Canal completed eighty-five years of service to the international maritime industry. On December 31, 1999, United States control of the canal ended. The formal transfer ceremony was scheduled for December 15 because

---

* Former Commissioner, Panama Canal Study Commission, United States Department of State.

M.H. Nordquist and J.N. Moore (eds.),
Current Marine Environmental Issues and the International Tribunal for the Law of the Sea, 319–327.
© 2001 *Kluwer Law International. Printed in the Netherlands.*

global millennium observances created schedule conflicts for many of the participants. More pragmatically, the earlier ceremony received more publicity than if it had to compete with the millennium for worldwide media attention. The Panamanian government welcomed publicity over the transfer ceremony while the United States downplayed the event in an effort to minimize the rekindling of the passions and resentment fostered in the United States when the Carter-Torrijos Treaty was signed in 1979. Secretary of State Albright was to be the highest ranking member of the Clinton administration to attend. She canceled, however, citing urgent demands elsewhere. It was widely regarded in Panama as an affront. Former President Jimmy Carter represented the United States at the ceremony.

The transition under the Carter/Torrijos Treaties of 1977 involved three aspects. The first was the operation and the administration of the Panama Canal. By 1999, almost all canal employees were Panamanians. The second transition regarded the reversion of properties: 5,000 buildings, 70,000 acres, and numerous military bases. The third transition regarded the defense of the canal.

When the United States negotiated the treaties, the assumption was that Panama's defense forces would assume principal responsibility for the defense of the canal, but these forces were abolished after Operation Just Cause in 1989 and the resulting ouster of President Noriega. The United States retains the independent right to defend the canal. This relieves Panama of tremendous military expenses. Panama does, however, have maintenance responsibility for the vast infrastructure of the former Canal Zone. While much has already been privatized, much still requires costly government maintenance.

Largely because of General Manuel Noriega and the U.S. invasion, Panamanian public attitudes toward a post-2000 U.S. presence have changed. Many who with nationalistic fervor opposed a U.S. military presence in 1978 came to favor some U.S. presence. A dramatic economic impact occurred as a result of the loss of the U.S. military payroll and other expenditures in Panama. Significant loss of employment resulted for the thousands of

Panamanians previously employed not just directly by the Americans, but also in many service jobs. There is apprehension over whether, and if so, when and how, that loss will be regained.

A poll published in the Panama City newspaper *La Prensa* in September 1999 found that over sixty percent of the Panamanians surveyed favored efforts to continue some form of U.S. military presence. There were intense negotiations to maintain Howard Air Force Base as a U.S. counter-drug facility. However, the Panamanian government has been ambivalent and divided on the issue. A U.S.-Panama agreement on specific terms was not reached, so beginning in 1999, the United States began operating counter-narcotics flights out of existing, host-country owned airfields in Aruba, Curacao, and Ecuador. A preferred site in Costa Rica has not been utilized because of provisions in the Costa Rica constitution that prohibit military activities.

There are significant continuing U.S. projects in Panama. In particular, USAID funds a program to develop sustainable management of the Panama Canal watershed. Distinct technical areas involved include: Economic Policy Development; Private Sector Development; Environmental Management; Participant Training; Municipal Development; and Administration of Justice (see Appendix II). Until recently, the United States and Panama were conducting joint maritime drug interdiction operations on Panama's coast as well. Those were canceled in early November over the issue of whether Panama will grant special status for the U.S. military personnel involved.

As bases were closed during the reversion process, departing U.S. military personnel left behind a legacy that is still an unresolved issue: children.

In the wake of the U.S. departure from Panama last May, Panama's Foreign Ministry opened a telephone hotline and an e-mail contact address to reach out to single parents seeking to register claims for child support. In the six months since it opened, the office has fielded around

321

1,500 calls from mothers seeking to lodge formal claims for support for school-age children fathered by U.S. civilian and military personnel. Almost all of the cases processed by the office come from the capital and the Caribbean city of Colon, alongside the former U.S.-controlled Canal Zone that was handed back to Panama under the 1977 canal treaties. . . . [T]he ministry has documented 658 cases of Panamanian children now of school age born to U.S. fathers.

While many are the fruit of happy marriages between Panamanian women and former soldiers and civilian workers during the final years of the U.S. era in Panama, the office says more than half have been dumped by absent fathers. Run by the U.S. government for more than 85 years, the Panama Canal Commission began forcibly deducting child support from Panamanian and U.S. employees' paychecks following a court ruling and 1988 accord.

But with transfer of the waterway at the end of last year, the only bilateral framework in place for awarding child maintenance disappeared, leaving single mothers and dependent children unprotected by any international accord. While Panama signed on to the Organization of American States-backed Inter-American Convention on Child Support last March, following five other regional states, Washington has yet to ratify it. The U.S. State Department has negotiated with more than 30 countries to establish the enforcement of reciprocal child maintenance agreements. . . .

"We want to find a way to make both the collection of child support and the recognition of paternity easier and more efficient," Foreign Ministry General Secretary Maria Alejandra Eisenmann told Reuters. "At the end of the day what interests us as a government is protecting children (by) giving them the right to an education, a name and food" (MSNBC/Reuters: November 14, 2000).

Another unresolved issue that has provoked considerable emotion is the remaining unexploded ordnance in some environmentally sensitive and/or difficult-to-access areas of the former U.S. military property. While there is concern over the safety hazard posed to local people, the United States contends that the cleanup was as thorough as possible given the terrain and the jungle. The position is that far more damage would be done by the clearing of vegetation that more complete cleanup would require. Extensive efforts were also made to educate local people about the hazards and the importance of notifying authorities when ordnance is found.

Panama has a service economy, with the tertiary economic sector comprising more than seventy percent of the Gross Domestic Product. The country is sharply stratified economically, so while it has approximately the same resources as neighboring Costa Rice, the poverty rate and other indicators of quality of life are much worse than rates for more egalitarian Costa Rica. Land ownership is quite concentrated, as is wealth in general. Urban/rural disparities and disparities between ethnic/racial groups are striking. Panama City/Pacific coast is much more affluent than Colon/Atlantic coast. Housing, medical care, and access to employment are areas where there are not only serious, but growing disparities. A more inclusive education system would make a major contribution toward redressing inequitable patterns.

Except for NAFTA, probably no treaties are more visible in this hemisphere than those with Panama. For the foreseeable future, there will be joint U.S./Panamanian economic and political interests. But other players are gaining prominence. As the United States' role in Panama diminishes, other nations are literally pouring money in. China, Taiwan, Thailand, Korea, and Mexico have all become very involved with the Panamanian government in numerous investments, loans, and business ventures such as export processing, luxury hotels, and casinos.

Fort Amador, the "jewel" of U.S. bases, is undergoing dramatic transformation. The Korean consortium that began the project is gone, but the plan is still for the site to become a resort complex with new passenger terminals and facilities for the growing cruise industry. Construction is currently underway. A world-class aquarium is planned.

A Melia hotel chain is developing Ft. Sherman and the former School of the Americas, a U.S. military academy that featured prominently in the Cold War activities of the United States. Plans include a 250-room hotel with a marina on Gatun Lake.

Ft. Clayton (former site of SouthCom, U.S. Army South Headquarters) is being transformed into the "City of Knowledge and Techno Park"—an educational complex and office center for high tech businesses and regional international organizations such as UNICEF. Albrook AFB has become the municipal airport for Panama City and a hub for intra-Panama flights. A second bridge (near the town of Paraiso) is planned across the canal to increase land transport efficiency. Currently the only major bridge (not counting the small one at Miraflores Locks) is the picturesque Bridge of the Americas at the Pacific entrance.

A third set of locks for post-Panamax ships is being planned, pending adequate financing for what will be an extremely costly project. The goal is to accommodate much larger ships than currently passable. The widening of the Culebra/Gaillard Cut is almost completed. This will allow two Panamax ships to transit simultaneously.

The ports at Balboa on the Pacific side of the canal and Cristobal on the Atlantic side have been leased for twenty-five to fifty years to a Hong Kong conglomerate, Hutchinson Whampoa, Ltd., which will become the gate keeper of the canal. This caused a storm of controversy. As a foothold in the Americas for the Chinese, some U.S. observers expressed concern because Hutchinson Whampoa has close ties to China's leadership and its armed forces. Others, including the Clinton administration, dismiss those concerns. Several other organizations are also operating terminal and loading facilities on the isthmus. HIT Terminals (Hutchinson Whampoa) and the government of Panama are reassuring all concerned that no foreign country will be able to exercise undue negative influence over the canal.

In addition, three new cruise ship terminals are being built, including one at Colon. These will allow tourists to disembark in-country for daytrips (particularly nature-oriented) and for shopping. Currently cruise ships pass directly through the canal without passengers ever setting foot on Panamanian soil (and without spending tourist money in Panama). The exceptions are the few ships that stop briefly in the San Blas islands.

The Kansas City Southern Railroad has entered into a twenty-five year operating agreement to finance, construct, and operate a railroad landbridge spanning Panama from the Atlantic to the Pacific oceans. There are plans to utilize the forty-seven-mile transcontinental rail service as an alternative to the waterway, particularly for transshipment of container cargo.

U.S.-Panama negotiation talks broke down on an agreement on the use of Howard Air Force Base, which has been an extremely important drug interdiction base. The U.S. Southern Command (SouthCom) has moved operations and equipment to Miami from Panama. The U.S. planes now operating from Miami, Ecuador, and Curacao cannot be maximally effective in the Colombian drug war, so the process of opening alternative airbases in Honduras or El Salvador is underway.

Colombia supplies three-fourths of the cocaine and much of the heroin consumed in the United States. The unstable situation in Colombia poses a tremendous worry for Panama, as it does not have the resources to keep armed Colombians out of the rainforest of Panama's sparsely populated southern region, the Darien. The Kuna Yala (territory of indigenous Kuna) extends on the Atlantic coast to the Colombian border. The situation is threatening to the integrity and security of the Kuna, a number of whom have been killed or injured by Colombian guerrillas. Others are drawn into aspects of the drug trade.

Plan Colombia, the U.S. funded anti-drug effort in Colombia, is extremely controversial in the region. It is seen by many as escalating a breakdown of Colombian society by contributing to the displacement of large numbers of rural Colombians, many of whom have fled into northern Ecuador. While Panama is not the primary recipient of refugees from the violence, it has become a conduit for gunrunning. Guns from the Cold-War conflicts in Nicaragua and El Salvador are smuggled through Panama into Colombia. Guerrillas seek safe haven from Colombian military by hiding in the Panamanian Darien jungle. Some fear that as Cambodia was to Vietnam, so Panama could become to Colombia if the level of conflict escalates. Ironically, there has been some small benefit of the neighboring strife to Panama's economy in that some wealthy Colombians have moved to Panama for security. That certainly does not outweigh the significant drop in exports to Colombia due to Colombia's weakened economy. Panama has publicly resolved to remain neutral and opposes the U.S. involvement that Plan Colombia entails.

Environmental changes are occurring as the rainforest protecting the canal watershed is diminished as privatization of the previously restricted land progresses. A colleague reported to me that in his visits with the Embarra Indians in the Chagras Lake region, they lamented the drastic reduction in wildlife due to hunting now that the U.S. military is gone and the area is under Panamanian control. Panama cannot afford sufficient patrols of protected areas. The Embarra were displaced by the Chagras Lake, created by a dam of the Rio Chagras to supply water for the canal. Those remaining in the lakeshore area report growing deforestation in the watershed due to lumbering. That raises concern over silting in of the lake, which supplies water for the canal. This also risks causing decreased rainfall, therefore reducing the fresh water needed for the canal. Concerns grow over future water quality and quantity. Coastal fisheries are also in need of protection from pollution such as agriculture runoff.

Resolution of the social, political, environmental, and economic adjustments facing Panama remain complex. Much depends on external developments that are not under the control of Panama or any other single country. It will, however, be crucial how Panama develops regional and hemispheric alliances and understandings. Through regional integration of communication, compliance with international law/standards, transportation, finance, industry, and commerce, Panama in concert with the other small countries of the region will be better positioned to compete successfully as globalization increases. As a small country with limited resources, Panama cannot realistically stand alone as an island and still achieve security and prosperity. With no army, the country is very vulnerable when neighboring countries are in turmoil. Renegotiating the longstanding special relationship with the United States out of mutual self-interest is possible if patience, mutual sensitivity, and respect are exercised.

Addressing domestic inequalities is vital to stability. Maintaining and strengthening democratic institutions must be a high priority. Greater government tolerance for the free press is necessary. The tourism industry has great potential, but an effective effort to promote a more positive international image will be necessary in order to attract the prerequisite capital investment as well as the tourists themselves. Addressing domestic issues such as crime, health, education, and housing will also enhance tourism development. Environmental protection must assume more importance.

As a new chapter unfolds in the history of the Panama Canal, there are high hopes for new opportunities, peace, and growth. It is expected that the canal will remain open to peaceful transit by vessels of all nations on terms of entire equality consistent with the principles of international law. The continued efficient functioning of the canal is also expected. Resolution of the social, political, environmental, and economic adjustments facing Panama remains a more complex matter.

OIL AND WATER: CASPIAN OIL AND TRANSPORTATION CHALLENGES FACING THE TURKISH STRAITS

Nilufer Oral[*]

PIPELINES TANKERS AND THE TURKISH STRAITS

The dissolution of the former Soviet Union and the emergence of the Newly Independent States (NIS) in 1991 opened new markets for western capital, but the jewel in the crown was the treasure trove of Caspian oil and gas. Caspian oil is not new and has played a significant role in petrol history since the Nobel Brothers launched the first bulk oil carrier, the *Zoroaster*, into the Caspian Sea in 1878. Through the circular route of history, over 100 years after its first discovery, Caspian oil finds itself once again faced with the very same problem: how to transport the oil out of the region and into the rest of the energy hungry world. Back then, oil was shipped in wooden barrels from Baku to Astrakhan and then down the Volga River in barges—a costly and slow means of transportation. The high cost of this method inspired Ludwig Nobel to come up with the idea of the first oil tanker.[1] Today, however, the oil tanker is not necessarily the solution but perhaps the problem itself. How is the new Caspian crude to be transported: by sea via tankers or pipelines or both?

If the matter was simply a question of pure accounting, the answer may have been simple: use existing pipelines in combination with Very Large Crude Carriers (VLCC) from the Black Sea through the Turkish Straits into the Mediterranean. Rarely, however, are matters so simple. The wild card in this gnarly basket of transport options is the Turkish Straits.[2] As the

---

[*] Assistant Director of the Maritime Law Research Centre, Istanbul Bilgi University. The author would like to thank Gündüz Aybay for his encouragement and guidance in the study of the Turkish Straits. The views expressed belong solely to the author and do not reflect the views of any institution, government entity, or organization.

M.H. Nordquist and J.N. Moore (eds.),
Current Marine Environmental Issues and the International Tribunal for the Law of the Sea, 329–364.
© 2001 *Kluwer Law International. Printed in the Netherlands.*

sole sea corridor linking the Black Sea to the Mediterranean, the Turkish Straits have for centuries carried a heavy historical burden. Today that burden comes primarily in the form of commercial vessels, as the number, size, and hazardous nature of the cargo have been rising rapidly. The Turkish Straits ranks among the three busiest straits in the world and is the only one that cuts directly through the center of a city teeming with over ten million inhabitants. Complicating calculations further is the position of the Turkish government, which has very plainly stated that the Turkish Straits would not become an alternative pipeline.[3]

There are various routing alternatives for Caspian oil, but for the purposes of the Turkish Straits, the following are important: the Baku to Supsa pipeline and the Baku to Novorossyk pipeline route, both of which would require transporting oil via tankers through the Turkish Straits; and the Baku-Tiblis-Ceyhan pipeline that would completely bypass the Turkish Straits by piping Caspian oil directly from Baku Georgia to the Mediterranean Turkish port of Ceyhan.[4] However, oil companies[5] have favored the routing alternatives using tankers through the Turkish Straits as studies have indicated this to be the cheapest routing alternative. Although, one of these studies also noted:

A large capacity pipeline that bypasses the Turkish Straits should be considered as a means of transporting projected increase in oil exports from the Caspian region. The economic viability of a bypass would be greater if shippers had to bear the true social cost of transiting the Turkish Straits (that is the expected value of damages borne by residents of Istanbul to either person or property as well as the cost of delays due to congestion). Measuring the true cost of tanker passage is very difficult since it requires the placement of a value on such "goods" as the integrity of historical buildings and locations.[6]

How Much Oil?

Although Caspian oil is not a new commodity for the Turkish Straits, the increase in oil being transported through the Straits has been steadily rising and has reached a critical level. Since 1991, shipment of oil through the Straits has doubled. Indeed, between 1995 and 1999, the number of tankers increased by nearly 1,300 per year. Simply between 1998 and 2000, the amount of oil and other dangerous cargo being shipped by tankers through the Straits has increased by almost fifty percent from sixty-eight million tons in 1998 to ninety-one million tons in 2000.[7] This existing increase pales in comparison with the prospective increase in tanker traffic once full production has been accomplished. If the excess production (oil not absorbed by the local economies)[8] is to be transported from the region to the rest of the world through the Turkish Straits, the number of tankers and size of these tankers will necessarily grow.

The estimated oil reserves in the Caspian Sea region vary between thirty billion barrels to two hundred billion barrels. However, recent discoveries support the upper estimates. In 1997, regional production averaged around 800-900 b/d of which a third was exported. Last year production from Supsa alone was five million tons (approximately 27.5 million b/a). This amount is expected to increase to ten to seventeen million tons (approximately 55-94 million b/a) by June 2001 when the Caspian pipeline from Baku-Supsa is completed. According to the U.S. Energy International Administration, total overall production by 2010 could reach around 3.9 million b/d (1,424 billon b/a).[9] In 1993, the OCIMF estimated that by 2005 the amount of oil being transported out of the Caspian Sea region through the Turkish Straits could increase by as much as 100 million tons per year.[10] According to one analyst, four high capacity pipelines (to carry one million barrels p/d) will eventually be needed from the Caspian Sea region via Turkey to the Mediterranean.[11] Another analyst explains that each ten million ton increment of Caspian oil shipped to the Mediterranean will require eight hundred trips through the Bosphorus by medium-sized oil tankers or two hundred trips by large tankers.[12]

PHYSICAL CHARACTERISTICS OF THE TURKISH STRAITS

It is essential to fully understand the geographical, morphological, and demographical hazards posed by the Turkish Straits for navigation. There are actually two separate straits separating the Black Sea from the Aegean Sea: the Strait of Istanbul (Bosphorus) and the Strait of Çanakkale (Dardannelles).[13] The Turkish Straits constitute an internal waterway of Turkey having only one coastal State and no waters, which, based on distance criteria, would constitutes high seas or even territorial seas. The Strait of Istanbul links the Black Sea to the Marmara Sea, which is an internal sea, and the Strait of Çanakkale links the Marmara Sea to the Aegean Sea.[14] The Strait of Istanbul measures 31 kilometers (km) and varies in width from a maximum width of 3.5 km to a minimum width of 700 meters (m). It takes approximately one to one-and-a-half hours for a vessel to traverse the Strait of Istanbul and twenty-two hours to complete the entire Turkish Straits trajectory. Measuring a mere 700 meters at its narrowest channel at Bebek and Kandilli, the challenges for the captain navigating the Strait of Istanbul are further enhanced by a 45 degree course alteration. However, the Bebek-Kandilli bend is only one of the total of twelve course alterations in the Strait of Istanbul alone, of which four require a 45 degree course alteration and one an 80 degree course alteration. As if nature had constructed an obstacle course, in addition to the sharp bends and narrow channels, navigation is furthered hindered by unpredictable and forceful currents sometimes as strong as six to eight knots[15] as well as the sudden changes in climatic conditions that can reduce visibility to less than one mile within a very short period of time. All of these risks factors are exponentially magnified by the fact that the entire route of the Strait of Istanbul snakes through one of the world's most crowded (ten to twelve million), historical,[16] and commercially active cities.

A brief comparison with other major straits used for international navigation underscores the enhanced navigational risks of the Turkish Straits. For example, the Strait of Gibraltar measures 36 miles (58 km) in length and narrows to 8 miles (13 km) in width. The Straits of Malacca measures 500 miles (830 km) in length and varies between 200 miles (328 km) and 11 miles (18 km) in width. The Strait of Dover (Calais) varies between 18 to 25 miles (30 to 40 km) in width and the Magellan Strait is 350 miles (560 km) long and 2 to 20 miles (3 to 32 km) wide. None of these straits is as narrow as the Strait of Istanbul, nor do any cut directly through the center of a crowded city where millions reside right on the coastline.

TRAFFIC AND ACCIDENTS IN THE TURKISH STRAITS

Currently, approximately fifty thousand vessels annually pass through the Turkish Straits.[17] That is, on a daily basis, approximately 150 vessels, of which fifteen to seventeen a day are tankers carrying oil, gas, or other hazardous or dangerous cargo. According to the Turkish Maritime Pilots Association (TUMPA), in 2000 a total of 4,937 tankers navigated through the Strait of Istanbul.[18] In addition to commercial vessel traffic, the Strait of Istanbul must support approximately 2,500 daily local intra-city commuter traffic carrying an estimated 2.5 million commuters, not to mention the innumerable small commercial fishing boats cluttering the waterway. Since 1936, the year when the Montreux Convention was signed, the characteristics of both the vessels and maritime traffic have changed significantly. In 1936, 4,500 vessels per year traversed the Turkish Straits. Today that number has increased by ten-fold. In 1936, the average vessel had an average weight of thirteen tons compared to the average weight today of 200,000 tons. Much of the dangerous/hazardous cargo created by modern science and know-how did not exist then. Likewise, the nature and magnitude of accidents have also become much more dangerous.

Between 1982 and 1994, a total of 205 serious maritime accidents occurred in the Strait of Istanbul alone. More notably, the frequency and severity of these accidents reached a state of emergency during the early part of the 1990s when the number of accidents had peaked at an average of forty per year.[19] But it is not merely the number of accidents but also the nature of these accidents that threaten the environs of the Straits. Tanker accidents may account for just a few of the total accidents, but they have been the most fatal and costly and pose the greatest immediate danger to the coast and the marine environment.[20]

In 1979, the *M/T Independenta* (160,000 GWT), a Romanian crude oil carrier transporting 95,000 tons of oil collided with a Greek freighter, the *M/V Evriali*, resulting in an explosion that rocked the city of Istanbul. Only three men of a total crew of forty-six survived. The collision caused a fire that burned for weeks and the wreck lay in the waters of the Strait for over ten years. The *Independenta* accident, ranked as tenth worst oil casualty in the world, spilled 95,000 tons[21] into the Strait of Istanbul, more than twice the amount of the Exxon Valdez spill (37,000 tons).[22]

In 1994, the tanker *Nassia*, *sailing from* Novorossiysk collided with the dry cargo carrier the *Shipbroker* and spilled 20,000 tons of crude oil into the Strait and closed it for nearly one week. Once again, tragically similar to the *Independenta* accident, there was a fiery explosion that took days to put out and twenty-six crew members lost their lives. The accident caused U.S. $1 billion in damages.

In 1998, the Greek tanker M/T *Crudegulf*, travelling from Russia to Italy, measuring 274 meters and fully laden with 140,000 tons of crude oil, lost steering ability due to a technical failure and ran aground in the Strait of Istanbul narrowly escaping a calamity.

On December 31, 1999, the Russian flagged *Volgoneft 248*, a river barge converted into oil tanker, just two days after the *Erika* accident,[23] broke in half in a fierce storm and spilled 950 tons of crude oil.[24] The 304-meter long giant tanker "IRIS STAR," fully-laden with crude-oil, lost power due to engine failure and drifted towards the narrow 700 meter Kandilli area of the Strait on July 27.[25]

Tanker accidents in the Strait of Istanbul have been explosive and fatal, whereas neither the *Torrey Canyon,* the *Amoco Cadiz*, the *Exxon Valdez*, nor the *Erika* accidents created an explosion and fire within a city. As noted by one observer:

> Turkey has been simply lucky that the most severe (accidents) have occurred near the ends of the Straits, thus reducing the threat to the densely-populated Istanbul coastline.[26]

But for how long can Turkey rely on luck?

LEGAL REGIME OF THE TURKISH STRAITS

The legal framework for the passage regime for the Turkish Straits was established by the 1936 Montreux Convention. However, the Convention itself has also been supplemented by practice, international conventions to which Turkey has become a party, such as COLREG, SOLAS, MARPOL, and most recently the Turkish Maritime Regulations for the Turkish Straits, as amended in 1998, along with the IMO issued Rules and Recommendations on Navigation Through the Strait of Istanbul, the Strait of Çanakkale and the Sea of Marmara.[27] Turkey is not a party to the 1982 United Nations Convention on the Law of the Sea (UNCLOS). However, even if it were, article 35(c) of the Convention expressly excludes the application of UNCLOS for straits covered in whole or in part by long standing conventions.[28]

What are the parameters of Montreux? Do the provisions of Montreux restrict Turkey from regulating vessel traffic through the Straits? Although Montreux does impose restrictions, such as preventing mandatory pilotage and tug, a careful interpretation of Montreux reveals that it actually recognizes more expansive regulatory authority to Turkey than the traditional regime of innocent passage, and certainly more than the new 1982 UNCLOS created transit passage regime for straits used in international navigation.

THE 1936 MONTREUX CONVENTION

Historical Background

The 1936 Montreux Convention holds a unique place in both diplomatic and legal history.[29] The Montreux Convention was created against the backdrop of a Europe on the precipice of a world war. Italian aggression into Africa threatened to spill into the eastern Mediterranean; Germany, steadily and quickly rearming, had unilaterally denounced the Treaty of Versailles; and Japan had withdrawn from the League of the Nations. The bubble of peaceful coexistence that had characterized the 1920s was about to burst. Turkey, uneasy with the *status quo* regime for the Turkish Straits as created by the terms of the 1923 Lausanne Convention, requested a conference to revise Lausanne on the grounds of changed circumstances (*rebus sic stantibus*).[30] Reluctant at first, Great Britain finally agreed to a Conference reuniting all of the Parties to the Lausanne Convention, except for Italy.[31] The Conference lasted for one month and left a rich record, an essential source for any full understanding and interpretation of the legal regime of the Turkish Straits.

The Montreux Convention consists of twenty-nine articles, four annexes, and one protocol. Articles 2 through 7 provide the rules of passage for merchant vessels and articles 8 through 22 for vessels for war. Of the three recognized longstanding treaties regulating passage through straits used for international navigation, without a doubt, the Montreux Convention is the most detailed.[32]

Freedom of Passage and Navigation

The Preamble of the Montreux Convention begins by reaffirming the principle of freedom of passage and navigation originally established in article 23 of the defunct 1923 Treaty of Lausanne Regime for the Turkish Straits. The principle of *freedom of passage*[33] *and navigation through the Straits* is reiterated in article 1[34] in general for all vessels and expressly for merchant vessels in article 2 of the Convention.[35] Nonetheless, virtually in the same breath, article 2 contains language that, in fact, restricts the very right of freedom of passage and navigation declared. While it is tempting to take the Montreux promise of complete *freedom of passage and navigation* at face value, the underlying reality of that freedom is, in fact, not so generous. Brüel noted in his analysis of article 2 that "the importance of these apparently liberal provisions is greatly lessened" by the exceptions created by article 3.[36] What then does *freedom* mean for a vessel undertaking voyage according to the provisions of Montreux: Is the regime a *transit passage* regime, a *non-suspendable innocent passage* regime, or something entirely different? The nature of the regime will clarify the extent of Turkey's authority, as recognized under international law, to regulate passage and take prescriptive action in the Straits.

For example, in his analysis of the Turkish Straits regime, Plant states that "the regime for *transiting* merchant vessels appears, *prima facie*, to be akin to the freedom of navigation, or at least to a form of the right of transit passage."[37] In a later article, Plant seems to modify his characterization of the regime by stating that "the customary law regime of transit passage governs 'residual matters' not covered by the Montreux Convention."[38] In their book on the Turkish Straits, Rozakis and Stagos basically describe it as a "freedom of transit and navigation" regime having a "peculiar nature" that was "shaped by local interests."[39] The authors also explain that the Convention imposed "severe limitations on that freedom."[40] Professor Toluner, along with other Turkish scholars on this issue, has long put forth the view that the regime of passage is a *sui generis* regime based on the international norm of innocent passage.[41] The present author would agree.[42]

During the Montreux Conference, the Turkish Delegation expressly stated that passage of vessels through the Turkish Straits was always to be innocent and inoffensive.[43] Mr. Menemencioğlu made it clear that vessels would not be able to freely navigate as they chose in the Straits and "to not come back one day and claim that ships can navigate as if they are on the high seas."[44] While at first blush this would indicate that passage through the Turkish Straits would be subject to the regime of innocent passage,[45] a careful analysis of the Convention shows that the regime created was a *sui generis regime*; that is, a regime different and unique from the norms of customary law for international straits at the time the Convention was adopted. In fact, the Convention actually recognized more rights to Turkey as the coastal State than was recognized to coastal States by the rules of innocent passage as understood in 1936.

First, it is important to recall that in 1936 the regime of transit passage as created by UNCLOS did not exist. Passage through territorial seas and straits used for international navigation was subject to the regime of innocent passage.[46] No distinction was made at that time between the applicable regime of passage through the territorial sea of a coastal State and the territorial waters that also formed part of a strait used for international navigation. Although there were discussions, the 1930 Hague Conference reflected the view that the regime of innocent passage applied to straits embraced by a single coast, the waters of which formed part of the territorial waters of the littoral or coastal State.[47] As explained by Brüel, the 1930 Conference was of the view that:

> the right of passage in straits for merchant vessels being generally looked upon as part of their right of harmless passage through the territorial waters in general, it follows that the condition for passage in territorial waters, viz. That the passage be harmless ("inoffensive," "innocent") towards the littoral state, must also apply to the passage of merchant vessels in straits.[48]

The right of innocent passage meant that the coastal State could not interfere with or place conditions on the passage of a vessel so long as the vessel, during passage, did not engage in activity harmful or prejudicial to the peace, order, and security of the coastal State. Although there was no agreed upon objective criterion as to what type of activity or nature of passage would constitute non-innocent passage, and thereby give the coastal State the right to interfere with that passage, under international law, as was affirmed by the 1949 *Corfu Channel* case, the coastal State was not to condition transit passage on the payment of fees and taxes, require prior notification or approval for passage, or make passage contingent on any form of inspection. Yet, the 1936 Montreux Convention recognized these rights to Turkey to impose as conditions of passage through the Turkish Straits.

Under the express provisions of Montreux, all vessels were obliged to report to a sanitary station for inspection before entering the Straits.[49] Ships were also made to report to the authorities "their name, nationality, tonnage, destination and last port of call."[50] Turkey was also given the right to collect taxes and fees from vessels passing in transit.

Another derogation of the Montreux passage regime from traditional innocent passage regime was the creation of different rules of passage for merchant vessels according to whether there was a war, whether Turkey was belligerent or neutral, or whether Turkey considered herself to be "threatened with imminent danger of war."[51] According to article 4 of the Convention, in time of war, if Turkey was not belligerent, merchant vessels enjoyed freedom of passage and navigation subject to the requirements of the Convention. However, if Turkey was belligerent, according to article 5, merchant vessels could still enjoy the same freedom of passage and navigation so long as they were not in any way assisting the enemy. However, passage would be during the daytime and only by routes prescribed by Turkey.[52] Furthermore, although article 2 of the Convention made pilotage optional, article 6 created an exception allowing Turkey to make pilotage obligatory (albeit free of charge) should Turkey consider herself to be "threatened with imminent danger of war."

In 1936, the regime for war vessel passage through straits was not as clearly defined as it was for merchant vessels.[53] However, in the *Corfu Channel* case, the International Court of Justice recognized that vessels of war also enjoyed the rights of innocent passage through "international straits." Under the Montreux

Convention, innocent passage rights for vessels of war were even further restricted than they had been for merchant vessels. The Convention created a very detailed and complicated passage regime for war vessels. It imposed limitations as to the nationality of ships that could navigate through the Straits,[54] the total tonnage,[55] and the type of vessel.[56] The Convention also made notification to Turkish authorities a precondition of passage favoring Black Sea Powers over non-Black Sea Powers.[57] Such restrictions were and are clearly counter to the regime of innocent passage as it applies to war vessels.

This brief, albeit compact, overview of the Montreux Convention shows that the regime of passage in the Turkish Straits for *both* merchant vessels and war vessels gives Turkey more authority to regulate the manner of passage, including interference with passage, than the traditional rule of innocent passage recognized. As was aptly observed in 1938, just two years after the Convention was concluded, by a scholar on the Turkish Straits:

> . . . Freedom of navigation, the only surviving provision of the Lausanne Convention also underwent profound changes: the waters of the Straits no longer formed an open corridor at all times . . . for the complete freedom of navigation of all foreign vessels. The Montreux Convention established limitations for both the passage of merchant vessels as well as war vessels.[58]

RECENT MEASURES TAKEN BY TURKEY

The Turkish Maritime Regulations for the Turkish Straits

Article 1 of the Maritime Traffic Scheme Regulations for the Administration of the Turkish Straits (as amended in 1998) (hereinafter, 1998 Regulations) provides that the Regulations were prepared with the purpose of ensuring safety of navigation, protection of lives, property, and the environment.[59] The Regulations consist of fifty-three articles[60] and six appendixes. The most notable aspects of the Regulations include the creation of a traffic separation scheme in accordance with Rule 10 of COLREG and provisions that provide for suspension of one-way and two-way traffic. In addition, the Regulations impose specific technical requirements that all vessels navigating through the Straits must meet (article 5) and an obligation to notify the Traffic Control Center if the vessel is unable to meet these requirements.

Article 6 of the Regulations also provides for a ship reporting system called TÜBRAP, according to which, depending on the size and nature of cargo, the ship's captain is to submit a Navigation Plan prior to entry into the Straits. According to the information provided, the Traffic Control Center will advise as to the manner and time of passage. However, as the suspension provisions were the most controversial, a more detailed examination is merited.

Article 20 provides for the temporary suspension of traffic through the Straits under enumerated circumstances, which include *force majeure*, hazardous conditions (such as fire, collisions, and pollution), large scale construction projects, and unexpected traffic hazards. Article 36 (Strait of Istanbul) and article 44 (Strait of Çanakkale) allow for one-way suspension when visibility is below one mile and in both directions when visibility is below one mile. Article 35 prohibits the passage of ships carrying hazardous cargo, large ships (200 meters and over), and deep draft vessels (15 meters and over) from entering the Strait of Istanbul and article 43 for the Strait of Çanakkale, when the currents are 6 nanometers (nm) or more.

Article 25, subsection (a) specifically applies to ships having difficulty navigating within the TSS. According to this article, ships having a length between 150 to 200 meters and/or a draft of between 10 to 15 meters are to submit an SP-1 report at least 24 hours in advance of their entry to the Straits; ships of a length between 200 to 300 meters, 48 hours. However, the article does not provide for what purpose the Traffic Control Center will use these reports, whereas, subsection (b) not only imposes a seventy-two hour advance SP-1 report for vessels 300 meters or greater but also requires that "the agent or operator . . . during the planning phase of the voyage shall provide information to the Administration regarding the characteristics of the ship and its cargo." Based upon this information, the Traffic Control Center is to advise the ship's operator, agent, or captain of any requirements or recommendations to ensure safe passage. Subparagraph (c) further imposes upon the Traffic Control Center the duty to take the necessary measures and may suspend the traffic separation lanes for subsection (a) and (b) vessels, as well as those carrying hazardous cargo, as part of its safety measures. Article (d) also prohibits the simultaneous passage of two or more vessels falling under (a) and (b), which are also carrying hazardous cargo.

Article 26 applies to ships operated by nuclear power transporting nuclear cargo or waste or other dangerous or hazardous cargo. There is no SP-1 report requirement, but there is a seventy-two hour advance reporting requirement for information to be provided to the administration regarding the cargo being transported and to provide documents as prepared by the Flag States showing that the ship meets IMO standards as well as other international conventions. The administration will provide "rules of passage" with which the captain has a duty to comply.

Article 29 provides a general prohibition against pollution.

Article 21 (c) is the only provision that expressly addresses the issue of enforcement measures.[61] It specifies that the Flag State and the IMO shall be notified if a ship does not comply with the traffic separation scheme. However, it remains to be seen whether or not the Turkish authorities will exercise coastal State jurisdiction in the form of criminal penalties, as provided under law No. 618 of the Istanbul Port law. The original 1994 Regulations had expressly made reference to law No. 608, whereas the amended Regulations make no express reference. The 1998 Regulations only expressly address the issue of violation of the traffic separation lanes and not the other remaining provisions.

The IMO Rules and Recommendations

The 1994 IMO adopted Rules and Recommendations on Navigation through the Strait of Istanbul, the Strait of Çanakkale and the Sea of Marmara (IMO Rules and Recommendations)[62] are parallel to the above cited provisions of the national Regulations but less detailed. The IMO Rules and Recommendations require that all vessels *shall* exercise full diligence and regard for the requirements of the traffic separation scheme (1.1). Those vessels not able to comply with the TSS *shall* give advance notice. The Turkish administration is authorized, then, to temporarily suspend two-way traffic and regulate one-way traffic to maintain a safe distance. Ships are in these circumstances advised to abide by Rule 9 of the International Regulations for Preventing Collisions at Sea, 1972 (1.2 and 1.3). Ships are *strongly recommended* to participate in the Turkish ship reporting system (TÜBRAP) (2.1) and are *strongly advised* to provide information about their characteristics and cargoes (2.2.). Transiting ships are *strongly advised* to use a pilot (3.1) and vessels having a length of more than 200 m and a draught more than 15 m are advised to navigate the Straits in daylight (4.1). Recommendations are also made for towing and anchorage (5.1 and 6.1).

BACKGROUND TO THE REGULATIONS AND THE IMO RULES AND RECOMMENDATIONS

The need for more effective regulations of vessel passage through the Turkish Straits dates back to a 1968 report published by the Merchant Marine Academy Association that presented a detailed study of the traffic problem together with recommendations.[63] The tragic and devastating 1979 *Independenta* tanker accident not only shattered thousands of windows when it exploded but also any illusion for the inhabitants of Istanbul that the Bosphorus was safe. Public sentiment was awoken and the need to improve the safety of the Turkish Straits began to be debated seriously.[64] In 1987, the Association of Turkish Ocean Going Masters prepared and submitted to the Ministry of Transportation a report and proposal for the creation of a traffic separation scheme in the Turkish Straits. In 1990, a Commission was established to conduct a detailed study of the matter of safety of navigation through the Straits. The Commission concluded that a traffic separation scheme was necessary to ensure the safety of the Straits as well as the bordering coastal area together with new regulations to replace the 1982 Istanbul Port Regulations, which were based on Rule 9 of the Convention on the International Regulations for Preventing Collisions at Sea, 1972 (COLREG). The Commission drafted the Regulations, which were ultimately adopted by the government and enacted as the 1994 Maritime Regulations for the Turkish Straits.[65]

At the same time, a decision was taken by the Turkish government to submit the proposed traffic separation scheme (TSS) for adoption to the International Maritime Organization.[66] On March 26, 1993, Turkey presented an information paper to the Sixty-second MSC on the existing maritime traffic problems in the Turkish Straits and a plan to introduce a TSS in the Turkish Straits in an effort to increase safety of navigation and protect the marine environment. Turkey also advised of its intention to enact new maritime Regulations.[67] Almost one year to the day Turkey had presented MSC 62/INF.10, the *Nassia/Shipbroker* accident shook Istanbul.[68] It was an alarm bell for the urgent need for a new traffic management system in the Straits. The IMO was quick to respond and at MSC 63 adopted the Turkish TSS and Associated *Rules and Recommendation on Navigation through the Straits of Istanbul, the Strait of Çanakkale and the Marmara Sea*, which were to go into force on November 24, 1994,[69] subject to confirmation by the Nineteenth General Assembly meeting (SN/Circ.166).[70]

National Regulations vs. IMO Rules and Recommendations

The *1994 Turkish Maritime Regulations for the Turkish Straits* (Regulations) proved to be controversial, and the IMO became an unwitting forum for what was often a political and legal debate.

Turkey had intended only to present the traffic separation scheme created by the 1994 Regulations for approval and adoption by the IMO. It was at the request for additional navigational Rules at NAV 39 that Turkey also presented a set of Rules for Navigation.[71] These Rules were taken directly from the draft national Regulation. The national Regulations in their entirety, however, were never brought to the attention of the IMO by Turkey for review. Nonetheless, the national Regulations found themselves to be the focus of debate, particularly by the Russian Federation, Bulgaria, Ukraine, Greece, Greek-Cyprus, and Malta. After a lengthy discussion, the MSC 63 Working Group agreed to a set of draft Rules and Recommendations, which eventually were adopted as the IMO Rules and Recommendations.[72]

However, the new draft IMO Rules and Recommendations contained provisions inconsistent with the Turkish national Regulations. For example, the Turkish national Regulations had defined a large vessel as 150 meters or more and a deep draught vessel as 10 meters or more, whereas the draft IMO Rules and Recommendations defined a large vessel as 200 meters or more and a deep draught vessel as 15 meters or more. This contradiction between the national Regulations and the draft IMO Rules and Recommendations drafted and adopted by the MSC resulted in objections being lodged against the Turkish national Regulations for being inconsistent with the IMO Rules, as well as general objections by certain member delegations that the national Regulations were in violation of the 1936 Montreux Treaty, LOSC, and *universally* accepted principles of international law, essentially placing the IMO, a technical organization, in the uncomfortable and legally questionable role of acting as a quasi-judicial forum.[73]

Russia specifically called upon the IMO Legal Committee to render an opinion by submitting a lengthy paper to the Legal Committee entitled "Unconformity [sic] of the Turkish Regulations for Traffic Order in the Area of the Straits and the Sea of Marmara to the Rules and Recommendations adopted by the

Maritime Safety Committee." The Russian Federation was essentially lodging a complaint against Turkey and requesting the Legal Committee to render a judgment,[74] a highly questionable action in light of the express Conventional mandate of the IMO to act as a technical forum[75] as well as the established function of the Legal Committee.[76]

The MSC eventually adopted, and the Nineteenth Assembly confirmed, the Turkish Straits TSS and Routeing system together with a set of Rules and Recommendations.[77] However, in doing so, the Assembly attempted to bridge the controversy between the Russian group and the Turkish Regulations by including in its preamble paragraph (2) that the Rules were *not intended in any way to affect or prejudice the rights of any ship using the Straits under international law, including the United Nations Law of the Sea Convention, 1982 and the 1936 Montreux Convention. National regulations should be in total conformity with the Present Rules and Recommendations.*

Despite adoption of the TSS and the Associated Rules and Recommendations by the MSC and confirmation by the Nineteenth General Assembly,[78] the Turkish Straits continued to be on the IMO agenda for another five years. This was partly, if not primarily, the result of *paragraph 5* of Resolution A.827 adopted by the Nineteenth Assembly. While confirming the MSC adopted Turkish TSS, the Resolution also requested the MSC

> to review, based on submissions from Governments, the operation of the Rules and Recommendations set out in Annex . . . and the conditions in the Straits of Istanbul, Strait of Canakkale and the Marmara Sea, to consider, as appropriate, any suggestions for changes in the said Rules and Recommendations.[79]

The request for a report opened the door to further discussions and further heated debates, primarily revolving around what was for Turkey the highly controversial NAV 43 Draft Report on the Turkish Straits prepared by the Working Group on Ships Routeing and Related Matter[80]

NAV 43 proved to be a watershed for the Turkish Straits at IMO. A Working Group was established to draft a report as requested by the Nineteenth Assembly Resolution. The draft NAV 43 Report included recommendations that the suspension of traffic be employed only in exceptional circumstances, such as in cases of *force majeure*, when visibility was below .05 miles or emergency situations, whereas the 1994 were far more detailed.[81] It is clear that the Turkish Regulations were far more detailed and much more likely to reduce the risk of an accident than the conditions proposed for the draft NAV 43 Report.

The NAV 43 Report also included a recommendation to replace Rule 10 (the TSS) with Rule 9 (Right-side passage). Yet, Turkey had adopted Rule 10 because Rule 9 had proven ineffective in preventing accidents. The recommendation that perhaps most raised the ire of the Turkish Delegations was the proposal that an international group of experts be sent to the Turkish Straits to study and analyze traffic movement. At MSC 67, Russia had originally proposed the creation of an international commission to oversee the operation of the Rules and Recommendations in the Turkish Straits, raising the specter of the Lausanne Treaty Commission.[82] Matters seemed to come to a head when Turkey objected to the NAV 43 draft report and refused to participate in the Subcommittee discussions. Turkey maintained its position that the Turkish Regulations had been prepared in conformity to international law and the Montreux Convention and repeated its objections that the IMO was exceeding its mandate as a technical organization. Fortunately the legal imbroglio that would have been created by the adoption of the NAV 43 Report over the objections of the coastal State was resolved when Turkey agreed to participate in the preparation of a new report on the condition that the NAV 43 Report be abandoned.[83]

Faster Passage or Safer Passage: Rule 9 vs. Rule 10

By MSC 70, discussions on a new draft report were primarily concerned with replacing Rule 10 with Rule 9 of COLREG. Russia presented a paper arguing for the replacement of the existing Rule 10 with Rule 9 and also complained that suspension of traffic in the Straits had been frequent and costly.[84] Bulgaria also presented a paper arguing for application of Rule 9.[85] The basic argument in the respective arguments was that Rule 10 caused frequent suspension of traffic. Turkey presented a number of papers, including its intention to accede to the CLC and FUND Conventions as amended by the 1992 Protocol,[86] an update on the VTS,[87] and a lengthy explanation for application of Rule 10.[88] The Turkish paper explained in detail how Rule 9 increased the likelihood of two vessels colliding in the narrow bends of the Straits. Furthermore, four years had passed since MSC 63 and statistics showed a significant decrease in maritime accidents in the Straits.[89] Turkey used this as proof that Rule 10 was successful and why it would maintain Rule 10.

The Turkish Straits matter seemed destined to a perpetual stalemate with each camp firmly entrenched in its demands. But MSC 71 brought about a dramatic change in events. It began with the submission by IFSMA,[90] IAIN,[91] and IMPA[92] of a paper recommending that the practice of suspending two-way traffic continue but that Rule 9 replace Rule 10. The Paper recognized that traffic incidents in the Straits had decreased significantly, but surmised that rather than the TSS, the suspension of two-way traffic had contributed to the noted decrease.[93] The paper also recognized that Turkey's stated intent to establish a modern VTS system would also further promote safety in the Turkish Straits. Turkey submitted a paper in which it outlined reasons for temporary suspension of traffic and for maintaining the TSS. The paper concluded that the *present ships routeing system in the Turkish Straits, as a whole, works well and has significantly enhanced safety of navigation.*[94]

The U.S. delegation in turn proposed that the Working Group finalize the draft report but that the emphasis be on "safety" and that an analysis of the *pros and cons* of the IFSMA, IAIN, and IMPA paper and the Turkish paper be made. Perhaps weary from six years of entertaining the matter of the Turkish Straits on his agenda, the Chairman of the MSC, taking heed of the statement of Joe Angelo, the head of the U.S. delegation, said that ". . . since 1994, we believe that discussions that have taken place in this committee have focused on everything but the safety issues of navigation through the Turkish Straits." With the approval of the MSC, he then went ahead and instructed the Working Group to examine the *pros and cons* of the application of Rule 9 and Rule 10 "taking into account the level of safety and protection of the marine environment which (had) been achieved under the existing IMO-adopted system. . . ." These terms were further narrowed to taking into account "the human element" thereby excluding all other factors, including economic and, of course, legal and political.

In light of the significant reduction of maritime accidents in the Turkish Straits since the implementation of the national Regulations and the IMO-adopted TSS and Associated Rules and Recommendations in 1994, a majority of the Working Group made amongst other things the following conclusion:

(1) Suspension of the two-way traffic was necessary within the context of the present routing system to prevent large ships from meeting in the narrow, winding part of the Straits of Istanbul and the Strait of Çanakkale;

(2) Vessels not taking advantage of available pilotage should;

(3) Vessels not particiapting in TÜBRAP should be more strongly encourage to; and

(4) Turkey should be encouraged in its efforts to implement a modern VTS.

Furthermore, a majority of the Working Group also noted that:[95]

(5) The existing IMO adopted routing system had been effective;

(6) After extensive technical discussions, the working group had not reached any conclusion that any change would make a clear and definitive contribution to safety of navigation in the Straits; and lastly,

(7) No changes could be made without the consent of Turkey, who had no intention of adopting any changes.

The Working Group recommended that there was no need for further discussion and, thus, no need for a new Report and recommended that the subject matter of the Turkish Straits be discontinued. This recommendation was adopted by MSC 71 and confirmed by the Twenty-first Assembly.[96] Safety carried the day.

THE OIL INDUSTRY IMO AND THE TURKISH STRAITS

When Turkey first introduced its proposal for the creation of a TSS in 1993, the Oil Companies Industry Maritime Forum (OCIMF) was quick to respond. In an action paper dated June 7, 1993, OCIMF revealed that it had already conducted a study on safety of navigation through the Turkish Straits.[97] The same paper raised the issue of future increase in oil and gas export from the Black Sea region and estimated that approximately 100 million tons of crude oil per annum, "a large percentage" of which would "probably be shipped out of the Black Sea" and through the Turkish Straits. The OCIMF paper included a map of the possible "former Soviet Union export options."[98] The map foresaw a total of *100 MTA–155 MTA* being transported from various parts of the Caucasian region to the Black Sea port of Novorossiysk alone—an original figure exceeding 100 million tons.

OCIMF, clearly aware of the hazards of navigating through the Straits,[99] put forth recommendations, some of which were not only in conflict with the terms of the Montreux Convention, such as recommending mandatory pilotage, but also with the principle of *transit passage* as envisioned in a post-UNCLOS world. For example, OCIMF *strongly* recommended that there be a *maximum vessel size for transit of these waters based on dimensions such as length overall, beam and draft.*[100] However, in return for what in the author's view were concessions, OCIMF wanted COLREG Rule 9 to continue applying in the Strait of Istanbul and Çanakkale and not Rule 10 (TSS).[101]

At MSC 67, the OCIMF presented a paper, which in many aspects supported the Turkish Regulations.[102] On the other hand, the Russian Federation had also presented a paper that was quite critical of Turkey.[103] OCIMF attempted to resolve the alleged conflict between the IMO Rules and Recommendations and the 1994 Turkish national Regulations by recommending a set of amendments, certain of which OCIMF stated *may conflict with the rights of free passage in an international strait allowed under Montreux.* The recommended amendments included compulsory pilotage, mandatory daylight transit of large or deep draught vessels,[104] mandatory reporting, suspension, and regulation of traffic for large vessels or vessels carrying dangerous/noxious/hazardous cargo, etc.

Despite the OCIMF stated concern for the Turkish Straits and its support for Turkish Regulations of vessel traffic through the Turkish Straits, the oil companies themselves continued to favor the Baku-Supsa or Baku-Novorossiysk pipeline option that would include transport by tankers through the Turkish Straits. However, by late 1999, there appeared to be a *volte-face* on the part of some of the major oil companies operating in the Caspian Sea region regarding their policy towards both the Turkish Straits and the Baku-Ceyhan pipeline.[105] The leader in this policy change was BP Amoco,[106] which had initially viewed the Baku-Ceyhan pipeline as not economically viable. In early 1999, BP Amoco made statements that the Azeri reserves would have to increase by one billion barrels in order for Baku-Ceyhan to be viable.[107] But in October 1999, BP made the surprising announcement that it was supporting the Baku-Ceyhan pipeline alternative.[108] In October 2000, BP Amoco, along with a group of other companies, signed an investors agreement with each other and transit agreements with

Turkey, Georgia, and Azerbaijan for the creation of the Baku-Ceyhan oil pipeline. As a major stakeholder in the AIOC, BP's position is important and, in the author's opinion, opened the way for others in the oil industry. In making this change in position, BP Amoco recognized the dangers additional traffic through the Turkish Straits would pose. In a presentation given on the subject matter at the CSIS, Captain Noel Hart of BP Amoco stated that BP Amoco's decision to support the Baku-Ceyhan pipeline ". . . in a large part is to relieve the burden on the Turkish Straits."[109] This is supported by an internal policy adopted by BP in 1998 for all its tankers according to which tankers on BP business were obliged to comply with Turkish transit guidelines.[110] BP's internal policy also mandated daylight passage and for all BP tankers to employ a pilot when passing through the Turkish Straits. BP Amoco has also submitted a request to the Navigation and Routeing Subcommittee of OCIMF to "assess the full spectrum of factors and develop an industry position on safety of navigation in the Straits." The Committee includes many of the major companies active in the Caspian.

Following BP Amoco, STATOIL, the Norwegian state-owned oil company, and a member of the AIOC also made a public commitment to Baku-Ceyhan and recognized the hazards of any increased tanker traffic through the Turkish Straits. Chevron[111] has also very recently announced its intention to join in the technical discussions relating to Baku-Ceyhan camp.[112] Chevron, who holds a fifteen percent interest in the CPC and forty-five percent of the TengizChevroil, is an important player, and its support of the Baku-Ceyhan project is quite important. However, of equal importance is its policy towards the Turkish Straits. Recently, Chevron indirectly aknowledged the traffic problems in the Strait of Istanbul by issuing a statement that the increased production from the Tengiz field being transported to the Black Sea port of Novorossiysk upon expected completion of the pipeline in Hune 2001 would not result in increased oil being transported through the Turkish Straits in the "near future."[113]

However, there are still many other players amongst the oil companies in the Caspian who have not expressed support for

Baku-Ceyhan or more importantly acknowledged the dangers of navigating the Turkish Straits. In comparison to the billions of dollars an oil casualty in Istanbul could cost, investing in a pipeline, such as Baku-Ceyhan, that would bypass the Turkish Straits seems to be both economically and environmentally a sound option.[114] There is, perhaps, the hope that Turkey, in improving its vessel management system with the implementation of a new U.S. $20 million Vessel Traffic System (VTS), will reduce the risks for a tanker casualty in the Straits. However, the VTS is not fail-safe. It requires full compliance by all vessels and also a well trained operating staff, both of which will take time and effort. A pipeline bypassing the Turkish Straits creates no risk to the Turkish Straits and so should be considered as an essential component of safety of navigation and protection of the environment for the Turkish Straits.

CONCLUSION

The existing traffic flow of nearly fifty thousand vessels, including tanker traffic, through the Turkish Straits creates a daily hazard, particularly for the densely populated Istanbul region. The projected increase of Caspian oil, if transported by tankers through the Turkish Straits, will only multiply those hazards. In the year 2000, nearly 100 million tons of oil and dangerous cargo was shipped through the Turkish Straits in tankers. This amount could double in the next decade and triple in the next fifteen years. Such an increase, if multiplied by 800 additional tanker trips for each 10 million ton increase, can only heighten the risk of a major casualty in the Straits even with the best vessel management system. Any calculation of the financial feasibility of a routing alternative for Caspian oil must include the environmental impact of an oil casualty in the Straits. It is entirely unacceptable that the difficulty in assessing value to such irreplaceable "goods" such as historical buildings or life itself should be resolved by simply omitting these very critical factors from the financial calculation. And while the existing legal regime of the Straits does offer Turkey an important degree of coastal State authority to regulate passage of vessels that pose a navigational hazard, it is not perfect. The 1998 Turkish Maritime Regulations has introduced a number of regulatory measures designed to reduce the risk of casualty in the Straits. However, there are limits on Turkey's ability to impose prescriptive measures. For example, even though in many ways it is a coastal State favorable regime, the Montreux Convention does impose restrictions, such as preventing mandatory pilotage.

The future of the Turkish Straits depends a great deal on the cooperation of the maritime industry to take the necessary safety measures to minimize the likelihood of a disaster. Otherwise, Turkey will probably continue to take further measures to prevent shipping disasters in the Turkish Straits. Recently, the Minister for Maritime Affairs made statements indicating the intention of the Turkish government to take further regulatory measures due to an anticipated increase in the transport of oil.[115] And such further actions, no doubt, could lead to tense relations. The Baku-Ceyhan pipeline must be assessed as an essential component of preserving the delicate marine and overall environmental integrity of the Turkish Straits.

Notes

[1] D. Yergin, *The Prize The Epic Quest for Oil, Money & Power* (Simon & Schuster, 1991), 59.

[2] At one point, there were as many as nine different pipeline route options. See T. L. Thomas and J. Shull, "Russian National Interests and the Caspian Sea," IV *Perceptions* 14 (Dec-Feb 2000): 75, 90.

[3] In its background note on the 1994 Regulations, the Turkish government stated that *the Turkish Straits cannot be considered as an oil transportation route. The Straits cannot carry the additional burden which will be brought by large amounts of oil shipments* <http://www.mga.gov.tr>.

[4] See <www.eia.doe.gov>.

[5] There are three main consortiums operating in the Caspian Region: the Azerbaijan International Operating Company (AIOC); Caspian Pipeline Consortium (CPC); and the Offshore Khazkhstan International Operating Company (OKIOC).

[6] R. Soligo and A. Jaffe, *The Economics of Pipeline Routes: The Conundrum of Oil Exports from the Caspian Basin* (1999) <http://riceinfo.rice.edu.projects/baker/Pubs/BakerPub/publications/studi.../pipelines.htm>.

The authors conclude, however, based on a purely economical basis, that all the routes to the Mediterranean designed to bypass the Turkish Straits are more costly than the use of tankers through the Straits.

[7] Source: Republic of Turkey Undersecretary for Maritime Affairs. According to official sources, most of the dangerous cargo consists of petroleum products.

[8] There is also the view that the growth of Black Sea economies creates a regional market for oil allowing local consumption thereby relieving some of the burden. Nonetheless, even with the most conservative estimates of future oil production, this would still result in 1.5 million b/d of oil needing an outlet to the Mediterranean. This argument also fails to take into consideration that the growth in the economies of these states will result in greater international trade, much of which will see transport through the Turkish Straits. (See UNCTAD Doc. A/53/331 *reproduced in* NILOS 14/1998, 126.) The problem of the Turkish Straits is not merely restricted to oil transport, the latter simply carries greater risks for catastrophic accidents.

[9] The Center for Strategic and International Studies (CSIS) of Washington, D.C., expects Kazakhstan, Azerbaijan, and Turkmenistan to reach a peak oil production level of about 3.5 million b/d sometime around 2010. In particular, CSIS expects Kazakh production to reach 1.9 million b/d from three main areas: the Tengiz field, the offshore Caspian shelf concession, and the Karachaganak field. The Tengiz Field, being developed by Tengizchevroil, has potential reserves of six to nine billion barrels of recoverable oil and is planned to reach peak production of 900,000 barrels per day in 2010. Some U.S. government

analysts suggest total Central Asian and Caucasus oil production could reach as high as 4.5 million b/d by 2010, absent political restraints.

[10] IMO Doc. NAV 39/3/10 (1993).

[11] A. Cohen, "U.S. Policy in the Caucasus and Central Asia: Building a New Silk Road to Economic Prosperity," *Backgrounder*, no. 1132 (The Heritage Foundation, 24 July 1997).

[12] E. J. Hicks, *Environmental Constraints on Development of Caspian Oil and Gas Resources: The Bosphorus and Caspian Sea* (1998) <http://www.wws. princeton.edu/~wws401c/1998/emily.html>.

[13] As the Strait of Çanakkale is not as narrow and does not go through a large metropolitan, the author has focused primarily on the Strait of Istanbul.

[14] The Marmara Sea is a large body of water (225 km) in which a vessel claiming to be traveling in transit, that is, non-stopover passage, can very easily disappear into the Sea of Marmara for days without any means of tracking the vessel. This raises an interesting issue as to at which point can a vessel claim to be "in transit" affecting the applicability of article 2 of the 1936 Montreux Convention for the Turkish Straits.

[15] The *orkoz currents* are especially problematic as they are counterclockwise currents that can cause a vessel to drift.

[16] Istanbul was named a World Heritage City by UNESCO.

[17] For detailed and up-to-date statistics on vessel movement and accidents through the Turkish Straits, see the Turkish Maritime Pilots website at <http://www.turkishpilots.org>.

[18] Of this total, LPG Carriers accounted for 474 passages, Chemical tankers for 682 passages, and LNG Carriers for (0) passages. Only forty percent of vessels used a pilot.

[19] Between 1952 and 1991, a total of 444 major incidents were reported, of which 332 occurred in the Strait of Istanbul. Thirty-five percent of these incidents took place since 1988, showing a steep progression (1988-7; 1989-16; 1990-38; 1991-57; and 1992-37). OCIMF IMO Doc. NAV39/3/10.

[20] In addition to these major oil accidents there have been many other serious accidents not involving oil tankers. For example, in 1982 a vessel struck a residence on the shore of the Istanbul Strait and killed a woman in her bed. Or, when in 1991, twenty thousand live sheep sank to the bottom of the Strait of Istanbul, where the effects of their decomposing carcasses still continue, after the Lebanese ship the *Rubunion* struck one of the bridges.

[21] The 1967 *Torrey Canyon* accident resulted in 117,000 tons of crude oil spilling into the Dover Straits.

[22] For the environmental effects of tanker accidents in the Turkish Straits, see B. Öztürk and A. A. Öztürk, "On the biology of the Turkish Straits system," *Bulletin Institut Oceanographique*. Monaco n° spécial 17 1996, CIESM Science Series, no. 2.

[23] The *M/T Erika* sank off the Brittany coast of France on December 28, 1999, and spilled 30,000 tons of heavy oil into the Atlantic Ocean. It was deemed the worst environmental accident in Western Europe in forty years.

[24] Both of these accidents involved aging vessels raising the issue of substandard ships and the need for stricter regulations.

[25] Turkish Pilots Maritime Association.

[26] E. J. Hicks, *Environmental Constraints on Development of Caspian Oil and Gas Resources: The Bosphorus and Caspian Sea*, *supra* note 11, 3.

[27] IMO Resolution A.19/827 (24 November 1994).

[28] Nonetheless, there are those who argue that the UNCLOS provisions on transit passage would apply as a residual source of customary law for aspects of navigation not covered by convention or treaty. See G. Plant, "The Turkish Straits and tanker traffic: an update," *Marine Policy*, 24 (2000): 193-214. However, Schachte and Bernhardt, in an analysis of the role of the transit passage regime as a residual source for straits regulated *in whole or in part by long standing conventions* take the view that each 35(c) strait regime is *sui generis* and that

> depending on the regime established under the particular "long standing convention" in question, the precise nature of the regime can most accurately be determined by the extent and nature of the navigational use developed therein. This usage is more indicative and determinant in cases in which the regime is imprecise.

W. L. Schachte, Jr., and J. P. A. Bernhardt, "International Straits and Navigational Freedoms," 33 *Virginia Jrnl of Int'l Law* 503 (1993): 544-45.

[29] The Montreux Convention was adopted in the City of Montreux, Switzerland, on July 20, 1936, and went into force on November 9, 1936. For an excellent history of the Convention, see A. R. DeLuca, *Great Power Rivalry at the Turkish Straits: The Montreux Conference and Convention of 1936* (New York, 1981).

[30] In 1935 Turkey sent a diplomatic note to all the signatories of the Lausanne Convention on the Regime of the Turkish Straits.

[31] The participating Parties at the Conference were: Great Britain, Australia, Bulgaria, France, Greece, Rumania, Japan, Yugoslavia, Russia, and Turkey. Italy eventually signed the 1936 Montreux Convention. After its defeat in World War II, Japan was removed as a Party.

[32] The Strait of Magellan, the Danish Straits, and the Ahvenanrauma Strait are regulated by Treaties or Conventions. Some also argue that the Strait of Gibraltar and the Strait of Tiran would also be article 35(c) straits.

[33] The official French text provides for "la complēte liberté de *passage* and navigation . . ." and not "complete freedom of *transit* and navigation . . ." as has been translated by the unofficial English text.

[34] Article 1 provides:

> The High Contracting Parties recognise and affirm the principle of freedom of passage and navigation by sea in the Straits. The exercise of this freedom shall henceforth be regulated by the provisions of the present convention.

[35] Article 2 provides in pertinent part:

> In time of peace, the merchant vessels shall enjoy complete freedom of passage and navigation in the straits, by day and by night, under any flag, with any kind of cargo, without any formalities, except as provided in Article 3 below. No taxes or charges other than those authorised by Annex I to the present Convention shall be levied by the Turkish authorities on these vessels when passing in transit without calling at port in the Straits. . . .

[36] E. Brüel, 1 *International Straits A Treatise on International Law* (1947), 393. Brüel observed that the "apparent liberality of the rules of passage contained in Article 2 is considerably modified by the fact that shipping is subject to sanitary control under Article 3 and the dues set out in Annex I." Ibid., 409.

[37] G. Plant, "Navigation regime in the Turkish Straits for merchant ships in peacetime," *Marine Policy* 20 (1995): 17.

[38] G. Plant, "The Turkish Straits and Tanker Traffic," *supra* note 27. The issue of whether the UNCLOS-created *transit passage* regime has become customary law is highly debatable and beyond the scope of this paper. Plant also argues that the Montreux Convention only regulates passage in part. However, the present author joins the view of other authors who do not view Montreux as being a Convention that regulates passage only in part. Schachte and Bernhardt, in their analysis of the Montreux Convention, put forth the official view of the United States that because "*the Convention is so detailed, it is a convention which regulates passage 'in whole', and the regime is sui generis.*" Schachte and Bernhardt, "International Straits and Navigational Freedoms," *supra* note 27, 547.

[39] C. L. Rozakis and P. N. Stagos, *The Turkish Straits* (Martinus Nijhoff, 1987), 105-106.

[40] Ibid.

[41] S. Toluner, "The Montreux Convention and the Authority to Regulate Passage Through the Straits," transl., *Review of Environment and Woodlands Protection Society of Turkey* (January 1980): 7; S. Toluner, "Rights and Duties of Turkey

Regarding Merchant Vessels Passing the Straits," *Turkish Straits: New Problems New Solution* (1995): 27-33: T. Tarhanli, "Innocent Passage Regime and Illicit Arms Trafficking Through the Turkish Straits," *Turkish Straits: New Problems New Solution* (Istanbul, 1995): 33.

[42] See N. Oral and G. Aybay, "The Meaning of Freedom of Passage and Navigation Under the 1936 Montreux Convention on the Regime of the Turkish Straits," 4 *Turkish Review of Balkan Studies* (1998-99), 179.

[43] S. L. Meray and O. Olcay, *Montreux Boğazlar Konferansı-Tutanaklar, Belgeler (Ankara*, 1976), 42.

[44] Ibid. at 164.

[45] See S. Toluner, "Rights and Duties of Turkey Regarding Merchant Vessels Passing Through the Straits" *supra* note 40, 28-29.

[46] In 1927, Judge Jessup wrote that the right of innocent passage required "no supporting argument or citation of authority" as it was "firmly established in international law." Cited in F. Ngantcha, *The Right of Innocent Passage* (1990), 9. See also E. Brüel, *Les Detroits Danois au Point de Vue du Droit International* Recueil des Cours 1936 (Tome 55), 610, stating that D*e nos jours les regles concernant les eaux territoriales sont en principe applicable aux detroits*; E. Brüel, *International Straits, A Treatise on International Law* (Copenhagen, 1947) 1:200; and R. R. Churchill and A. V. Lowe, *The Law of the Sea*, 3d ed. (Manchester Press, 1999), 102 Cf. G. Plant rejects the author's argument as being based on "the, perhaps, false premise that innocent passage was the regime accepted in customary international law in 1936." However, Plant's quotation from Rozakis and Stagnos regarding customary law for international straits was actually meant to apply to the nineteenth century and not the 1930s by the original authors. G. Plant, "The Turkish Straits and Tanker Traffic," *supra* note 27, 201 (citing Rozakis and Stagnos, 63, n. 67).

[47] J. A. de Yturriaga, *Straits Used for International Navigation, A Spanish Perspective* (Netherlands, 1991), 25-26. The main issue of debate at the 1930 Hague Conference concerned the breadth of the territorial sea. B. B. Jia, *The Regime of Straits in International Law* (Oxford, 1997), 90-105; M. Giuliano, "The Regime of Straits in General International Law," 1 *The Italian Year Book of International Law* (1975).

[48] E. Brüel. *International Straits, A Treatise on International law* (Copenhagen, 1947) 1: 217.

[49] Article 3. During the Montreux Conference, Lord Stanhope, the head of the British delegation, remarked that he had been informed that the Strait of Çanakkale was the only strait where sanitary fees were collected from vessels engaged in transit passage. *Montreux Bogazlar Konferansi-Tutanaklar, Belgeler* (1976), 51.

Professor T. Scovazzi, in his analysis of the Montreux Convention provision for sanitary inspection, observes that the concerns that made Turkey insist upon maintaining this provision could be "transferred from the sanitary field to the environmental field" today. T. Scovazzi, *The Evolution of the International Regime Concerning Passage of Ships Through the Black Sea Straits*, Paper presented at the Athens Conference of the "Passage of Ships Through Straits" (1999).

[50] Article 2.

[51] These provisions were also included in the 1923 Lausanne Convention on the Regime Regarding the Turkish Straits. Article 6, on the other hand, introduced an entirely new limitation on the freedom of merchant vessel passage.

[52] This provision implicitly appears to give Turkey the authority to inspect (stop and detain) vessels it suspects of rendering assistance to an enemy force.

[53] The 1930 Hague Conference drafted an article recognizing the right of innocent passage for war vessels.

[54] The Convention created three main categories of war vessels according to nationality: Turkish vessels, Black Sea Power vessels, and non-Black Sea Power vessels.

[55] For example, Article 14 restricted the maximum aggregate tonnage of foreign naval forces that can transit the Straits to not exceed 15,000 tons. Article 11, however, allows Black Sea Powers to send capital ships through the Straits of a greater tonnage so long as they pass in single file and are not escorted by more than two destroyers. Article 18 provides details of the limitations on the passage of non-Black Sea Power war vessels.

[56] For example, the Convention does not limit the number of auxiliary vessels that can pass through the Straits but does forbid the passage of aircraft carriers.

[57] Article 13.

[58] M. C. Djonker, *Le Bosphore et les Dardenelles Les Conventions des Detroits de Lausanne (1923) et Montreux (1936)* (1938 These de Doctorat), 146 (transl. by author).

[59] Aybay-Oral, *Turkish Straits Maritime Traffic Scheme Regulations*, Engl. transl. (Istanbul, 1998).

[60] Originally, the 1998 Regulations were comprised of fifty-four articles. However, article 50 was subsequently repealed.

[61] Article 51 of the 1998 regulations is vague in that in very general language it provides that "ships captains and crew members determined to have acted in violation of the Regulations shall be subject to those provisions of the law as required."

[62] IMO Doc. Resolution A.19/827.

[63] Gunduz Aybay, "On the Power of Turkey to Regulate Free Passage Through the Straits," *New Problems New Solutions*, 53.

[64] *The Review of Environment and Woodlands Protection Society of Turkey* devoted a special volume in 1980 to the safety hazards in the Bosphorus and also of tanker fires (January 1980, vol. 3). See also the special issue on the

Bosphorus, 14 *The Review of Environment and Woodlands Protection Society of Turkey* (October 1982).

[65] The Regulations went into effect on July 1, 1994.

[66] For varying views of the Turkish Straits experienced at the IMO, see G. Plant *supra*, n. 66; M. Dyoulgerov, "Navigating the Bosphorus and the Dardanelles: A Test for the International Community," 14 *Intl Jrnl of Mar and Coastal Law*, no. 1 (1999); A. Scharfenberg, "Regulating Traffic Flow in the Turkish Straits: A Test for Modern International Law," 10 *Emory Int'l Law Review*, no. 1 (Spring 1996); N. Unlu, *The Montreux Convention and the Development of the Legal Regime of the Turkish Straits* (1999), Ph.D. Thesis (unpublished).

[67] MSC 62/INF.10.

[68] On March 13, 1994.

[69] The national Turkish Maritime Regulations went into effect on July 1, 1994.

[70] MSC 63/WP.5/Add.1; MSC 63/WP.17.

[71] IMO Doc. MSC 63/7/2. The Rules were taken directly from the national Regulations.

[72] IMO Doc. MSC 63WP 11.

[73] For details of the objections, see, for example, Russian paper MSC 63/7/15; MSC 63 WP11/Add. 2.

[74] The Russian document once again put forth the view that the national Regulations put into effect by Turkey on July 1, 1994, were in contradiction with the 1936 Montreux Convention and international law in general, including the 1982 UN Convention on the Law of the Sea and not in conformity with the IMO Rules and Regulations as adopted by the Sixty-third MSC and issued as SN/Circ. 166. The Russian paper requested the Legal Committee to give a direct opinion as to whether the Turkish Regulations were in conformity with IMO Rules and Recommendations, and specifically, the Russian Federation objected to those provisions of the national Rules which:

> envisaged in some cases de facto the imposition of an authorization procedure for the passage, other unreasonable restrictions for navigation including its suspension under certain circumstances or even a ban for certain classes of ships for passing through the Straits.

See IMO Doc. LEG 71/12. The Legal Committee concluded that the national Regulations were not in compliance with international law and IMO Rules and Recommendations but that the matter should be resolved by the MSC.

[75] Article 1 of the IMO Conventions states, *inter alia*, as its purpose:

> (a) to provide machinery for co-operation among Governments in the field of governmental regulation and practices relating to technical matters of all kinds affecting shipping engaged in international trade; to

encourage and facilitate the general adoption of the highest practicable standards in matters concerning maritime safety, efficiency of navigation and prevention and control of marine pollution from ships; and to deal with administrative and legal matters related to the purposes set out in this article; . . .

[76] For a detailed discussion of the Legal Committee, see R. P. Balkin, "The Establishment and Work of the IMO Legal Committee, E. Maritime Safety Issues," M. H. Nordquist and J. N. Moore, eds., *Current Maritime Issues and the International Maritime Organization* (1999), 291-325.

[77] Routeing Measures Other than Traffic Separation Schemes Rules and Recommendations on Navigation Through the Strait of Istanbul, the Strait of Çanakkale and the Sea of Marmara, IMO Doc. SN/Circ. 166 and A.19/827.

[78] Res.19.A/ 827.

[79] The Turkish delegation objected to this paragraph, which has not been included in the draft Rules and Recommendations, accepted by consensus by NAV 40. Turkey also objected that the IMO was creating a permanent oversight mission in the Turkish Straits. In fact, at the following MSC 67, the Russian delegation proposed the creation of an international commission to oversee the operation of the Rules and Recommendations in the Turkish Straits (IMO Doc. MSC 67/7/12).

[80] The NAV 43 Draft Report (NAV 34 WP. 1), included recommended amendments to the existing TSS in the Turkish Straits as well as to the Rules and Recommendations. The Draft report was based on papers prepared by Turkey (NAV 43 INF.5 and 6), Russia (Nav 43/3/1), Bulgaria (NAV 43 INF.8), and the OCIMF MSC 67/7/12.

[81] Turkish Regulations provided for the temporary suspension of traffic under a variety of circumstances: such as during construction work, extinguishing fire, drilling, scientific and sports activity search and rescue operations, prevention and removal of marine pollution, and pursuit of criminal and accidents (article 24); for the passage of large vessels or vessels carrying hazardous cargo when visibility was 1 nm or less, for all vessels 100 m or greater when visibility was 0.5, and for all vessels when 0.5 or less (article 41.); for large vessels, deep draft vessels, or vessels carrying hazardous cargo traveling at 10 nm when the current force was 4 nm or more (articles 40 and 50); and regardless of traveling speed for large vessels and deep draft vessels when current force was 6 nm or more (articles 41 and 51). Article 42 also prohibited two large vessels carrying hazardous cargo from navigating the Strait of Istanbul at the same time. Article 52 prohibited two large vessels carrying hazardous cargo from navigating in opposite directions in the Straits of Çanakkale and imposed a minimum distance of 20 nm for vessels traveling in the same direction.

[82] One of the goals of Turkey at the Montreux Conference was to abolish the Lausanne Treaty-created international commission for the Turkish Straits, which it succeeded in accomplishing.

[83] Although the Chairman of the Working Group repeatedly noted that amendment of the TSS could not be done without the consent of the coastal State (Turkey), discussions on the report continued without the participation of Turkey.

[84] IMO Doc. MSC 70/11/11.

[85] IMO Doc. MSC 70/11/13.

[86] IMO Doc. 70/INF.21.

[87] IMO Doc. 70/INF.22.

[88] IMO Doc. 70/INF.20 and IMO Doc. 70/11/16 (response to Bulgarian paper).

[89] By 1998, accidents in the Straits had fallen to 5 per annum from a high of 49.

[90] International Federation of Shipmasters' Association.

[91] International Association of Institutes of Navigation.

[92] International Maritime Pilots' Association.

[93] IMO Doc. 71/22/8.

[94] IMO Doc. MSC 71/22/9.

[95] Russia, Greece, Bulgaria, Ukraine, and Greek-Cyprus noted their reservations.

[96] During the Twenty-first Assembly, Turkey was for the first time elected to category "C" of the IMO Council.

[97] NAV 39/3/10 (1993).

[98] Annex 2.

[99] *Navigation through the Bosphorus Straits, Sea of Marmara and the Dardanelles presents an increasing potential risk to shipping, safety, the environment and the well being of the local community* (NAV 39/3/10 para. 33).

[100] Other recommendations included compulsory reporting for all vessels exceeding a specified size, upgrade of navigational aids, introduction of a Vessel Traffic System (VTS), upgrade of tugs available, and review of oil spill contingency planning per article 6 of the OPRC Convention.

[101] OCIMF did not object to the introduction of Rule 10 in the Sea of Marmara.

[102] IMO Doc. MSC 67/7/12.

[103] IMO Doc. MSC 67/7/8.

[104] OCIMF proposed adopting the IMO definition of a large vessel as 200 m or more and deep draught as 15 m or more.

[105] It is purely speculative, but tempting, to associate any part of this change with the decision of the IMO in May 1999 to stop further discussions of the Turkish Straits. Sir John Browne, CEO for BP Amoco, explained the change of policy by saying:

> BP-Amoco's decision to endorse Baku-Ceyhan as the right route for an East-West pipeline is an important milestone. By endorsing the route,

BP-Amoco acknowledges the three issues recognised by the Caspian governments at the signing of the Ankara Declaration last October: *The Bosphorus is not, for environmental reasons, a long-term solution for the export of Caspian oil; Baku-Ceyhan is the best alternative*; [and] Eastern and Western Caspian shippers need to aggregate their volumes on an equal basis to make this project work.

C. Coe, "Is BP-Amoco really committed to Baku-Ceyhan?" (emphasis added) 4 *Alexander's Gas & Oil Connection* 22 (December 24, 1999).

[106] The BP Amoco consortium, named Azerbaijan International Operating Co. (AIOC), includes Exxon Corp. and Unocal Corp. of the U.S., Statoil A.S. of Norway, and OAO Lukoil Holding of Russia. BP Amoco holds more than thirty-four percent of AIOC.

[107] J. Dorsey, "Oil Companies Rejecting U.S.-Turkish Plans to Bypass Iran Pipeline to Transport Caspian Oil," *Washington Report On Middle Eastern Affairs* (Jan/Feb. 1999).

[108] "BP Amoco backs $2.5 billion Caspian pipeline," *United Press International* (October 19, 1999).

[109] In full quote, Captain Noel Hart said: "Let me assure you that BP is putting leadership, resources and capital behind this project which in a large part is to relieve the burden on the Turkish Straits." "BP's View of the Turkish Straits," *CSIS* (November 28, 2000).

[110] See "BP's View of the Turkish Straits," *supra* note 106.

[111] Chevron holds a fifteen percent equity interest in the CPC and a forty-five percent interest in Tengizchevroil, operator of the Tengiz Field. The Tengiz Field has potential reserves of six to nine billion barrels of recoverable oil and is planned to reach peak production of 700,000 barrels per day in 2010.

[112] "Turkey says Chevron interested in Baku-Ceyhan line," *Reuters* (February 9, 2001).

[113] Turkish Pilots Association.

[114] Exxon, which had to pay over U.S. $5 billion in damages and fines after the Exxon-Valdez spill, has not yet indicated support of the Baku-Ceyhan pipeline or acknowledged the navigational hazards of the Turkish Straits.

[115] B. Sellars, "Turkey ponders further curbs on Bosphorus tankers," *Lloyd's List* (March 29, 2001).

PANEL VII

Perspectives on Maritime Disasters

WELCOMING REMARKS TO PANEL VII

Michael Lodge[*]

Good afternoon everyone. I hope that you had a good lunch. Welcome to our final panel, the topic of which is the perspective of the legal advisor on maritime disasters. We have heard very good presentations in this morning's session about various types of maritime disasters, so I am happy that the theme of this panel seems to follow quite logically from the discussions today.

There is a slight change to the program. There will be one less speaker than advertised, and we also have a substitute. Unfortunately, Dr. Breitzke is unwell, and we shall have instead a presentation on the same theme from Dr. Klaus Ramming, on my right, whom I shall introduce in a few minutes.

The whole theme of the conference has been on environmental concerns, and, of course, maritime disasters are a major concern to all of us who are involved in law of the sea issues and environmental issues. And, indeed, there is a whole section of the Convention that addresses the question of protection and preservation of the marine environment. Those provisions address the general duties of States in respect of the marine environment. They have been elaborated upon through numerous conventions and regional agreements that, taken as a whole, form an extremely large and complex corpus of international, regional, and domestic law that may be relevant in the case of a maritime disaster.

The focus of the presentations this afternoon will be on maritime disasters in the context of shipping, and we have two expert individuals to present papers on the subject. My own perspective is slightly different. As you probably know, I am the legal advisor to the International Seabed Authority. Over the last few years, my particular interest in this subject has been from the point of view of seabed operations; that is, seabed mining and exploration in very deep waters. In addition to the general

---

[*] Legal Advisor, International Seabed Authority.

M.H. Nordquist and J.N. Moore (eds.),
Current Marine Environmental Issues and the International Tribunal for the Law of the Sea, 367–370.

provisions in the Law of the Sea Convention, there is a very specific emphasis in the 1994 Implementation Agreement on the importance of the prevention of pollution and the reduction of damage to the marine environment. This emphasis has been reflected in the work of the International Seabed Authority since its commencement in 1996 and is reflected in the regulations recently adopted by the Authority that the Secretary-General spoke about at the dinner on Saturday evening, which I believe many of you attended. It is very interesting to see this growing awareness of environmental concerns, particularly in the seabed context where we are only just beginning to appreciate the possible consequences to the marine environment of a disaster arising from seabed mining operations.

Seabed activities are still in their infancy. Most of the activities involve exploration at very great depths. These exploration activities are relatively non-invasive, and we feel reasonably confident that they are unlikely to result in any harmful or deleterious effects on the marine environment. All those conducting activities in the deep seabed are required as a matter of law ever since the 1994 agreement to submit environmental impact assessments and to carry out baseline studies against which to assess the likely effects of their activities on the marine environment. In short, it is a reflection of the precautionary approach that we discussed at some length in Saturday's presentations.

I believe that this is an area that will continue to preoccupy us in coming years. From my own perspective, as seabed activities progress, there are all sorts of potential environmental consequences that may arise when people begin operations at great depths. We have very little idea of the consequences of those activities in terms of creating, for example, sediment plumes that will persist in the oceans for very lengthy periods of time. In respect of disposal of slurry and sediments from mineral exploitation and, indeed, from leakage of the very minerals and heavy metals themselves into the world's oceans, the potential consequences of an incident involving these kinds of issues are very far-reaching. We need to do a great deal more study and research before we can come to any definitive conclusions. In that context, an area that will need to be examined in greater detail in the future is the relationship between the very general provisions in Part XII of the Convention that impose on States the duty to protect and preserve the marine environment, and regulation of specific activities that take place in the marine environment. In some sectors, as I mentioned, there is already a large corpus of international law relating to those issues. In other areas, such as seabed mining, there is very little.

I would like to introduce our first panelist, Mr. Davis Robinson. He has a very eminent career, which I will try to summarize briefly. As a graduate of Yale and Harvard Law School, he started his career as a Foreign Service Officer with the U.S. Department of State. Currently Mr. Robinson is a partner in the firm of LeBoeuf, Lamb, Greene & MacRae in Washington, D.C., where he specializes in international transactions, transnational litigation, international arbitration, and, in particular, international maritime and land boundary law. His recent activities have included comprehensive advice to a major Middle East government on all of its international boundary disputes. In addition, he has worked as an advocate in international contract arbitrations. From 1981 to 1985, before going into private practice, Mr. Robinson was the Legal Adviser to the U.S. Department of State. He was an assistant secretary of state and chief counsel to the secretary of state on international matters. During that time, he had broad responsibility for the international application of U.S. securities, banking, antitrust, and export laws. However, for the present gathering, the most interesting activity was, perhaps, that he was responsible for the representation of the United States before the Iran-U.S. Claims Tribunal in The Hague and in a number of other cases before the International Court of Justice. We are extremely fortunate to have such a distinguished presenter.

Our next and, in fact, our final speaker this afternoon, will be Dr. Klaus Ramming. He is from the firm Lebuhn & Puchta, a private law firm in Hamburg. Dr. Ramming was born in San Francisco but grew up in Hamburg. He is a qualified master mariner as well as a lawyer admitted in the Hamburg courts, including the Hamburg Court of Appeal. He specializes in maritime law, including collision and salvage cases as well as carriage of goods, including multimodal transport, charter party disputes, and detention of vessels by port States. He has written numerous articles on maritime and other transport issues including a thesis on speed and consumption claims, and he is also in the process of writing a major book on carriage of goods by sea. This afternoon, Dr. Ramming will give us the private law perspective of a lawyer specializing in collision cases. So it is a great pleasure to introduce Dr. Klaus Ramming.

RECOURSE AGAINST FLAG STATES FOR BREACHES OF THEIR INTERNATIONAL OBLIGATIONS UNDER THE 1982 LAW OF THE SEA CONVENTION

Davis R. Robinson[*]

Good afternoon. I would like to begin by thanking the International Tribunal for the Law of the Sea and the judges of the Tribunal for the opportunity to visit this wonderful facility and this very historic town that is so important to the development of the Law of the Sea and commercial shipping. I would also like to thank my good friends, John Norton Moore and Myron Nordquist, as well as the staff of the Center for Oceans Law and Policy at the University of Virginia, for their invitation to participate. I have certainly learned a lot in the last few days, and I have enjoyed the opportunity to see old friends and make new acquaintances. I hope that in my remarks this afternoon, I will add a few thoughts that will contribute to the Conference.

The topic of this panel is "Perspectives on Maritime Disasters." First, I must issue a disclaimer that admits that I am *not* an expert in the field of maritime disasters. So some intensive homework was in order. However, as I conducted my research and began to prepare my remarks, I discovered that I could find very few answers to the questions that came to mind during my review of the 1982 Law of the Sea Convention (LOS) and its negotiating history. This realization led me to wonder how best to approach the assigned topic. I determined that play-acting within a role with which I am familiar might serve best, so I chose the perspective of the legal adviser to a ministry of foreign affairs. It also seemed that in light of United States views on these matters, I should *not* assume my former role as the Legal Adviser to the United States

---

[*] Former Legal Adviser, U.S. Department of State; Senior Partner, LeBoeuf, Lamb, Greene & MacRae, L.L.P. I am indebted in the preparation of this paper to my colleagues, David Colson and Aimee Ibrahim.

M.H. Nordquist and J.N. Moore (eds.),
Current Marine Environmental Issues and the International Tribunal for the Law of the Sea, 371–383.
© 2001 *Kluwer Law International. Printed in the Netherlands.*

Department of State, but rather pretend that I am a legal adviser here in Europe to a foreign minister.

For a factual context, we selected the maritime disaster resulting from the break-up of the ship *Erika* off the coast of France in late 1999. We then decided to address the issues that the lead attorney in the Quai d'Orsay in Paris would likely immediately confront.

Let us assume that the legal adviser is informed of this matter by his staff, which reports that the Foreign Minister is in a hurry to speak to the legal adviser. The facts are as follows: a tanker flying the flag of Malta has broken up 40 to 50 miles off the French coast and has dumped 3 million gallons of heavy crude oil into the sea before sinking. The legal adviser is told: (i) the owner of the ship is an Italian company; (ii) the crew is Indian; (iii) the charterer of the vessel is a Franco-Belgian company; and (iv) the owner of the cargo is a French company. As an experienced practitioner in public international law, the legal adviser has some working knowledge about the conventional and customary Law of the Sea and about such related institutions as the International Maritime Organization, but the legal adviser is not an expert.

With these facts and considerations in hand, the legal adviser marches off to the Foreign Minister's office. The Foreign Minister announces that this maritime disaster involving the *Erika* is a matter of critical national interest and that the people and political power centers of France are demanding prompt answers. The Foreign Minister tells the legal adviser that the President of France wants a report on his desk in just a few hours before appearing on the national evening news to explain what took place, who is to blame, and what the solution is. The Foreign Minister instructs his legal adviser immediately to address two central questions. The first is what France's international legal options are in seeking to impose liability and to recover all the costs of clean-up and related damages. The second question is what France's international legal options are to try to ensure that this kind of maritime catastrophe does not happen again in French waters.

The legal adviser then returns to his office and calls in the specialists who work on the Law of the Sea, International Maritime Organization affairs, and international environmental law issues. Before the specialists arrive, the legal adviser considers as best he can what the French national interests are in this matter. On a personal basis, the legal adviser, as counsel to a major maritime power, is by no means a rabid environmental regulator, but his country is now faced with a tragedy that threatens its fishing industry, its ecology, and its tourism. He operates from the basic legal proposition that if there is damage, someone is at fault in the absence of an act of God, and compensation is due. In this instance, France has suffered injury from what appears to be human error and negligence, and international law should provide a means by which France will recover adequate compensation for that injury.

The legal adviser also reflects on the fact that France is a maritime nation with major shipping interests. The international system of maritime commerce is important to France. That is how it exports and imports many important products as a major trading nation. France maintains a blue water navy, and, thus, the freedom of navigation and overflight on the high seas throughout the world is a matter essential to France's national security.

The legal adviser also recalls from history that the Law of the Sea has evolved from the time of Grotius to the present. This evolution has tended to increase the power and legal rights of coastal States at the expense of those maritime powers that want to use the seas freely without restriction. And he knows that many of the changes that have occurred in the Law of the Sea over the years have come about because those States that sought to use the seas freely without limitation did not always behave responsibly. These are the thoughts traversing the legal adviser's mind as he awaits his colleagues.

With the specialists, the legal adviser then outlines the task in front of them and asks them initially to focus on the first question: what does France do to impose liability and to recover its costs?

He first asks the specialist on the 1982 Law of the Sea Convention for his/her thoughts. International conventions generally create rights and obligations between States alone, and, thus, the legal adviser can only wonder how the LOS Convention would help France impose State-to-State liabilities in the fact pattern of the *Erika* disaster. Obviously, the first State to consider in this regard is the flag State, Malta.

The specialist then recounts the factual history of this particular ship in recent years. The legal adviser learns that the *Erika* was inspected in Rotterdam in 1997 where deficiencies were found, but apparently nothing was done. In May of 1998, the vessel was inspected in Norway where deficiencies were found again, but the ship sailed away from port without all deficiencies rectified. Only one month later in June 1998, the *Erika* was inspected in France itself by a classification society that found the ship in such poor condition that it was only authorized to undertake one unladen voyage without a more comprehensive inspection. Later, another classification society inspected the *Erika* and regarded the vessel to be in such poor condition that its superstructure was close to collapse. Evidently, these inspections had some beneficial effect, because the ship went into a shipyard in Montenegro for six weeks of repairs in the middle of 1998. Following that service, a classification society deemed the ship to be seaworthy, but a year later, inspections in Russia again found deficiencies. Then, just a few days before the disaster, a classification society noted various problems but allowed the ship to go to sea provided that repairs were made before the end of January. However, the ship never made it to the end of January and later reports indicate that the repair work was carried out in a slipshod manner.

As these facts unfold, the legal adviser thinks to himself that if this were a purely domestic situation, there is no doubt that whoever was responsible for this ship's condition would suffer liability under French law and would have to make whole those on the receiving end of the damages. But this is not a purely domestic situation, and along with the Law of the Sea specialist, the legal adviser thus begins to review the complex provisions of Part XII of

374

the 1982 Law of the Sea Convention on the "Protection and Preservation of the Marine Environment" and other relevant articles. He quickly realizes that the Convention may hint at answers but not in what appears to be a conclusive manner.

The LOS text requires flag States to take measures to ensure the seaworthiness of ships flying their flag. Article 94(3)(a), for example, says: "[e]very State shall take such measures for ships flying its flag as are necessary to ensure safety at sea with regard, *inter alia,* to: (a) the construction, equipment and seaworthiness of ships. . . ." The legal adviser understands that there is a limit to what governments can do to compel private parties, be they individual ship owners, corporations, or persons, to behave in a responsible manner, but here, given the recent history of the ship, somebody in the Maltese government should have become aware of its decrepit state and should have done something about it. However, when confronted with the facts, most probably Malta would say that it had complied with the terms of the LOS Convention because Malta had conformed to general international shipping practice through its reliance on the services of classification societies, which, over a period of months, had subjected the ship to a number of inspections. Yet none had said, "stop."

However, the LOS Convention contains some strong language regarding the duties of flag States. Article 217(2) provides, for example, that

> States shall, in particular, take appropriate measures in order to ensure that vessels flying their flag or of their registry are prohibited from sailing, until they can proceed to sea in compliance with the requirements of . . . [and here the provision refers back to paragraph 1 relating to "the international rules and standards for the prevention, reduction and control of pollution of the marine environment," and then it continues] . . . including with the

requirements in respect of design, construction, equipment and manning of vessels.

If this language is to be followed in these circumstances, it seems to allow only one of two possible legal conclusions: either Malta breached its duties to France under the LOS Convention with legal consequences flowing therefrom, or the technical language and detailed requirements of the various international rules to which the Convention refers are so convoluted or weak as to render its provisions fundamentally meaningless.

The LOS specialist next calls attention to article 235 of the LOS Convention, which falls under section 9 of Part XII entitled "Responsibility and Liability." The language of article 235—which applies to all States—contains a lot of high-sounding, hortatory words, but the drift of the article is unclear. Paragraph 1 of article 235 seems simple enough when it declares:

> States are responsible for the fulfillment of their international obligations concerning the protection and preservation of the marine environment. They shall be liable in accordance with international law.

Paragraphs 2 and 3 of this same article cause the legal adviser to wonder whether they are intended as weakening modifiers of paragraph 1 or as supplements to that provision. Paragraph 2 requires a State to ensure that its internal legal system provides recourse for marine pollution caused by a vessel under its jurisdiction. Does that mean that coastal States damaged by an incident *must* seek redress in the flag State's court in a situation such as the *Erika*? Paragraph 3 seems to require States to resort to established or developing methods of compensation under international law. Included among these would be compensation funds (like the Civil Liability and Fund Conventions) and compulsory insurance. Does this mean that France's remedies are limited to such schemes? It is not clear.

The discussion then turns to Part XV of the LOS Convention on the "Settlement of Disputes," which is often heralded as a major advancement in international law and which provides the LOS Tribunal with its mandate. The specialist first refers the legal adviser to article 286, which appears to provide for compulsory jurisdiction between France and Malta for disputes arising under the Convention, subject to sections 3 and 1. The specialist informs the legal adviser that some interesting events relating to article 286 recently took place in the Bluefin Tuna case.

Upon a quick review, it does not appear as if any of the limitations or exceptions to jurisdiction provided in section 3 are applicable in the facts of the situation. If France has a dispute with Malta about whether Malta has breached its duties to France under the LOS Convention by not fulfilling its flag State responsibilities, then it appears doubtful that Malta can escape by calling upon article 297 or 298 in section 3.

More interesting and difficult questions arise upon examination of section 1, however. Article 286 creates jurisdiction but only "where no settlement has been reached by recourse to section 1." Section 1 of Part XV requires, among other things, that States must settle their disputes by peaceful means. It also requires States to expeditiously exchange views regarding their dispute (article 283), and article 282 allows in some circumstances for regional, bilateral, and multilateral agreements with dispute resolution provisions to operate in lieu of the procedures in Part XV. Moreover, article 281, entitled "Procedure Where no Settlement has been Reached by the Parties," was applied in the Bluefin Tuna case to defeat jurisdiction of the *ad hoc* arbitration tribunal. Could Malta escape by calling on these various requirements of section 1? This is by no means clear. Certainly the specialist is able to conjure up arguments that Malta's lawyers could make to seek to defeat jurisdiction under Part XV.

This quick survey of the 1982 Law of the Sea Convention leads the legal adviser to the following points of conclusion. First, he thinks France can make a good case that Malta breached its flag State duties to France in connection with the *Erika*. Second, he is concerned that Malta may have a defense in arguing that it acted in accordance with standard international shipping practice, which incorporates the international rules and standards to which Part XII refers, and which, as far as the legal adviser can tell, are surprisingly lax. Third, while France may have non-conclusive grounds to initiate proceedings against Malta, its co-Contracting Party under the Law of the Sea Convention, France, as a prerequisite would first have to try to negotiate a settlement of the dispute, which would take time. As a final point, the legal adviser worries that Malta would seek to use section 1 of Part XV to defeat jurisdiction under the LOS Convention.

In summary, as the legal adviser contemplates the contents of his rushed advice to the Foreign Minister, he unfortunately finds no clear answers under the LOS Convention to satisfy the immediate political imperative confronting the Foreign Minister and the President of France. About all the legal adviser concludes he can legitimately say to the Minister is that the LOS Convention provides some "maybes" as answers but that considerable further study is necessary before any firm legal opinions are supportable. The legal adviser is more than aware that this kind of answer is *not* going to sit well with his boss because a "wishy-washy" report from the Foreign Minister will *not* please the President.

During the course of examination of section 1 of Part XV of the Convention, the specialist also mentions the two Civil Liability and Fund Conventions to the legal adviser. The Civil Liability and Fund Conventions were negotiated in the late 1960s in order to deal with the exact kind of problem with which France is now confronted. Those 1969 Conventions, in turn, were later amended by protocols. The specialist and the legal adviser discuss whether an international tribunal might regard any French treaty relationship with Malta under these protocols as providing the full and exclusive remedy for France in this circumstance, particularly given articles 281 and 282 and paragraph 3 of article 235 of the LOS Convention.

In describing the terms of the original 1969 Convention on Civil Liability, the specialist emphasizes that its jurisdictional scope was limited to damages suffered in the territorial sea and the internal waters of France. The legal adviser also notes that the damages available under the 1969 Fund Convention were modest in the extreme, indeed, a mere pittance in relation to the actual scope of loss caused by the *Erika* disaster. The legal adviser learns that it was because of the low level of compensation provided under the 1969 Conventions that the new protocols resulted. The protocols extended the territorial scope of the Civil Liability Convention to the exclusive economic zone (EEZ) and increased the compensation available; however, the possible present level of compensation may still be clearly insufficient to cover the consequences of the *Erika*, particularly when consequential economic damages to the French tourist and fishing industries are considered.

The legal adviser can only conclude that the Civil Liability and Fund Conventions are inadequate and their legal relationship to Part XV of the Law of the Sea Convention is by no means clear.

As time is fleeting, the legal adviser hurriedly begins to formulate his written response to the Foreign Minister's first question. The legal adviser experiences a keen sense of disappointment in recognizing that the international community had to date failed to create an effective process whereby France would with confidence recover its clean-up costs and other damages resulting from the *Erika*. Furthermore, the only other useful step that the legal adviser and the specialist can visualize is a suggestion that the Minister of Justice of France consider ways of claiming in French domestic courts against the owner of the vessel, the charterer, the owner of the cargo, the classification societies, and/or the international insurance companies. Any such advice goes against the legal adviser's grain as an international lawyer, and he is concerned that any such suggestion might be regarded by some international lawyers as overreaching. But with so few options available, it is simply unacceptable to the legal adviser that France not take every possible step in seeking to impose liability and to recover the costs of clean-up and compensation for other damages.

The legal adviser and the staff specialists quickly turn to the second question, namely what can France do to prevent such a disaster from happening again in French waters? The first thought that enters the legal adviser's mind is to insist that before any ship enters French waters, French authorities must inspect it. But he knows immediately that such a system is not possible for practical reasons and would not be consistent with France's general interests in promoting a proper balance between maritime navigation rights and coastal State protections.

The legal adviser and the specialists discuss the possibility of using the *Erika* incident to create pressures, of a public, legal, and diplomatic nature, to compel proper performance by all flag States. If a country is going to allow a ship to fly its flag, then it has certain responsibilities. And if that nation fails to meet those responsibilities, then there is no valid reason why it should not pay the consequences. That would be the gist of the diplomatic blitz. The response that flag of convenience countries do *not* have sufficient financial wherewithal to make it practical to perform their duties would not be accepted. Surely, the legal adviser asks, why is adequate insurance coverage not required when a State registers a vessel so that other States are indemnified for any damages that the activities of the flag vessel may cause?

Also, the legal adviser asks, if a flag State does not perform its duty, at what point do other States no longer respect that flag? The sanctity of a flag vessel on the high seas is not necessarily absolute. Over the years, high seas freedoms have been eroded as the right of coastal States to impose certain conditions has increased. The commercial shipping and military sectors are especially concerned about this erosion in the necessary balance of interests, a process that some have labeled "creeping jurisdiction." But why, asks the legal adviser, should the international community allow a flag State to breach its duties with impunity and provide no acceptable recourse to States that are damaged or threatened because of the flag State's failures? The legal adviser sees no radicalism in suggesting that at a given point States will stop recognizing the rights of vessels from such States. Instead, he speculates, the time may come when the international community will regard such ships as Stateless vessels against which States can proceed in accordance with their national laws. The legal adviser knows this is not the traditional view of his country, but there is no reason why irresponsible flag States must be respected simply as a cost of doing international trade.

The specialist and the legal adviser also conclude that the port States that the *Erika* recently visited could and should have done more. Many of them did take the initial step of inspecting a ship that was in a derelict state but then did little else. But the legal adviser appreciates that there are reasons for this lack of activism. The practical problem is that port States are not likely to have allocated the necessary resources to inspect every foreign flagged vessel that comes into their harbors. Second, when port States do find vessels that are unseaworthy, they often encounter reluctant owners who are unwilling to spend the money needed to remedy the situation immediately. The ship owner, even a responsible one, often will cite numerous reasons why immediate repairs are neither necessary nor feasible. Furthermore, the longer that the vessel is held by a port State, the more the costs mount, some of which the port State itself may incur in berthing the vessel. There is the "who pays" problem for any government holding a foreign flagged vessel and, once again, international law is unfortunately not satisfactorily developed in this regard.

Another legal problem that port States confront arises out of article 219 of the LOS Convention. Article 219 allows the port State only to take "administrative measures" in connection with foreign flagged vessels. Just what this means is unclear. It is particularly unclear when article 226 is examined and its implications considered. For example, would such "administrative measures" include condemnation of a foreign flag vessel in a situation where the owner did not come forward with a plan that would both ensure the seaworthiness of the vessel and the protection of the marine environment? The legal adviser sees it as eminently sensible that port States should have more leverage and more effective responses than are available under the current state of international law and practice. In this regard, the specialist points out the mounting disgruntlement within the international community about flag State compliance and the resulting movement toward greater port State control over vessel condition. He speculates that this movement will lead to new international understandings in order to ensure that vessels and their flag States meet their responsibilities.

The legal adviser recognizes that his time to prepare his written advice to the Foreign Minister is about to expire. He is confident that maritime disasters like the *Erika* will inevitably start a process that will likely change the Law of the Sea as we know it. Irresponsible international fishing brought about the creation of the 200 nautical mile exclusive economic zone (EEZ) and likewise the failure of flag States to perform will lead, in his opinion, to growing erosion of their prerogatives. In fact, if flag States "don't get their act together," the notion of civilian vessels having a flag identity may one day disappear. If the flag State does not accept responsibility, why should any other State honor it? All this speculation about the future provides little comfort to the legal adviser in addressing the need to provide some practical, currently available remedies to the Foreign Minister.

As the legal adviser forms his answer to the second question, he sees basically two points for transmission to the Foreign Minister. First, coastal States and port States need to use all means at their disposal to compel flag State compliance with flag State responsibilities. Second, changes are in the wind that time honored traditions of the sea are not likely to constrain. Compliance with sound legal obligations is what ultimately matters. If the traditions of the sea do not prevent vessels from plying their trade with impunity while creating massive losses for others, then those traditions have become an unacceptable way of doing the world's business. If our domestic legal systems do not allow such an ineffectual result in an internal case, why should international law allow such conduct in an international case? Someone is harmed, someone is liable, and someone should pay. It is as simple as that. There is no reason, the legal adviser concludes, why the international system cannot address and correct the unsatisfactory status quo while balancing the multitude of interests that are implicated.

I will now remove my hypothetical French legal adviser's hat and say that I, of course, do not know how the French government and its legal adviser might, in fact, have privately deliberated during this *Erika* incident, nor do I intend to be hypercritical of Malta. However, the facts of the *Erika* case clearly illustrate the current deficiencies of international law in dealing with maritime disasters. There is too much ambiguity, there are too many holes, and there is too much leeway to avoid liability. Undoubtedly, there are many responsible international shipping companies, many responsible classification societies, and many responsible States with commercial registries. However, if they want to maintain their place, these groups must in my view participate in an effort to ensure that those States and other parties that are responsible face the consequences. The status quo is simply unacceptable and poses too many risks for our citizens and for our ecologies. Change must and will come.

Thank you for this opportunity to speak at this most useful colloquium. I am confident that the International Tribunal for the Law of the Sea will itself in the future contribute to the development of the law with respect to maritime disasters. I look forward to hearing from the other panelists and to responding to any questions.

COPING WITH A MARINE DISASTER:
A CHALLENGE FOR THE MARITIME LAWYER

Christian Breitzke[*]

The final working session of this conference deals with various aspects of major maritime disasters. Given my background, I would like to look at the subject through the eyes of a maritime lawyer.

Nearly ninety years ago in April of 1912, the passenger vessel *Titanic* sank after a collision with an iceberg in the northern Atlantic. On board were 1,136 passengers and 885 crew members. Of these 2,201 people, only 711 survived, which is less than one third. Looking at the number of lost lives, this was the largest maritime disaster of commercial shipping. At the time, it received considerable media coverage, and it still continues to touch people to this day. Also, owing to a major movie, public interest once more has focused on the incident.

Compared to the significance and publicity of the incident, dealing with the legal aspects at the time was relatively simple.

The United States Senate commenced an investigation under its General Investigative Powers. The report of Senator Smith recommended the passing of a bill known as "The Smith Act." Its provisions referred, *inter alia*, to government licensing of wireless operators, a sufficient number of lifeboats to carry all passengers, horizontal as well as vertical bulkheads in the construction of vessels, and many other requirements mirroring the failures found in the *Titanic*. Finally, a resolution was passed urging an International Conference for the Safety of Life at Sea, which was held in 1913 and 1914 in London. The SOLAS Convention— Safety of Life at Sea—remains the most prominent of the ship safety conventions we have today.

---

[*] Dr. Christian Breitzke is a partner of the Hamburg law firm Lebuhn & Puchta. This paper was presented by Dr. Klaus Ramming, also of Lebuhn & Puchta.

M.H. Nordquist and J.N. Moore (eds.),
Current Marine Environmental Issues and the International Tribunal for the Law of the Sea, 385–390.
© 2001 *Kluwer Law International. Printed in the Netherlands.*

The British Board of Trade under the chair of Lord Mersey, the former General Counsel to the White Star Line, the owners of the *Titanic*, conducted a formal investigation, which exonerated the White Star Line and the master (Captain Smith) from negligence and any liability in the sinking of the *Titanic*.

Claims in the amount of approximately U.S. $17 million were settled in the United States, based on the limitation of liability, at an amount of approximately $300,000. The amount of the fund was, in fact, much less, $97,000.

The *Titanic* had a tonnage of 46,000 gross tons. Under U.S. law today, the limitation amount would be approximately $19,500,000.00. Compared to what is being heard about liability claims and amounts in the United States, these were golden times, at least from the owners' and the insurers' perspective. However, this, of course, is not the view of the maritime lawyer. Shipping and maritime environmental disasters comparable to the loss of the *Titanic*, will usually not only require the involvement of dozens of lawyers, but they have also become so complex that looking solely at the legal interests of the parties involved is not sufficient. The lawyers play only a minor role in what might be referred to as a defending battle the owners and their insurers must get involved in to minimize risks, damages, and losses to an acceptable limit. Contingency plans are required that provide for activities and measures at all levels.

There can be no doubt that a loss such as the one of the *Titanic* today would result in considerable coverage from the world's media. One of the first and most important points is to make adequate arrangements to deal with the media. Big shipping lines have their own PR-department. Medium and smaller companies must rely on their P&I Club's assistance. Most clubs have an emergency response team that will consider the appropriate steps required. The assessment of the situation must include facts such as the type of vessel, her cargo, the nationality of the crew and the passengers, the location of the accident, and the environment. Therefore, the first objective is to establish a line of information to allow a proper strategy to be adopted in terms of PR, of initial and subsequent investigations into the cause of the disaster, in terms of employing professional media relation companies, salvors, technical experts, surveyors, and—last but not least—qualified maritime lawyers.

Another important aspect involves expected or pending inquiries, including criminal proceedings against the persons involved. There will no doubt be a media-driven desire to find fault, to blame individuals, and to urge the criminal prosecution of the persons involved. The U.S. Congress investigation into the *Titanic* case has already been mentioned. The authority of political and administrative agencies to conduct investigations utilizing the processes of the courts to compel testimony is part of the U.S. legal system. The U.S. Congress has the legal authority to conduct an investigation, subpoena witnesses, and make recommendations.

The U.S. Coast Guard is the administrative agency that has jurisdiction over American flag vessels and foreign flag vessels within the U.S. territorial waters and has discretionary jurisdiction over certain passenger vessels outside territorial waters. Within this scope the Coast Guard may conduct investigations, detain and inspect vessels, and impose penalties.

The growth of the oil and chemical trades has exponentially increased the risk of pollution. Domestic laws in many countries—most dramatically in the United States—make pollution an expensive problem for ship owners, who will be exposed to potential civil and criminal liabilities in relation to environmental damage. Such sanctions, together with respective media coverage, can destroy personal and professional reputations, can financially ruin companies, and even deprive responsible individuals of their personal liberty. Mere accidents resulting from human error can give rise to criminal charges. The applicable legal provisions provide a strict criminal liability even without negligence in some cases.

Criminal sanctions arising out of environmental casualties are, however, not unique to the United States. In the Sea Empress incident, which occurred off New Haven, the British port authority was fined £ 4 million for the way the salvage of the Sea Empress was handled. At the same time, this affects the professional salvor's motivation to assist.

This leads to the third aspect of relevance, that is, whether and how further damage to vessel and cargo and, in particular, to the environment could be prevented or minimized. Also in this respect, considering the public interest, the owner is best advised to involve a recognized and qualified salvor. In respect of the PR aspects and also in relation to beginning public inquiries and criminal proceedings, the services required of a lawyer are of an advisory nature. However, when a salvage contract is negotiated, genuine legal services are required at the time and at the center of the disaster.

The modern law of salvage as evidenced by the 1989 Salvage Convention, the new edition of the Lloyds Standard Form of Salvage Agreement (LOF 2000), and last but not least, the much discussed Scopic Clause (Special Compensation P&I Club Clause) does not any more focus on the principle of "no cure—no pay," but to a considerable extent also on the prevention and limitation of environmental damage. Scopic, the new special compensation system, is the salvage, ship owning, and insurance industries' response to a genuine public interest need. The traditional law of salvage had one specific shortcoming, because it did not aim at avoiding or minimizing the effects of oil pollutions and the threats to the environment. Once the Scopic Clause has been formally invoked, the "no cure—no pay" principle will be superseded and the salvor will become entitled to pre-agreed tariff payments that allow the salvor to take the necessary steps for the protection of the environment.

The question of whether or not the Scopic Clause should be invoked by the salvor is a risky one. In the extreme, he receives the full salvage award plus a special compensation if he managed to prevent or minimize environmental damage, while in the alternative possibly he gets nothing. In such a situation, obtaining proper legal advice is fundamental.

The next aspect that has to be taken care of is the securing of evidence. This includes involving experts and surveyors, taking statements of the individuals involved, and approaching authorities with a request to inspect their files.

Finally, the handling of disaster litigation claims is the most prominent field of activities of international maritime lawyers. All issues, which at a later stage may affect the jurisdiction as well as the law applicable to the relevant parties' claims for damages, must be considered. In this respect, the flag and the port of registry of the vessel, the location of the accident, the fate of the vessel or wreck, the agreements made with the salvor as well as security provided, and all related agreements made must be looked at. American courts show a tendency to accept American jurisdiction in order to protect national interests. This requires an investigation into the connections the owner and his business may have with the United States, as well as in the case of passenger vessels, the American nationality of crew members and/or passengers.

By commencing limitation actions including establishing a fund according to the 1976 Convention on Limitation of Liability for Maritime Claims, or by applying for a declaration of non-liability, the parties may influence by way of a forum shopping both jurisdiction and the relevant law. On the other hand, an owner these days, being under considerable pressure from the media, may be forced to waive his right to limit liability and to either effect immediate payment or to pay a compensation exceeding the limits provided by the law. Early down payments of a preliminary nature may in many respects prejudice the respective party's liability, the limitation thereof, jurisdiction, and the applicable law. These steps should be used not only in this respect, but possibly also to agree on an amicable settlement with the respective claimants.

The call for generous flat rate payments to all victims, regardless of the merits of the claim, appears to have become more common in relation to major disasters. The liable party may make use of this effect and make down payments contingent on entering into agreements with the potential claimants. This has, for example, happened in relation to the Estonia Incident in which my firm also was involved.

Last but not least, the maritime lawyer involved in a major disaster must make sure that his clients' rights as to indemnity claims are protected. Depending on the cause of the incident, the client might seek to obtain indemnity from crew members, the pilot, cargo interests, stevedores, traffic control authorities, the shipyard, the classification society, or other persons involved in the operation of the vessel, which possibly may have played a part in the incident. It may be that claims must be secured and pursued in many countries, which requires appointing different lawyers and applying the law of different states.

It is quite obvious that major maritime disasters nowadays may be of such a complex nature that experienced maritime lawyers are not able to deal with them without outside assistance. Hull Insurers, P&I Clubs, PR-agents, technical experts, surveyors, salvors, and maritime lawyers—often many lawyers of different countries—must work as a team hand in hand to cope with major maritime disasters. The qualified maritime lawyer's job in the first place is, in view of his clients' liability, to coordinate and guide the efforts made in order to limit his clients' exposure to liability to a reasonable limit.

CLOSING REMARKS

CLOSING REMARKS

Alexander Yankov[*]

Thank you Myron, ladies and gentlemen, dear colleagues, and friends.

Today I have to accomplish an honorary mission to address this closing session of the Conference at the request and on behalf of the President of the Tribunal, H. E. Mr. P. Chandrasekhara Rao, who is indisposed and cannot be with us today.

The President of the Tribunal asked me to convey to you his most sincere gratitude for deciding to hold this Conference at the new premises of the Tribunal in the Free and Hanseatic City of Hamburg. We take pride of the fact that Hamburg has been known as one of the major seaports in the world. Its role in shipping and seaborne international trade as a focal center for marine affairs stretches back to the thirteenth and fourteenth centuries. Moreover, it is well-known that the Senate of the City of Hamburg, on many occasions performed the role of arbitral institution in maritime affairs. Perhaps the location of the International Tribunal for the Law of the Sea is a coincidence with symbolic significance.

This Conference is the first international gathering of experts from various walks of oceans law and policy, and its general theme is directly related to the International Tribunal for the Law of the Sea, which corresponds to its mission in the judicial settlement of current marine environmental issues. Therefore, the convening of the Annual Conference of the Center for Oceans Law and Policy here, in Hamburg, seems to be well-founded.

The deliberations in the eight panels and roundtables have been marked by a lively exchange of views between academics and practitioners. Interesting discussions and suggestions have covered a wide range of topical issues, such as the activities of ITLOS and its future prospects, judicial procedures, and practices, based on the assessment of the cases handled by the Tribunal since its

---

[*] Judge, International Tribunal for the Law of the Sea.

M.H. Nordquist and J.N. Moore (eds.),
Current Marine Environmental Issues and the International Tribunal for the Law of the Sea, 393–395.
© 2001 *Kluwer Law International. Printed in the Netherlands.*

establishment only five years ago. The other current issues have centered on the legal and environmental aspects of marine disasters, including insurance, classification and accidents, obligations and responsibilities of oil producers and shippers, as well as legal advisers' views on maritime disasters.

This comprehensive program of crucial issues is characteristic for the objectives of the Center and its dedication to the promotion of viable legal order over the world's oceans. I have in mind the key idea advanced by the founder and Director of the Center, Professor John Norton Moore, in his opening remarks, referring to the need to strengthen the rule of law on the oceans and seas. The Conference has been guided by this fundamental principle of the law of the sea throughout its deliberations. This has been the consistent policy of the Center since its establishment at the height of the negotiations at the Third United Nations Conference on the Law of the Sea in 1976. That Conference served as a generator of many developments in the policy of states and the lawmaking process on marine affairs, such as the establishment of the exclusive economic zone, introduction of new criteria and parameters for the outer limits of the continental shelf, the regime of the seabed beyond the limits of national jurisdiction, the legal status of the archipelagic waters, protection and preservation of the marine environment, regime of marine scientific research, and elaboration of a system for settlement of disputes. Ambassador Pardo of Malta and the U.S. delegation initiated the incorporation into the Convention on the Law of the Sea, a system of dispute settlement provisions.

The Center for Oceans Law and Policy has contributed also to the elucidation of the complexity of the above-mentioned novel issues through its annual conferences, scientific research, and international meetings.

However, the greatest input of the Center to that effect, has been the initiative of the Center for the preparation and publication of the *Commentary on the United Nations Convention on the Law of the Sea of 1982*. The reviews of this fundamental work have appraised the *Commentary* as the most authoritative source of information on the new law of the sea, both for legal practitioners and publicists. In addition, it may be emphasized that this work is based on the most reliable documentation reflecting the negotiations that took place at the Law of the Sea Conference, having in mind the lack of the traditional *travaux préparatoires* of the diplomatic codification conferences.

In conclusion, I should like to point out that the Twenty-fifth Annual Conference of the Center for Oceans Law and Policy has not been confined simply to current issues of immediate interest. The discussions very often have gone beyond the present status of marine affairs and contained ideas and suggestions, which have direct bearing to future measures aimed at the improvement of the marine environmental situation.

I cannot miss the opportunity, in these closing remarks, not to pay special tribute to the late Elliot Richardson who made an exceptional contribution to the conduct of the complex and difficult negotiations that took place at the Third United Nations Conference on the Law of the Sea. His competence as a head of the U.S. delegation, political vision, human touch, and exemplary integrity, had a decisive role in the search for generally acceptable solutions at the most critical moments of the negotiations.

Finally, I wish to express my best wishes to all participants in this Conference for a happy journey home. Now that you know the premises of the Tribunal along the Elbe River in Hamburg, and its address in German "Am Internationale Seegerichtshof," I wish to assure you that you will always be welcome here, and I hope that we may meet again.